T0375660

HEALTHY SENSE OF SELF

The Secret to Being Your Best Self

ANTOINETTA VOGELS

BALBOA.PRESS
A DIVISION OF HAY HOUSE

Balboa Press books may be ordered through booksellers or by contacting:

Balboa Press
A Division of Hay House
1663 Liberty Drive
Bloomington, IN 47403
www.balboapress.com
844-682-1282

Print information available on the last page.

ISBN: 978-1-9822-6308-9 (sc)
ISBN: 978-1-9822-6309-6 (e)

Balboa Press rev. date: 06/16/2022

HealthySenseOfSelf Publications

HealthySenseOfSelf
www.healthysenseofself.com

Email: contact@healthysenseofself.com

Disclaimer/Notice

The content of this book is presented for informational and educational purposes only. Nothing in this book is intended or presented to, in any way cure, prevent, treat, or diagnose any physical, mental, emotional, spiritual, psychological, psychiatric, or medical disease or condition of any kind. If you have a problem or challenge of any kind, please consult your doctor.

The use of this material is no substitute for, nor is it intended in any way to be used in connection with health, psychological, psychiatric, medical, legal, or other professional services. The author of this book is not a trained or licensed psychologist, or psychiatrist, or professional health care practitioner of any kind. Everything presented in this book is based on personal experience and anecdote, and has not been tested or verified (yet) by scientific research.

Dedication

To our mothers and fathers, who could not help but pass along the suffering they inherited from their parents.

To parents like me who break the vicious cycle.

To our children, who still have to deal with a lot of processing, but who now are able to develop a healthier Sense of Self.

To our children's children in turn, whose suffering and wars may hereby be prevented.

You only have one life to live; make sure it is yours!

~ *Antoinetta Vogels*

Table of Contents

Disclaimer/Notice 3

Dedication 5

Foreword to the Third Edition 15

Introduction 19

The Start of My Inner Quest 19

Something Was Missing: My Sense of Self 23

Putting My Insights to Use 25

My Vow as a Little Girl 27

What This Book Presents: The Sense of Self Method 27

Who Might Benefit from Working with This Method? 29

What Is Required from You? 30

Benefits of a Healthy Sense of Self 33

The Twelve SoS Reconditioning Statements 37

PART I. THE SENSE OF SELF THEORY 39

Chapter 1. The Sense of Self Theory & Method 41

A Lack of Sense of Self Causes a Substitute Sense of Self 42

Characteristics of a Lack of Sense of Self 42

Detecting a Lack of Sense of Self 43

A Brief Summary of the Sense of Self Theory 44

The Importance of a Sense of Self 46

The Importance of the Parent/Caregiver. 47

Parents and Caregivers 48

An Influence Throughout Life 49

There Is No Perfect Solution 51

Summary and Looking Ahead 51

Chapter 2. Environmental Input 53

A Strict Sequence 53

Absence of Crucial Input 57

The Metaphor of the Tree 58

Summary and Looking Ahead 66

Chapter 3. Mirroring 67

Mirroring from Caregivers 69

Is Mirroring Always Accurate and Neutral? 70

The Distorted Mirror 72

Becoming a Distorted Mirror 74

The Challenges of Being a Parent 76

An Eternal Vicious Cycle 78

Summary and Looking Ahead 78

Chapter 4. Fear of Annihilation –Approval versus Acknowledgment 79

Experiencing Annihilation 81

Healthy and Unhealthy Aspects of Your Self 81

Fearing Annihilation 81

The Fear of Annihilation Generates Many Other Fears 81

Fearing the Fear of Annihilation 81

Approval and Acknowledgment: An Unfortunate Mix-Up 87

Becoming Hooked on Approval 88

Thoughts on Workaholism 91

Thoughts on Alcoholism 91

Thoughts on My Insomnia 92

Thoughts on Suicide 93

Summary and Looking Ahead 94

Chapter 5. Early Childhood Survival Strategy and the "Feel-good-about-self" State 95

Early Childhood Survival Strategy 95

"Feel-good-about-self" 98

How "Feel-good-about-self" Relates to Early Childhood Survival Strategy 100

The Internalized Parental Voice (IPV) 103

Life in a Substitute Sense of Self–oriented Way 105

Every Child has the Right to Develop a Healthy Sense of Self 106

Summary and Looking Ahead 109

Chapter 6. Motivation & Substitute Sense of Self 111

Introduction to Motivation 111

Discovering Your Motivations Is Not Easy 112

How Do Your Motivations Develop? 113

Labeling Motivation as Direct and Indirect 114

What Is Motivation? 114

Why Is Knowing the Root of Your Motivation Important? 115

Specifying Motivation 115

"Things Are Seldom What They Seem" 116

Indirect Motivation Aims at a Hidden Agenda 119

Questioning Your Behavior 120

Direct Motivation 121

Indirect Motivation 122
Transference 124
The Hidden Agenda 125
Vehicles 126
The Hidden Goal versus the Hidden Agenda 128
Aspects of Indirect Motivation 130
Emphasis on Proving You Can and its Result 130
Indirect Motivation and the Sense of Self 131
Summary and Looking Ahead 132

Chapter 7. Ego-References and Enmeshment 133
Ego-References 135
Origin of the Term Ego-References 136
Conditions That Become Ego-References 138
Reactionary Ego-References 140
Ego-References and Vehicles 141
Examples of Ego-References 142
Ego-References and Inner Conflict 144
Erica's Situation: An Example of an Inner Conflict 146
Enmeshment and the Addiction to Approval 151
The Castle of Enmeshment: An Analogy 154
Summary and Looking Ahead 158

The SoS Comparison Chart: Do I Have A Substitute Sense Of Self? 159
How to Use the SoS Comparison Chart 159
SoS Comparison Chart: Natural Sense of Self, Substitute Sense of Self, and Restored Sense of Self 163

PART II. THE EFFECTS OF THE DEPENDENCY ON A SUBSTITUTE SENSE OF SELF 173

Chapter 8. Substitute Sense of Self–Oriented Behavior 175
Substitute Sense of Self–oriented Behavior 177
Emotional Complexity 180
The Soup of Substitute Sense of Self-Related Goals and Emotions 180
Principles at Work in Making Soup 182
Suffering and Stress 183
Compulsiveness and Addictive Behaviors 184
Smooth-Floor Syndrome 185
A Personal Example of Self-Sabotage 186
Teasing Thoughts/Solo Syndrome 187
Self-Sabotage: A Sign of Substitute Sense of Self–oriented Activity 188
Summary and Looking Ahead 189

Chapter 9. Harmful Effects of the Addiction to Approval 191
Anger and Rage 192
Substitute Sense of Self–oriented Fears 196
Anxiety 197
Fear of Your Own Emotions 198
Fear of Your Own Behavior 199
Fear of Not Being Able to Function 201
Fear of Change 202
Fear of Failure 202
Stage Fright 203
Summary and Looking Ahead 206
Chapter 10. Impact on Your Life 207
Unhealthy Motivations 207
A Lack of Integrity – Body Language 209
Indirect Motivation and a Career in Classical Music 210
Limited Access to Achieving Success 211
Know *WHY* you do what you do! 213
Pleading for Compassion and Early Understanding 214
Summary and Looking Ahead 215
PART III. RECOVERY 217
Chapter 11. The Restored Sense of Self 219
What Is a Restored Sense of Self? 220
A Restored Sense of Self versus a Natural Sense of Self 221
The Benefits of a Restored Sense of Self 222
How a Restored Sense of Self Feels 223
Quality-of-Life Experience 224
Measuring Stress Levels as an Indicator for Approval-Oriented Activity 224
The Challenges to Restoring Your Sense of Self 227
The Pull of the Black Hole 228
The Magic Cane 229
Habits and Backsliding 229
Beware of Denial 230
An Addiction 231
My Own Recovery Process 234
Fear and Blame 234
Special Challenges in Recovering from the Compulsion to Perform Ego-References 235
Discover Your Stressors 237
Tools and Time Are Needed 238
Achieving a Restored Sense of Self *Is* Possible 239
Looking Inward 239
Willingness to Be Honest with Yourself 241

The Aggressive Nature of Indirect Motivations 241
The Challenge of Being Honest 241
Summary and Looking Ahead 243

Chapter 12. Recovery from the Addiction to a Substitute Sense of Self 245
Motivation Check A Tool to Detect Indirect Motivation 245
Indirect Motivation is Highly Personalized 246
How Do You Recognize Indirect Motivation? 254
Helpful Tip 256
The Stages to Restoring Your Sense of Self 256
The Stages of Change 256
Stage 1: Pre-contemplation 257
Stage 2: Contemplation 257
Stage 3: Preparation 259
Stage 4: Action 259
Stage 5: Maintenance 260
Recovery from the Addiction to a Substitute Sense of Self 263
A Word of Caution 264
Summary and Looking Ahead 265

Chapter 13. Learning to Sense Your Self 267
The SoS Method 269
Preparing for the Twelve SoS Reconditioning Statements 271
The Twelve SoS Self-Assessment Statements 272
The Twelve SoS Reconditioning Statements 273
Summary and Looking Ahead 275

Chapter 14. The Twelve SoS Reconditioning Statements 277
I. My Life and My Body Are Mine 278
The Three M's: Master, Manager, Maintenance 278
Sense Your Body Activity 279
Variation 1 281
Variation 2 281
Variation 3 281
Variation 4 282
II. I Experience Myself Directly 282
Direct Relationship with Self Activity 284
III. I Am Present to the Here and Now 285
Reality Awareness Activity 286
IV. I Think for Myself 287
Think for Yourself Activity 287
V. I Am Consciously Aware of My Senses 289
Primary Senses Activity 289
VI. I Have Access to My Own Feelings, Preferences, and Opinions 290
Discover the True You Activity 291

VII. I See Other People for Who They Are 292
People Living in Their Own Bubble 293
Being Egocentric Is Okay 294
Direct Motivation Creates a Better World 294
Personal Bubble Activity 295
VIII. I Have Conversations to Transfer Information or to Connect with Others 296
Awareness of Your Problem 297
I Am Already 297
Compulsion to Endlessly Prolong Phone Calls 298
Conversation Awareness Activity 298
IX. My Work is Aimed at the Obvious, Direct Outcome 299
Work for Work's Sake Activity 300
X. Relapse Is Always Lurking 300
Sidestepping the Black Hole Activity 302
XI. I Am Ready to Share My Life with Others 303
Warning 304
Centering Activity 304
XII. I Am Ready to Be a Part of and Contribute to a Healthy Community! 305
Reconditioning Activity 306
Summary and Looking Ahead 307

CHAPTER 15. ON THE THRESHOLD … AFFIRMATIONS, AWARENESS EXERCISES, AND ADVICE 309
Affirmations 309
I Already AM 310
I Accept That Others Create and Have a Life, Just as I Do 310
I Feel Good about Myself No Matter What! 310
I Practice Constant Body Awareness 310
I Am Aware of the Always-Lurking Suction of the Black Hole 311
I No Longer Need to Comply with Other People's Wishes Because I No Longer Fear Rejection. 312
Awareness Exercises 313
Try to Reconstruct the Path to Your Substitute Sense of Self Aloud 313
Practice Mindfulness and Being in the Moment 314
Methods of Self-Optimization and Problem-Solving 315
Advice on the Threshold … 315
Hold On to Your Newly Restored Sense of Self Using Arts and Crafts 316
Learn Your List of Ego-References Using the Motivation Checklist 317
Become Fluent with the Glossary Terms 317
Know What You Are All About! 317
Create a Short Overview of Your Former Indirect Motivation 317
Pay Attention to the Lurking Relapse 318

New Freedom, New Now 319
Being Happy for No Reason! 320
Visualization 320
The Magic Formula 320
Summary and Looking Ahead 321

PART IV. THOUGHTS AND CONCLUSIONS 323

CHAPTER 16. SELF AND SENSE OF SELF 325
What Is the Self? 325
Lack of Sensing, Not a Lack of Self 327
The Layers of Self 327
Layer 1: The Unconscious Spiritual Self 327
Layer 2: The Layer of the Incarnated (Body) Self 327
Layer 3: The Self Experienced as a Conscious Thought-Form 328
Layer 4: The Psycho-Emotional Functions 328
Layer 5: The Social Self 329
Layer 6: The Conscious Spiritual Self 329
Healthy Layers Form a Healthy Sense of Self 330
The Sense of Self 330
The Natural Sense of Self 331
The Substitute Sense of Self 332
The Layers of the Substitute Sense of Self 333
The Substitute Sense of Self – A Natural, Inevitable Development 337
Defining *Sensing* 338
A Direct Relationship with Your Self 338
An Indirect Relationship with Your Self 339
A Sense of Self Is an Action, Not an Object 340
Self-Esteem Requires a Sense of Self 340
Summary and Looking Ahead 341

CHAPTER 17. MAPS FOR RESTORING YOUR SENSE OF SELF 343
Introduction of the Maps for Restoring Your Sense of Self 343
Do These Maps Apply to You? 344
The Maps as a Tool in Your Healing Toolkit 345
Map of a Natural Sense of Self 346
Map of a Lack of Sense of Self 346
Map for Restoring your Sense of Self 349
Summary and Looking Ahead 350

CHAPTER 18. THE SOS SOLUTION 351
Insomnia 352
The Way out of Insomnia 353
Encouragement to Look Within 354
Depression 354
Root Causes of Common Depression 355
Depression Due to Changes in Circumstances Outside Yourself 356

A Few Illustrative Scenarios 356
Warning for People in Recovery 358
Hope 358
The Way out of Depression 359
Addiction to Alcohol 360
Dual Problem 361
The Way out of Addiction 362
Implement Sense of Self Method in Treatment Centers 362
Resources 363
Compulsiveness 363
Compulsive Training 363
My Own Dependency 364
Closing 365
AFTERWORD 367
GLOSSARY 371
ACKNOWLEDGMENTS 379
SHORT OVERVIEW OF THE SENSE OF SELF METHOD 383
ABSTRACT OF THE SENSE OF SELF METHOD 385
Introduction 385
The Problem 386
The Method 386
The Results 387
Conclusion 388
ABOUT THE AUTHOR 389
VISION AND MISSION STATEMENT OF HEALTHYSENSEOFSELF ® 391
Vision 391
Mission Statement 391
OVERVIEW HYSOS RESOURCES 393
KIRKUS REVIEW 397
Title Information 397
Book Review 397
INDEX 399

Foreword to the Third Edition

A decade has gone by since the first edition of this book was published under the name: *Healthy Sense of Self, How to Be True to Your Self and Make Your World a Better Place!*

That title seemed long, but it summed up the topic. The content of the original version of the book has been trimmed since then, as it is clearly a challenge to explain a new theory in such a way that people immediately resonate with it. Especially for someone like me who is not an academic writer and who is untrained in verbalizing scientific theories.

The term Sense of Self was rarely used (if at all) when I originally began writing on this topic. Back then, the term even seemed to be a stumbling block for people who thought it sounded too "touchy feely." To circumvent this issue, we decided on another, more robust title for the second edition: *The Motivation Cure, the Secret to Being Your Best Self.*

Today, at the time of this writing (May 2020), the concept of the Sense of Self is much more widely understood and accepted, and it's become a hot topic among therapists and other psychology professionals. So, we restored the original title while preserving the subtitle from the second edition. This is a fortunate combination, if you ask me. I hope you agree and enjoy the revelation of the Sense of Self Theory and Method on your own personal journey to becoming your best Self.

Antoinetta Vogels
Bellevue, WA, May 24, 2020

"If a positive model of desire is established early, then the baby will grow up with natural desires that match its true needs. A psychologically healthy person, in fact, can be defined as someone whose desires actually produce happiness. But if the baby is imprinted with the opposite notion, that its desires are shameful and are only grudgingly met, then desire won't develop in a healthy way. In later years, the adult will keep searching for fulfillment in externals, needing more and more power, money, or sex to fill a void that was created in his or her sense of self as a baby; the person's very sense of being is judged to be wrong."

Deepak Chopra, *The Way of the Wizard*

Introduction

The Start of My Inner Quest

The development of the Sense of Self Method began nearly thirty years ago as my personal quest, as a new mother, to end insomnia. Little did I know that it would be an ongoing discovery of misconceptions I had about life and living. I had to face them one by one while I was finding out that they were mainly based on one thing: the absence of awareness that *I was my own person*. As such, what I did or did not do had consequences mainly for myself and for nobody else. I needed to learn – to understand – that *my* quality of life was the only thing at stake. Somehow I had developed the anxiety-provoking point of view that my *being seen by others* (read: truly existing as a person) depended on the outcome of my achievements or behavior. In other words, I was not present to myself.

To get access to and make sense of what was playing on a subconscious level, I had to dig deep into myself. Reading on, you too must be prepared to leave behind most of your everyday thoughts and feelings. Imagine you are going down a spiral stairway that leads into the dungeons of your mind. As you descend, you are continuously turning yourself around to inevitably face your inner demons chained to the walls of ill-lit compartments. With the determination needed to pursue this route, it may happen that you'll come to a point where you are so in touch with your Self that you almost pick up on the sound of your own blood gently rushing through your veins.

To begin your experience of the Sense of Self Method, you can select an action or activity that has been keeping you preoccupied. For this purpose, you may choose a particular exercise you often perform or a piece of music you play. Other activities, such as staying on good terms with your children or students, or the effort of becoming successful in business may also be selected. In short, select any challenge in your life right now that requires your complete devotion. Record your thoughts and feelings about this action or activity, and measure the results you get with it in a given moment. Whatever action or activity you choose, you will notice a considerable positive difference after successfully completing the work in this book.

This book is meant to be the solid foundation for a growing business, as well as for ongoing research and future educational projects. The Sense of Self Method, as well as the theory behind it, is my contribution to a better life for each individual on a personal level and, on a bigger scale, for the world at large. Here is how it all started:

It was 1985 and my daughter was three months old; it was time for me to return to work. I was a bassoonist in the Amsterdam Philharmonic Orchestra (The Netherlands), and my extended maternity leave had come to an end.

Why was I suddenly unable to drift off into a well-deserved and refreshing sleep, just when I needed it most? Being a new mother is quite a challenge by itself; it was even more challenging because my first-born child came prematurely, and she was as tiny as a Barbie Doll. Caring for my baby and getting back to work as a musician required a clear mind and a well-rested body, but no … I couldn't sleep!

"No doubt I'm having trouble adjusting to my new situation. I trust it will gradually resolve itself," I thought reassuringly. But it didn't. One night I would sleep reasonably well, and the next two nights I would get little to no sleep at all. Not that I actually worried about anything while lying in bed; no, my mind was totally blank. Nothing stirred. I had no idea what was going on.

In the months that followed the onset of my insomnia, I tried to cope in many ways. "Have a glass of hot milk before you go to bed," was my mother's advice. "Try a glass of red wine," a well-meaning friend suggested. "Stop doing anything an hour before you go to bed and practice relaxation exercises," was someone else's advice. "No coffee for you," I was summoned by many people. "No garlic and no peppers," was the remedy offered by a Tibetan healer, along with his prescription of a great number of bitter brown pills that made no difference. My doctor provided me with sleep medications, and yes, they did put me to sleep. However, the moment I stopped taking them, it was over. I could not sleep anymore. As medical causes for my constant insomnia were ruled out, I despaired: "What else is left for me now but a lifetime of medication?"

I refused to start that journey. I believed that sleeping is a natural process, and if my sleep was being thwarted, there *had* to be a reason. So I chose my path of trying to find the cause and the cure for what kept me awake at night, which was damaging my quality of life. It affected my ability to mother my child, maintain my health, and resume my career, not to mention what it was doing to the lives of my other family members.

In hindsight, I can say that I had more problems than just insomnia. This included an extreme temper: if things did not go the way I wanted, I would erupt in anger and blame everybody and the world for it. My co-musicians complained that they felt I lacked team spirit. I had frequent colds on crucial performance days and a sore throat whenever I made a commitment to sing. "Your timing is off in ensemble-playing," my colleagues pointed out candidly. Even my best friend expressed her concern about my behavior.

I tried changing things *outside* myself: practicing like crazy, taking more lessons, and getting help at home. Nothing I tried produced the desired result. Looking *outside* of myself didn't really help with the problems, so gradually I began to notice what was going on *inside* of me. I started to observe my thoughts and behavior. I delved deeper into all the things I was worrying about instead of pushing them away. "What are my motives for what I do or for what I try to avoid?" I wondered. "What is the underlying reason for my explosions of rage, which seem so out of proportion with what actually takes place in those moments?"

A MiniDisc recorder became my confidante. I began to record my thoughts and feelings; later, I listened to what I had said. For twenty-five years, I talked to my recorder and studied myself, trying to make sense of what motivated me. I discovered that rather than making conscious decisions, my choices were based on subconscious motives. Decades later, an understanding of what was really going on in my mind began to emerge – I started to notice things that had previously been totally outside the spotlight of my awareness. I was shocked to find that I had what I later came to call a **Hidden Agenda**.

I discovered that I had underlying motives and that some of the emotions I experienced on a daily basis were actually reactions to these things instead of to the things that happened in my everyday reality.

To my surprise, I realized I had many fears. So I followed the trail back to its starting place, and I finally learned what kept me imprisoned. I started to understand that certain motives that stemmed from my early childhood and adolescence were still active in me *as an adult*. However, I still had yet to understand the reasons for my fears or for my insomnia. At that point, all I was able to create was a map, and as we all know, "the map is not the territory."[1] However, this map proved very useful to me in changing the territory of my life, both internally and externally.

Many years later, I was able to describe the root of many of my problems; they stemmed from an unhealthy relationship with my mother. Unknowingly, an enmeshment had formed between myself and the woman who had raised me. Trying to live up to her conditions kept me spellbound. This state of enmeshment prevented me from developing any sense of being my own unique and potentially autonomous Self. As my situation became clearer, I came up with ways to change the effects of my childhood experiences. I more or less reconditioned myself. Restoring my **Sense of Self (SoS)** took all of my time and energy, and filled my waking hours for many years, as if it were my day job.

Paradoxically, the sleepless nights, as annoying and disruptive for my life as they were, also brought me valuable insights. Desperate

[1] Quote attributed to Alfred Korzybski, founder of the field of study of General Semantics.

and determined to survive, like an antelope trying to free itself from the claws of a lion, I held on to my scripted reconditioning statements, which you can find in Chapter 14.

Finally, I was sleeping better, and many of my other problems diminished as well. Ultimately, they vanished, and my quality of life and that of my loved ones improved accordingly.

As I came to understand my own inner workings, I suspected I was not unique. I was sure others had similar problems and similar inner workings. That was when I realized that my solutions might help others, and I decided to write them down.

Thus, in this book, I share with you the deviations that formed my perceived and misguided reality, which I call the Sense of Self Theory, as well as how I enabled myself to get my power back, which I call the Sense of Self Method. I hope that others may benefit and that my insights speed up your processes toward a better quality of life.

Something Was Missing: My Sense of Self

In my search for the truth, I made an unexpected discovery – one that I dreaded to even say aloud. It was the hardest truth I ever had to face, and even now, it chills my heart.

What in life is more sacred than a mother? The role and function of a mother is revered and idealized by most people in most cultures. Therefore, I had great difficulty finding support among my family (father, brother, and sister) or even among friends, when contemplating the possibility that there might be any fault in the relationship between my mother and me. Even the Bible protects her: *"Honor your father and your mother."* But how could I respectfully find a solution for my problem if I were not allowed to question the commonly accepted picture of the all-encompassing motherly love: deeply loving her child while allowing and encouraging them to be his/her Self?

Could I even allow myself to look at my mother and conclude that she, like everybody else, was just a person who had her own demons to fight?

What I found was that I had never felt acknowledged, respected, or valued as a unique human being, which had thwarted the development of my own Sense of Self. I started to see how this Lack of Sense of Self was then reinforced during other critical moments in my life. I realized that I had made poor decisions because they were never based on a healthy sense of my own personhood. I began to consciously understand that something fundamental was missing within me.

Sense of Self (SoS)

A conscious and/or subconscious awareness of existing independently as a unique and potentially autonomous human being.

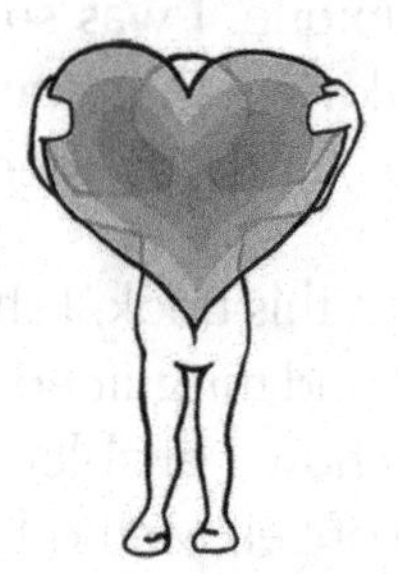

With a shock, I became aware that the overall goal of my life, so far, had been to try to find *what* was missing. I was always busy trying to get a hold of that unknown factor that set me apart from others and incorporate it into my life. I studied the behavior and inner workings of others by asking them to describe how they perceived themselves: what their Self felt like and how they were sure their motivations stemmed from that source called Self.

I learned that many other people had a completely different inner framework and were less anxious and frantic. I compared what they clearly had to my own condition to figure out what I was missing. This was when I discovered that having a **Healthy Sense of Self** was essential for leading a happy and productive life.

Instead of having an inner home base for my "me-ness," I depended on getting approval, mainly from my mother and other significant people in my life, such as teachers, bosses, and colleagues to whom I had given the power to allow or deny me my right of existence.

I had internalized most of my parents' opinions and judgments about myself after having focused on them throughout my life. I call that the **Internalized Parental Voice (IPV)**. I used to mistake that IPV for my own voice; I had no idea that my caregivers' influence was so overwhelming that it dominated my mind. Only in the moments after I had gained the approval of my IPV, could I experience a sense of safety.

Internalized Parental Voice (IPV)

The often-repeated verbal and nonverbal messages that parents, knowingly or unknowingly, transmit to their children becomes (almost?) hardwired in the child's mind so that it is perceived as an unquestionable truth (about and) by the child.

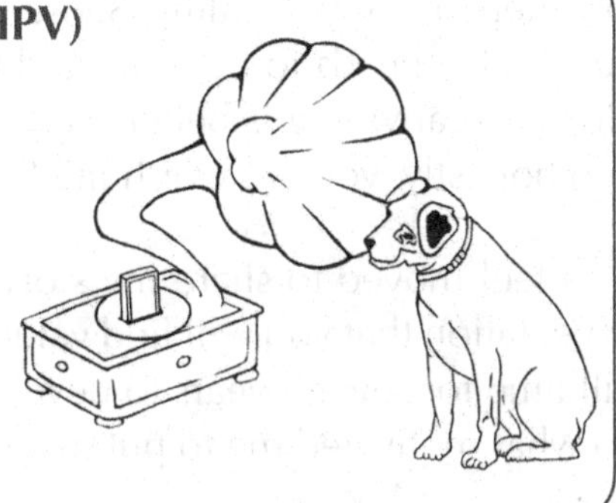

Eventually, I became more and more aware of the fact that these brief moments of "Feeling-good-about-myself" were not only unhealthy; they were a poor substitute for a Healthy Sense of Self. I diagnosed myself as having a "Lack of Sense of Self" and began investigating what I used to rely upon for my self-experience.

Putting My Insights to Use

The picture looked pretty bleak, but at least I had a picture. I now understood I had to come up with my "real" Sense of Self. What I had to do was to find out what having a Healthy Sense of Self actually meant. What was it that I had to implement within myself to restore my own truncated, thwarted Sense of Self?

Out of my inner nothingness (the Lack of Sense of Self), I embarked on a journey seeking to generate some kind of inner core of "me-ness" that would not be dependent on the approval of others or on the approval of my IPV.

Since then, my quality of life has greatly improved. I am happier, healthier, more playful, and more successful. Initially I fell back into my old way of thinking quite a bit, and I still need to refresh my reconditioning every so often. By doing that, I am able to reach again, on the deepest level, the certainty that my being and my doing are separate. In order to be, I do not have to do; in order to do, I first have to be, then I have the choice of doing or not doing. My being is no longer dependent on my doing.

I can say wholeheartedly that getting into the right mindset and experiencing my Healthy Sense of Self comes more easily every day. It also needs to be indicated that my method is not a quick fix. However, anything is better than skipping your own life altogether – and honestly, you are worth the time it takes to do this right!

I feel moved to share my story and my findings in the hope and expectation that you will find value in it. I have devoted myself nearly full time for several years to developing the materials in front of you. So what motivated me to put in so much effort?

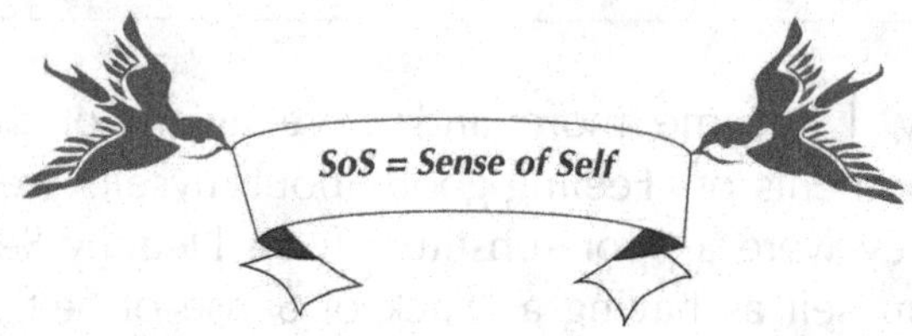

In the course of my healing and recovery process, I have come to see that by making your own Sense of Self healthier, you can break the vicious cycle of passing down an unhealthy SoS from one generation to the next within your family. Once you have taken care of your own Sense of Self, you will be able to effectively facilitate a Healthy Sense of Self in your children. If this could be achieved on a worldwide scale, everyone's quality of life would improve drastically, as there would be less violence, less war, and less human suffering.

I take pride in my life's journey and hope you can learn from my experiences and then join me in my mission to make this world a better place. Sharing my findings with you, and with the rest of the world, fulfills a vow I made as a four-year-old girl looking at the ruins of World War II.[2]

[2] The logic behind this reasoning will become clear as you read on. Once you understand the impact the absence of a Healthy SoS has on people's behavior, choices, and actions, you'll see how that can have a major impact on the lives of everyone around them.

My Vow as a Little Girl

I was born in the Netherlands right after World War II. Even though I was not alive *during* the war, I vividly recall listening to my father's stories about the horrors of the Holocaust. I remember walking with him over the ruins of the city in which he was born and raised, Groningen. The atrocious acts of war I learned about, in detail, as a four year old, are forever stored in my memory. Is it any wonder that I made a firm decision, a vow to myself, that I *had* to do something to make wars stop?

Little did I know at the time that life would offer me an opportunity to contribute to the understanding of human behavior by having me grow up with a Lack of Sense of Self. Through the task of figuring out what was off in my life, I gained a deep understanding of what is off with the world and, with that, what could be done to heal it.

Ending the *war within* yourself by restoring your Sense of Self will lead you to a happier and more productive life. Finding your "inner home" may also help prevent the small personal wars that you might experience between family members, coworkers, or neighbors.

I have a dream that the widespread application of the Sense of Self Method can help prevent war on a larger scale. Let me start with hoping, though, that the Sense of Self Method will help you and your loved ones become more peaceful and successful on a personal level, as well as allow you to live up to your potential.

This is how this book was born. Now get ready to work your way toward the goal of reducing and hopefully eradicating your suffering!

Figure I.1: Me at age four, with my father in my birthplace: Boskoop, Netherlands.

What This Book Presents: The Sense of Self Method

This book offers a holistic theory as the foundation for a self-help method based on the belief that many symptoms of human suffering are rooted in a Lack of Sense of Self. Symptoms of a Lack of Sense of Self can show up in your physical, mental, and emotional health, as well as various dysfunctional social and societal aspects of your life.

This work addresses the child in every person. It hopes to shed a light on how your development into a healthy, fully functioning adult can be hindered during childhood. Distortions in your psycho-emotional system are the result. These abnormalities, in turn, can result in physical, psychological, emotional, and social problems. This work is not a general theory of psychology but rather an expanded first-person case study of abnormal development. The method is holistic (integrated) in the sense that it talks about the mind, emotions, and body as mutually interactive and interdependent.

This method is not an abstract exercise; it aims at improving your quality of life. The purpose of this work is to:

1. Help you recognize whether you rely on a **Substitute Sense of Self** for your self-experience.
2. Find the cause of why and how this happened.
3. Have you accept and face your condition based on these insights.
4. Eliminate the power your unhealthy past has in your present.
5. Ultimately replace your Substitute Sense of Self with a **Restored Sense of Self**.

This book consists of four parts:

• **Part I**: An introduction to the Sense of Self Theory and Method with a focus on how the various concepts link together, providing a full picture of the unhealthy mental and emotional makeup of a person with a Lack of Sense of Self.

• **Part II**: Descriptions and examples of how this situation plays out in the life of a person with a Lack of Sense of Self.

• **Part III**: This section is dedicated to the recovery from the dependency on a Substitute Sense of Self. It includes a procedure for you to follow – The Twelve SoS Reconditioning Statements – plus more exercises and educational suggestions to restore your Sense of Self.

• **Part IV**: Some explicit and more in-depth elaboration of some of the foundational concepts of the Sense of Self Theory and Method.

Who Might Benefit from Working with This Method?

It is likely that you will be able to improve your quality of life if any of the following describes you:

- Something is "off," but you are unable to figure out what it is.
- You know you are not living up to your potential.
- Doctors and therapists don't seem to make you better.
- You have relationship challenges: marriage, children, social, and/or professional.
- You are addicted to work or other activities or behaviors.
- It is difficult for you to stay sober.
- You are in pain physically or emotionally.

Who would think that there are people walking around in this life without a Sense of Self? What does that actually imply? Please, don't discard the idea too quickly just because you think it's unusual and therefore it doesn't apply to you – or because you don't like the idea of applying it to yourself. The degree to which denial plays a role in all this is impressive. There *are* many people walking around *without* a Healthy Sense of Self.

The solution is to restore or strengthen your Sense of Self. Then you will no longer be ruled by unhealthy (and, in hindsight, completely obsolete and unnecessary) subconscious motivations. Based on my experience, I have found that an astounding variety of issues that affect a person's well-being and quality of life seem to all come down to the root cause of lacking a Healthy Sense of Self. Some of these problems include, but are not limited to, the following:

Addiction	Learning problems/lack of focus in children
Anger issues and rage	Marital problems
Anxiety	Nervousness
Being easily upset	Relapse during recovery from addiction
Depression	Relationship problems
Fatigue	Self-sabotage
Headaches	Too much drama
Insomnia	Work-related problems

Depending on the person, the symptoms and problems show up differently and vary with circumstances. The strength of the Sense of Self Method is that it functions as an umbrella for the solution of a great number of ailments and dysfunctions.

No pills, potions, doctor's visits, new religion, or new technology are needed to help yourself through the Sense of Self Method, though some people might benefit from or even require professional assistance. Understanding and applying the Sense of Self Method can suffice to give you the tools to solve a variety of issues and deeply enhance your life!

What Is Required from You?

Finding the answers to your unique challenges requires your open-minded willingness to explore your thoughts and feelings and being honest about what you find. I offer you suggestions of what to look for and solutions that worked for me. The method is logical and easy to understand. There are stories and examples, and the basics are repeated every so often. Once you understand the ideas presented here, you are well on your way to your own healing!

If you already have a (Natural) Healthy Sense of Self, you can use this book to help yourself understand your clients, friends, or family members who are suffering from symptoms that can be caused by a Lack of Sense of Self.

Healthy Sense of Self

The ability to experience and be present to your own person and to your own life and recognize both as uniquely owned by YOU. That includes the right to live and be as your Self and experience your innermost core as your ultimate home from where you live your life.

The Sense of Self Method will remain a living work in progress for some time to come. I invite you to share your thoughts with me at research@healthysenseofself.com, thus helping to turn this work from a theory into an even more practical healing method so we can reach more people and give them a chance to improve their quality of life.

I salute our journey together. I invite your participation. Please share whatever you think can help others cultivate a Healthy Sense of Self, so that together, we cause a positive ripple on the ocean of the lives of all of us amazing people.

Benefits of a Healthy Sense of Self

Below is a list of benefits the Sense of Self Method claims to help people achieve when they successfully restore their Sense of Self. For the purpose of clarity, I've arranged these benefits into categories based on the topics they're most aligned with.

Addiction

- Less substance abuse
- Fewer cravings
- Less compulsion to give in to addictive behavior
- Less desire to escape reality

Aging

- Potentially less susceptible to age-related diseases
- More feelings of fulfillment
- Less worried about/more accepting of aging appearance
- Greater enjoyment found in retirement and the golden years
- Greater desire to maintain health for improved longevity

Anxiety and despair

- Fewer panic attacks
- Fewer rages
- Decreased depression
- No suicidal thoughts or acts

- Less erratic behavior
- Increased feelings of joy, happiness, and contentment
- Increased vitality and success
- More self-acceptance and acceptance of others

Child rearing

- More patience
- Better parenting skills
- Fewer family upsets
- More respect for children's needs
- Improved overall well-being for the child
    - Less distracted
    - Increased desire to learn
    - Better performance in school
    - Better relationships with teachers and peers
    - Less rebellion

General health and well-being

- Better overall health
- Better sleep
- More awareness of personal health needs
- Healthier habits
- Less stress, which leads to fewer stress-related ailments
- Less eyestrain
- Fewer migraines and headaches
- Better functioning digestive system
- More relaxed nervous system
- Less prone to accidents caused by a lack of focus or awareness
- More vibrant and active

Harmful or destructive behavior

- Fewer outbursts
- Less uncontrollable behavior (i.e. temper tantrums, meltdowns)
- Less over-reactive
- Less retaliation or desire for revenge against perceived wrongs
- Less violence
- Fewer fights and arguments
- More responsible, controlled behavior
- Less careless spending and fewer issues with money
- More in tune with common sense
- Greater desire to be part of a healthy community
- Greater desire to be a functioning member of society

Professional success

- Clearer understanding of talents, abilities, and limitations
- Better focus at work
- Less prone to workplace injuries
- Less vulnerable to workplace bullying
- Better relationships with coworkers and managers
- Better equipped for teamwork
- Better equipped to deal with criticism
- Better able to communicate and defend ideas
- More confident when asking for a raise/promotion
- More in tune with personal goals
- More likely to achieve goals
- Less fear of failure

Relationships

- Better chance to find, give, and receive love
- Less controlling of others and situations
- Increased comfort with being around others

- Increased comfort with being alone
- Better companion
- Better social skills
- Better communication skills
- Better able to recognize healthy and unhealthy relationships
- Lower chances for divorce (in a healthy marriage)

Self-realization

- Higher overall quality of life
- More self-confidence
- Less self-critical
- More self-accepting
- No self-sabotage
- More realistic – more real
- Better balance between head and heart; genuine and integrated feelings
- More compassion and empathy
- Less self-sacrificing
- Better able to define and defend personal boundaries
- More comfortable with self-expression
- Clearer sense of personal preferences, tastes, and opinions
- Better sense of personal desires
- Better aligned with personal "blueprint"
- More inner peace
- Able to self-realize and live life to the fullest

The Twelve SoS Reconditioning Statements

The Twelve SoS Reconditioning Statements are the keys to curing your **Motivation** and unlocking your best Self.

Please take a moment to familiarize yourself with these statements now. Eventually, you will come to know them by heart. However, you first need to learn how to identify the nature of your motivation and gain enough insight into your early childhood experiences. Then you will be ready to shake off the shackles of your old self. In Chapter 14, we will delve into the details of how to put these statements to positive use so you can begin living life with more mental and emotional freedom.

I	My life and my body are mine.
II	I experience myself directly.
III	I am present to the Here and Now.
IV	I think for myself.
V	I am consciously aware of my senses.
VI	I have access to my own feelings, preferences, and opinions.
VII	I see other people for who they are.
VIII	I have conversations to transfer information or to connect with others.
IX	My work is aimed at the obvious, direct outcome.
X	Relapse is always lurking.
XI	I am ready to share my life with others.
XII	I am ready to be part of a healthy community.

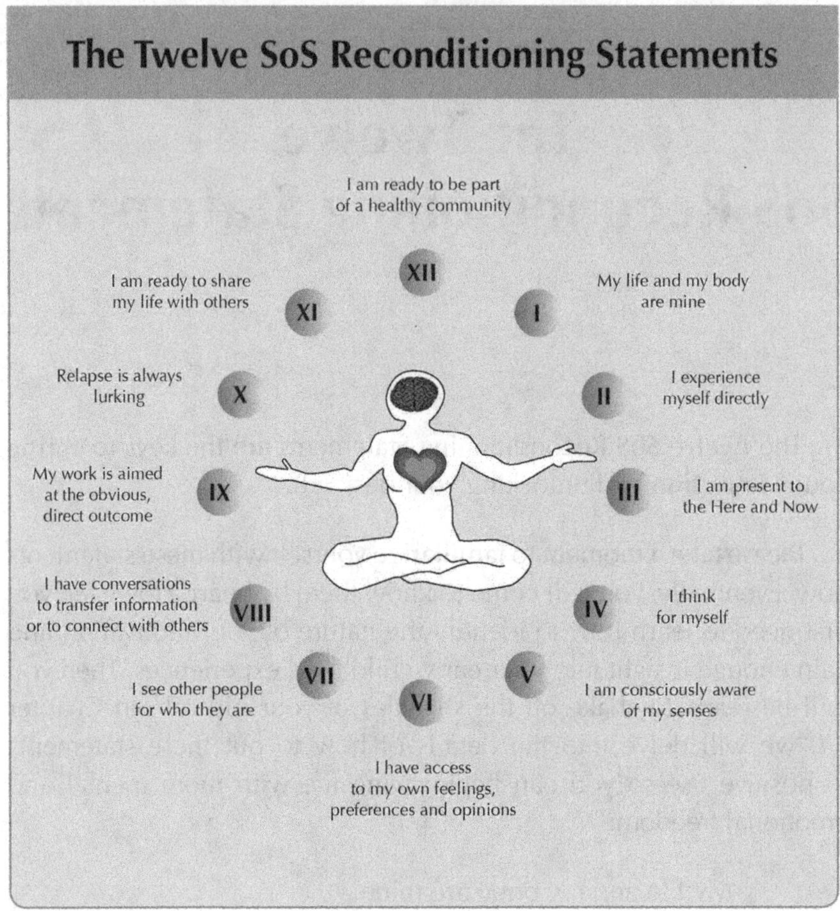

Figure 0.1: The Twelve SoS Reconditioning Statements.

Part I

The Sense of Self Theory

Chapter 1

The Sense of Self Theory & Method

What is it like not to have a **Natural Sense of Self**? The question is hard to pose, let alone to answer. How is it possible to explain the lack of something you never had in the first place? In the Introduction, I described how I found out I lacked something other people seemed to have. Here is an example of a situation that helped me to see a small light that grew into a beacon in my jungle of darkness.

> *"Please don't be mad at me," I begged my husband every time I vented my annoyance at him when I was unable to fall asleep. "I'm not really angry at you, but I am angry at the fact that I don't sleep. I can't keep myself from getting upset and I need to let it out."*
>
> *He understood, and so we went on like that for many years. However, at some point he said, "I don't quite understand you. Are you not the one in control of this anger? You choose to either be angry or not. Then, if you choose to be angry, you also choose how to express yourself."*
>
> *I simply could not find within myself any power, force, or will that was capable of such a choice. Based on this and other similar conclusions, I deduced that he must have something inside himself that I did not have. So I started to pay attention and look more closely at this concept.*

Natural Sense of Self

The subconscious sense – developed normally in childhood – of being alive as a "real," definite person, with the unconditional right to exist as who you are, regardless of what others think, feel, or say about you.

A Lack of Sense of Self Causes a Substitute Sense of Self

When a Natural Sense of Self does not develop, there is a Lack of Sense of Self. In its place, another structure develops: a Substitute Sense of Self. It fills in (substitutes) for the functions and services that a Natural Sense of Self would provide and masks the Lack of Sense of Self.

Characteristics of a Lack of Sense of Self

If you lack a Sense of Self, you don't have the sensation of being at home within your very own being – you have no anchor that keeps you from drifting, no source to base your decisions on, other than the criteria of the Substitute Sense of Self that has developed in its place.

Lack of Sense of Self

Characteristic of a person who never developed a natural, ongoing inner knowing that he or she is truly alive as a "real," independent human being.

People with a **Lack of Sense of Self** are, among other things, highly sensitive to criticism and extremely irritable. They have a great need to perform to perfection because they have to live up to expectations, called **Ego-References** (more on those in Chapter 7).

A deeply felt restlessness leads them to extremes in many aspects of life – for example, not settling down, not being able to stay with one partner, and not staying in one field of study or work. There is a continuous changing of jobs, an inability to be a good parent, and an overall lack of focus and consistency. In short, people with a Lack of Sense of Self do not know where to go, what to do, or why they should do something. It might appear that they are extremely motivated, but deep down, they are driven by their compulsions that are based on their fear of **Annihilation**.

Ego-References

Subconsciously accepted requirements to feel and behave in certain ways and achieve certain results in order to feel approved of, as a substitute for a healthy way of experiencing the Self.

Annihilation

A strong perception of being overlooked, not being seen and heard, not being taken into account, and not having any impact in one's environment, which is experienced as non-existing.

Detecting a Lack of Sense of Self

Drawing conclusions from my self-exploration was hard. Identifying a lack of something when I had no information on what that something looked or felt like was almost impossible. My Lack of Sense of Self was therefore inferred and/or detected through the presence of a Substitute Sense of Self.

To find out whether or not you have a Lack of Sense of Self, you need to list your issues – the types of ailments or dysfunctions you are plagued by. Next, with your list in hand, take a moment to review the SoS Comparison Chart on page 159. You can also get a quick assessment by completing the Healthy Sense of Self Quiz, available online at www.healthysenseofself.com/the-healthy-sense-of-self-quiz.[1]

To identify a Lack of Sense of Self, you have to pay attention to the presence in your life/body of any of the symptoms that you find in Figure 1.1. This overview highlights some of the states of mind mentioned in the SoS Comparison Chart and serves to measure your Sense of Self. These symptoms and/or dysfunctions can namely result from the stress and exhaustion that accompany a Substitute Sense of Self.

Symptoms of Lack of Sense of Self

- Emotional Roller Coaster
- Excessive Need for "High"
- Fear to Face Your Self
- Out of Touch with Reality
- Inner Turmoil
- Absence of Straight Focus
- Compulsive, Obsessive Behavior
- Insomnia
- Panic Attacks
- Migraines
- Suicidal Thoughts
- Relationship Problems
- Unreasonable Anger, Violence
- Unmanegeable Chronic High Stress
- Chronic Fear of Failure
- Controlling Behavior
- Prone to Motion Sickness
- Fear of Crowds
- Easily Aggravated, Offended
- Highly Sensitive
- "Fluttering" in Nervous system
- Absence of Happiness + Love
- Cramped Muscles
- Issues with Money

Figure 1.1: Symptoms of a Lack of Sense of Self.

A Brief Summary of the Sense of Self Theory

The SoS Theory comprises an integrated approach to understanding an important part of the human condition and offers potential improvements. The body, mind, and emotions are in continuous

[1] The Quiz consists of a series of simple statements that you will quickly rate in present time as true, false, or partly so. Taking the quiz and reviewing the SoS Comparison Chart will enhance your ability to identify the state of your Sense of Self.

communication with one another during all developmental and maturational phases, which impacts the way each person manifests him- or herself in the world at any given moment in time.

Here is what I believe: you are born (as is everyone) with certain qualities and characteristics that define who you truly, uniquely are, but you can only express those qualities when you are free to be yourself. To that purpose, the environment in which you grow up needs to allow that to take place. In other words, if there are fewer obstacles to your developing a healthy mind and body, then your circumstances allow you to live up to your potential. But what happens if there are too many obstacles? What happens to your potential when your development, as it should naturally go, is blocked or distorted by certain circumstances?

I always felt I could have been so much more successful if I hadn't been distracted for such a long time by doing things for the wrong reasons and hadn't been forced to look within to find out what was off with me. If I could have spent all that energy and focus on my profession, I would have been much better at it, and I could have gotten more value from my education. Perhaps I would not have chosen to become a professional musician at all and would have found great satisfaction as a psychologist. I would have had, possibly, a lot more people who wanted to be friends with me because I had something to offer instead of being needy and fearful of rejection.

A Sense of Self is one of the most important things that human beings need to develop. The SoS Theory addresses what happens when infants and small children fail to receive sufficient input that is fundamentally necessary to develop a Natural Sense of Self.

If this growth/health-promoting input is missing during infancy and early childhood, a survival mechanism kicks in to help the body, mind, and emotions compensate for that lack. This theory describes how those compensations turn into compulsions that aim at making a person **"Feel-good-about-self"** when, without a Sense of Self, that is not their natural state. This "Feel-good-about-self" functions as a Substitute Sense of Self but causes mental, emotional, and physical suffering. The SoS Theory describes how to overcome these compulsions and their ill effects.

Compulsions are natural, instinctive responses to unmet needs during the critical period when a child should be developing their Natural Sense of Self. At a very young age, coping conclusions are drawn, which eventually lead to the development of a survival mechanism: **Early Childhood Survival Strategy (ECSS)**. This survival mechanism is so overwhelming that you could say it takes over a person's life. That means the major part of what a person wants evolves around fulfilling those compulsive conditions for fear of feeling annihilated or nonexistent.

The SoS Theory deems the absence of a Natural Sense of Self to be a root cause of many ailments and dysfunctions. A Lack of Sense of Self can lie at the bottom of your inability to manifest yourself fully and live up to your inherent potential.

The theory has been developed into a self-healing method that gives you tools to recover from what otherwise would be a lifelong predicament.

The Importance of a Sense of Self

This theory maintains that:

- The development of a Natural Sense of Self is a core aspect of healthy, normal psychological maturation.
- The maturation of a Sense of Self is subject to either healthy or unhealthy development based on behavior of the primary caregiver(s) toward the child.
- A lack of a Natural Sense of Self leads automatically to dependency on a Substitute Sense of Self for self-experience, which is one of the root causes of human suffering.

To improve the human condition, it is crucial that all people be educated in developing, strengthening, or restoring a Healthy Sense of Self in themselves as well as fostering a Natural Sense of Self in their children.

Human suffering refers to the array of issues that create a lack of well-being, from personal unhappiness to war. It includes physical disease, from the common cold to serious illnesses; conflicts and disagreements; psycho-emotional ailments and mental challenges of all sorts such as depression, insomnia, learning disabilities, moodiness, and attention deficit/hyperactivity disorder. Human suffering includes family dysfunction, child abuse, suicide, violence, crime, and war!

It may be unrealistic to believe we could eradicate all disease and dysfunction or all aggression, violence, conflict, and war from human behavior, because some of it might be evolutionarily innate to the human species. Whether we like it or not, humans are part of the animal kingdom, and animalistic traits will always pop up in our behavior. But if we, as individuals and as members of our families and communities, improve our sense of ourselves, it will change how we relate to one another, and that will ultimately help the world at large.

My own experience has led me to believe that a great deal of human suffering could be reduced or even eliminated if every person were thoroughly in touch with his or her Self. It would lead to more responsible and more self-respecting behavior and, as a consequence, to more respectful behavior toward others. Based on my inner research, I have come to believe that if everyone had a Healthy Sense of Self, everyone's quality of life would be enhanced and world peace would be within reach!

I have a vision in which the awareness, knowledge, and specific skills provided by the SoS Theory and Method ripples out to everyone on the planet. If that were to really happen, the odds of parents establishing a Healthy Sense of Self – first in themselves and then in their children – would be so much better. Once established across two generations, it will take increasingly less effort to make the world a better place for future generations.

The Importance of the Parent/Caregiver

Throughout this book, by "parent," "caregiver," or "primary caregiver," I am referring to whomever provided most of your care from birth on, whether that person is a relative or not. These terms are used interchangeably. At later ages, these positions can include teachers, nannies, sports figures, religious leaders, and other authority figures who may influence a child's Sense of Self.

Whoever raised you and whoever the most important or influential people were in your life can be understood as being your caregivers.

A Sense of Self is something that either develops or does not. That process depends mainly on the nature of the input from the primary caregiver. And because the Sense of Self is so foundational to an individual's ability to function on all levels, I state that the role of the caregiver is crucial to the world. The people who are with the child from birth on are the ones who make the greatest impression on the individual. They are the ones who determine whether a Natural Sense of Self develops in the child. With that, they (unknowingly) more or less determine this person's future quality of life and the impact he or she will have in the world.

So you see, the importance of the primary caregiver in this process is major!

> *Note: Even if you are not a caregiver, the following section pertains to the child in every person, adult or not! When having been given the building blocks to a Healthy Sense of Self, a person becomes emotionally free and independent and consequently a better parent themselves!*

Parents and Caregivers

A caregiver's most positive contribution to society includes having the skill, patience, and psycho-emotional healthiness to connect with their children in a "real," responsible, and truly loving way. Ideally, future parents would spend time working out their issues with their caregivers before having children of their own. This might assure their ability to be fully present for their offspring, not only physically but also psychologically. Only those who feel they have come to terms with their own issues are able to sufficiently care for others.

I am aware that this book presents a rather utopian vision of possibilities in childcare, but I am just pointing in a specific direction, and, as I mentioned before, "the map is not the territory!" If each caregiver could live up to between just 5 and 15 percent of this ideal image, there would be a considerable improvement in this world.

If anybody can make a change in what children become later on in life, it is the primary caregivers. Kindergarten and elementary school teachers are included because their early influence will stay with the children well into their adulthood. The caregivers' behavior toward a child largely determines a very important aspect of their future characteristic: Will they grow up to be helpful and tolerant, or frustrated and violent? Will they be forgiving because they've been blessed with the opportunity to develop a Natural Sense of Self or will they be full of suppressed rage because they were thwarted in developing a connection to their own Self? Will they feel they were "not allowed to be" when unable to live up to specific conditions, which lead to a Substitute Sense of Self taking over their lives?

A Sense of Self, whether healthy or lacking, is the crucial determinant of that difference. Just about anyone can be a parent in name only. Biologically, becoming a parent is not hard, but *being* a parent, especially in today's hyper-connected society, is extremely challenging.

However, if we truly want to change the world at large, more caregivers would assume responsibility and start by gaining insight about themselves. They would learn to "introspect," to look inside, get to know themselves, find out who they actually are, and deal with their own issues. They would then stand a much better chance of lovingly bringing up the next generation.

An Influence Throughout Life

As you grow up and become more autonomous, the direct influence and impact of your caregiver's behavior normally diminishes. This is true for children who have developed a Natural Sense of Self. Yet, if you live in an **Enmeshment** with your caregiver, an unhealthy degree of dependency continues through adulthood and even into old age. In adulthood, the caregiver's influence becomes less visible, less obvious, and is less traceable, but it may still be present in the background – for example, through emails and phone calls. (See Chapter 7 for more on Enmeshment.)

Enmeshment

An unhealthy relationship between child and primary caretaker. The child's identity remains under- or undeveloped and his or her motives stay geared toward getting the adult's approval, which leads to extreme dependence on approval.

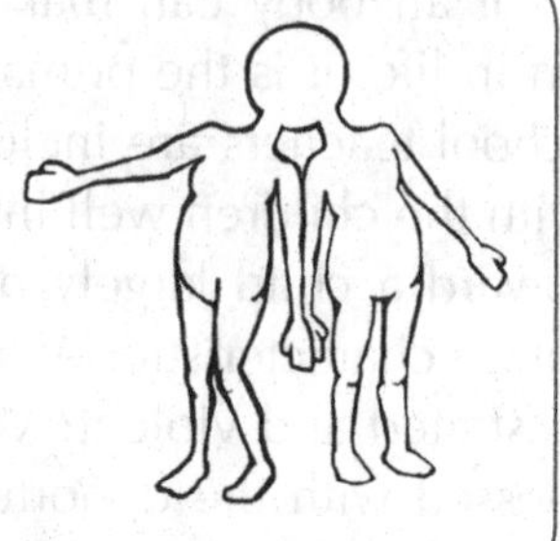

Too often, even as a full-grown adult, you can become terribly stressed when visiting your parents because you feel you are not who your parents want you to be, yet you still need your parents' approval and validation because of your Lack of Sense of Self.

It can be similarly stressful when your parents come to visit. For example, you may find yourself cleaning and organizing like a madwoman because your house never seems to be good enough for your mother. The funny thing is that if someone were to point this behavior out to you, you might prefer to stay in denial and not look at what you are doing and why. You need that approval so desperately that you would prefer to justify your behavior. However, when the stress levels are so much higher than is justified by the actual event, it is likely that deep down inside you feel your Substitute Sense of Self is at stake.

At any age, grown children can be needy whether their parents are alive or not. Adults with a Lack of SoS still hope that by living up to their parents' expectations, they might finally see (even virtually) their deepest wish come true. That wish is to be unconditionally loved, which would make them feel accepted for who they are and thus acknowledged as valuable human beings.

Even if an ocean lies between parents and their grown children, the parents' influence can be just as present as ever within the child's inner life. The parent's standards and criteria still reverberate in his or her head and form the Internalized Parental Voice (IPV), see page 103.

This is valid for the child in every person,
including the child in every parent!

Recently, I once again fell into the trap of thinking I had to behave in a certain way to be a good mother to my children. I was convinced I was a failure as a mother if I had my own personal projects going on. To resolve this conflict, I had to look deeper into the issue because it was causing me to lose sleep.

Through introspection, I found that I was using my mother's criteria instead of my own. Being unable to live up to those *internalized parental conditions* brought me feelings of great fear and anger; you could almost call it terror. Distinguishing what I really think of things for myself and putting aside with peaceful conviction the other voice in my head was what was needed, and it was not as easy as it might sound.

Unfortunately, most adults in this situation are unaware that they have internalized their parents' criteria and reasoning, and that they are still seeking their parents' approval. These adults are bound to let their parents' expectations run their lives instead of developing their own standards.

There Is No Perfect Solution

For many of the problems and choices we face in life, there simply isn't a one and only best solution. Sometimes we need to set priorities or give in to the limitations of our personal circumstances. But one thing every caregiver *can* do is this: *Consider your children as independent, autonomous human beings and not as extensions of yourself!* Having a Healthy Sense of Self enables you to do just that. Find the courage to undertake the steps necessary to work your way to a healthy *Restored* Sense of Self. It will enable you to create a better future for yourself, for your children, and for the world at large!

Summary and Looking Ahead

In this chapter, you became more familiar with the term Sense of Self. You've learned how personal independence is the ultimate good a person can reach and how that is enabled by a Healthy Sense of Self. A Lack of Sense of Self leads to dependency on approval and outside validation. This can turn you into the slave of trying to achieve the best possible results in anything you do.

All in all, this is a very good reason to investigate what it will take to restore your Sense of Self if you don't already have one.

In Chapter 2, you'll discover what role nature plays in the process of developing – or missing your chance to develop – a Natural Sense of Self, and thus a Healthy Sense of Self.

Chapter 2 Environmental Input

This chapter focuses on the environmental conditions during childhood and how they affect the development of a Natural Sense of Self. Your motivation to read this book may have to do with academic interest, or you may want to solve some issues for yourself, or perhaps you are a parent who would like to do the best job on child-rearing. Whatever the case, this chapter clarifies a complex psychological concept by using the analogy of how a tree grows and applying it to the human infant. This approach allows for a few illustrations that say more than a thousand words.

A Strict Sequence

When a Sense of Self starts to develop in a person, it follows a particular pattern with particular input at particular times. If this is not met within the critical window of time, the child can be in trouble. Children who do not get the input they need at the right time grow up locked into self-destructive overcompensations that cause all kinds of suffering.

Let us explore the natural, healthy process of how a person ought to grow up and compare it with what happens when that process is distorted. First, though, here are some general thoughts about growth processes that occur in nature:

Every living being goes through a formation process. Even after a seed has sprouted or a baby has been born, its anatomical and functional systems are still developing. This process follows a strict sequence that is pretty much predetermined by nature. However, the *interactions* between nature-influences and nurture-influences (or lack thereof) also play an important role.

The genes of each living being are its "nature" aspect. The circumstances in which the being exists are its "nurture" aspect. These two factors influence each other, such that genes or circumstances may reinforce or distort the growth and development of a plant or animal in one direction or another.

Certain processes need to take place before others can. If some part of a living being's physiology does not develop fully and appropriately at its given time, the clock marches on anyway. When this critical time passes, the being is abnormal in some way, unable to live up to its full (initial) potential.

As it is with plants and animals, so it is for people. So much of who you are as a person and how your life unfolds are initiated in your childhood. So let's take a brief look at what happens in childhood.

You do not stop developing after you are born. Development follows certain patterns; for example, you crawl before you learn to walk, you walk before you learn to run, and you babble before you learn to talk. Another important but often overlooked rule is that specific kinds of input are required at certain times for development to occur as it is meant to. If the right input happens at the right time, a child's development will be normal and healthy. If a child does not experience the correct conditions, it will grow in an unnatural and limited manner. It might be alive, but it struggles to function.

Figure 2.1: A tree thwarted in its development while being deprived of space.

During the process of formation, an infant needs various kinds of physical and environmental input, such as adequate food, water, and warmth, as well as specific interpersonal, psychological, and emotional input. It is essential to realize that both physical and psychological input affect both body and mind.

The *natural* in Natural Sense of Self means a person has a Sense of Self that developed adequately at the natural time and in the required natural order. It indicates the development was "normal" – that the human consciousness was able to do what it was programmed to do. If the required input is not present or provided at the appropriate time, the development of a Natural Sense of Self cannot take place, and the result is a person with a Lack of Sense of Self.

When developed in a distorted manner, just like trees, we often need others to support us.

Figure 2.2: A crooked tree.

So having a Sense of Self is not implied in "existing." It's not something you are born with or that you develop automatically. You do have an inborn drive to develop it, but unless certain kinds of feedback are provided and processed in infancy and early childhood, a Sense of Self won't develop naturally and normally.

A core sense of "me-ness" – the sense that "I exist independently from others" – is part of normal, healthy human development. However, that normal, healthy development requires a specific attitude from the primary caregiver toward the child: the person who rears the child needs to communicate certain information to the child about his or her "being." This specific attitude, called **Mirroring**, is what provides the building blocks for the development of a Healthy Sense of Self.

Absence of Crucial Input

When this required piece of environmental input is insufficient or the timing is off for normal development to occur, the child (and later the adult) will suffer the consequences in very unpleasant ways. Their functional systems, physical and/or psychological, will be weak, distorted, or stunted and may work in abnormal ways. Because the necessary functions for supporting a normal existence do not operate adequately, this situation will lead to a painful life experience and possibly to an earlier death.

Many studies and experiments have been done to find out what happens when the necessary input is not given at the right (crucial) time. One such study, led by René Spitz,[1] observed infants deprived of touch during the early stages of development. His results are a prime example of the devastating effects of deprivation: the neglected infants withered physically and emotionally, and died very young.

This example is directly related to how I grew up; my mother felt utterly inadequate to the task of caring for her firstborn baby (me) so my father, who was nine years her senior and somewhat authoritarian, took over my care in specific instances. He had a spartan philosophy concerning child-rearing, a common approach in the Netherlands, which, in 1945, had just been freed from German invasion and domination. That meant that I was left alone in my crib – not picked up or hugged by anyone – just left there until it was time for me to be fed, all for fear that I would grow up weak. This example is not intended to convey the message that this is the only reason I didn't develop a healthy sense of my Self – but you can certainly look at it as a symptom of my mother's inability to establish a healthy attachment to me, her child.

[1] René Spitz, developmental psychologist. The film *Psychogenic Disease in Infancy* (1952) shows the effects of emotional and maternal deprivation on the infant's development. http://www.youtube.com/watch?v=VvdOe10vrs4 (March 2011).

For now, let us remember that the development of a Natural Sense of Self requires specific input at the appropriate times. If adequate input is not provided, a child's development cannot proceed normally, which then results in a Lack of Sense of Self. Later in this chapter and the following chapter, we will take a look at what necessary environmental inputs are related to the development of a Natural Sense of Self.

The Metaphor of the Tree

Because they are immobile, plants and trees are limited to using whatever they can get from their environment, regardless of whether the right type of input is available in the right amounts at the right times. If the developing tree has limited options to get its needs met, it may grow crooked and end up underdeveloped. For example, a seedling will grow in the direction of light, and it will extend its roots in the direction of water – even if these stretches and bends weaken the seedling.

The same laws of adjustment apply to human beings. If your needs were not met, your growth was thwarted, and your Sense of Self became crooked in some way. Just like a tree, you grew in the direction you perceived would better meet your needs. The formation of your brain and its wiring was stimulated in certain directions, even if this led you away from your own innate abilities and characteristics. Children will bend over backward, psychologically and neurologically, in their adjustment toward getting what comes closest to the environmental input they need for the development of a (Natural) Sense of Self: to be acknowledged as a *real* person.

Figure 2.3: The well-balanced development of the roots is easy to spot.

The roots of a tree are sometimes visible (see Figure 2.3). Observing them, we can see how the sapling was forced to compensate for environmental deprivations. Unfortunately, we cannot study the brain of a person in the same way, so what happens there on a physical level remains a mystery.

The analogy of how a tree grows may help, though. Let's look at trees a little closer to better visualize how the human psyche compensates for lacks in input. It is important to understand how that process brings about permanent changes in the (physical) structure of the brain.

Comparing the way in which a tree forms itself to the way the human mind forms itself helps give a clearer mental picture of what happens in the psycho-emotional development of a child when raised in specific circumstances.

Look at the branches of the tree as representing the mental-emotional structures of your consciousness, or, more precisely, the physical manifestation of your brain's wiring. When you learn something or mature in some way, a neurological pathway is created in the brain that is either reinforced through repetition, falls latent if rarely used, or disappears with disuse. For the sake of comparison, I propose that these neurological pathways be considered the physical manifestation of our mind, which in turn influences our entire psyche.

This description of the brain processes is intended to be a very simplistic approach for the complex subject of brain wiring. I hope it helps you recognize and accept certain growth deviations that might have happened in the wiring of your brain as you encountered obstacles or lacked essential nourishment for healthy psycho-emotional development as you were growing up.

Just like the brain, a tree develops following its blueprint (nature) and the influence of environmental factors on its development (nurture). When there are a number of unfavorable circumstances, both a person's and a tree's development may become unbalanced or lopsided.

A seedling grows into a healthy, strong tree when all its needs are met (nurture). The seedling's natural inclination is to grow up straight and tall and with branches evenly spread on all sides. But imagine a building, a fence, other trees, or wires obstruct the pathway of that seedling's growth. Where there are obstacles, the seedling must bend to avoid them (see Figure 2.4). Changing its direction of growth permanently affects the shape of the trunk, leaving it bent or crooked.

Figure 2.4: Bending over (backward) to avoid obstacles, this tree is making the best of its limiting circumstances while growing up.

In some cases, this means that the roots grow sideways instead of deep down into the soil. Some trees develop mostly to one side (see Figure 2.5); their trunks may develop more branches on the side that receives a lot of sun and fewer on the shady side.

Figure 2.5: Some trees develop branches only on one side ...

Strong, continuous winds often result in trees with branches on only one side (see Figure 2.6).

Figure 2.6: The trunk and branches of a crooked tree.

Due to such outside influences, some trees are doomed to never live up to their proud potential of being straight and symmetrical. Roots, too, if unimpeded, grow naturally in certain directions so they can best balance the weight and shape of the tree. A root may grow out of proportion in a certain direction compared to others, or, if the tree needs to avoid an obstacle, the root may be thwarted in its growth and a different one may develop instead.

Now, imagine the tree bending over backward to get its necessary supply of nutrients and how that affects the physical body of the tree. That is exactly what happens in your brain. Imagine that your brain's neurons (see Figure 2.7) are similar to the branches of a tree. Specific brain wiring develops as you shift to fulfill unmet needs. Some of that specific wiring may inhibit the development of other neural pathways and become dominant in areas where it normally would not even exist. What happens to the original blueprint of the person who, under better circumstances, would have fully developed? Maybe you can relate to the question it evokes: *Is that maybe what happened to me? (I feel like I'm functioning far below the level I think I am capable of.)*

Taking into consideration that what you went through in the past had an impact on your physical brain also sheds a light on why it is so terribly hard to change certain behavior that was learned early on. I do not say it is impossible, but it takes dedication, time, and serious effort to change.

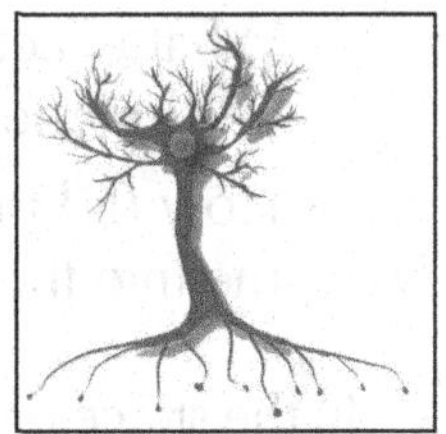

Figure 2.7: Neuron.

If only our brain wiring was as visible as the branches of a tree during the cold season ...

Figure 2.8: The branches of a tree.

Keeping in mind all the different shapes and directions the trunks, roots, and branches of trees can take, you may find it easier to visualize what happened during the development of your brain's wiring (your entire psyche).

Now would be a great time to do some self-exploration by asking yourself the following questions:

- What was the environment I grew up in like?
- What obstacles were in my way?
- How did my inner "brain-tree" adjust to that?

- What effect did that have on the shape and form of my mind and emotions?
- How did that development influence my potential and make me into the person I am at this very moment?

In the space provided below, sketch how you imagine your "brain-tree" grew. Obviously, there is no right or wrong way to do this. Enjoy the creative process of shaping this image of your own mental and emotional growth and development. Take the time to think over any questions, impressions, and/or memories that may arise.

Figure 2.9: Draw your own brain tree.

Figure 2.10: Would your brain tree look like this?

Figure 2.11: Or maybe more like this?

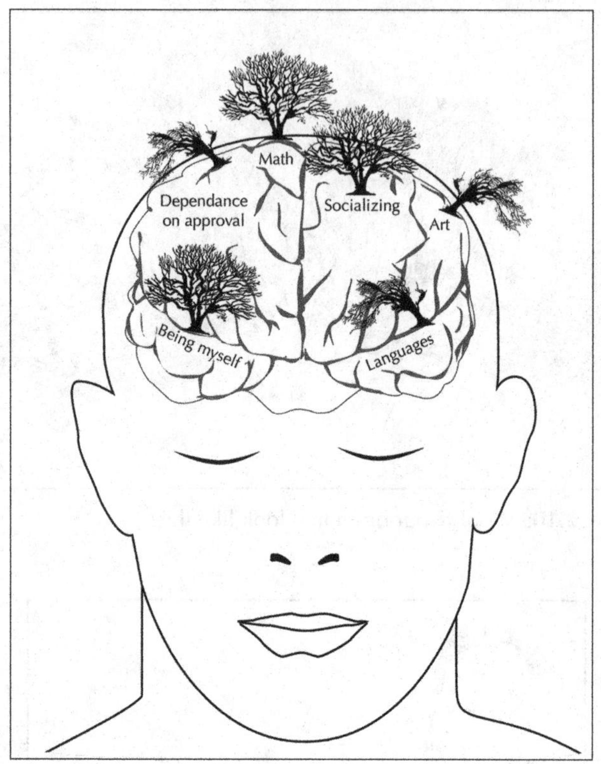

Summary and Looking Ahead

In this chapter, we discussed what happens to children's growth when they are deprived of essential input during childhood. In the next chapter, we will look at the most crucial element of our development: Mirroring.

Chapter 3
Mirroring

In the preceding chapter, you saw that children need to receive specific feedback as a prerequisite for the development of a Natural Sense of Self. They need to know they're seen for who they are and that they have every right to be their true Self. Keeping a child in limbo about whether or not they are good – just as they are – can prevent them from coming into their own way of being later in life.

A person who needs to spend his life searching for his Self is unable to resolve his own problems, let alone contribute to our common human quest of finding solutions for bigger issues such as hunger and war. Not getting the necessary ingredients for developing a Natural Sense of Self is a disaster for a person's future as a self-sustainable human being. You need a Healthy Sense of Self to fully be yourself and live up to your potential.

- Only when you have a Healthy Sense of Self can you fully be yourself.
- Only when you can fully be yourself can you function independently and interdependently.
- A Lack of Sense of Self leads to neediness and dependency. Only when you can interact without neediness can you effectively contribute to society and help make the world a better place.
- A healthy society consists of people who are psychologically and emotionally independent so they can function interdependently and build community with others by assisting and supporting one another.

So the fundamental difference in environment that leads to a Healthy Sense of Self or a Lack of Sense of Self is the *presence* or *absence* of the right kind of input during the critical period of infancy and early childhood. When parents do not provide the required input, the development of a Natural Sense of Self does not occur. For the young person, this means there is no way of having a concrete inner knowing that "my life is about me."

This chapter aims at giving you a deeper understanding of what could have played out in your childhood. It focuses on specific issues that arise in infancy and childhood that affect the development of a Sense of Self.

Obviously, not every child gets the right kind of Mirroring at the right time. What happens then? Nature's Plan B comes into action: the need for a Substitute Sense of Self is generated. In this chapter, you will see how a Substitute Sense of Self develops, where it comes from, what it does, and how it feels. The role of the primary caregiver will be discussed as well as the conclusions we draw as children when our needs are not met. We will find that these conclusions are internalized and become part of who we think we are. Then we will study how a Substitute Sense of Self differs from a Healthy Sense of Self and how to recognize it.

Mirroring

The mutual and subconscious verbal and nonverbal processes by which the primary caretaker conveys basic feedback to the child about whether the caretaker relates to the child as an independently existing individual or as a means to fulfill the caretaker's emotional needs.

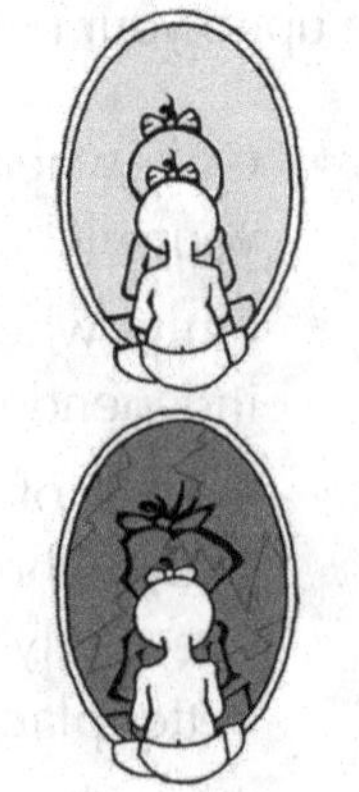

Mirroring from Caregivers

Mirroring is feedback that parents, caregivers, or others provide unconsciously to children; the way this process evolves is vitally important during the critical stages of a child's development, as it is part of the foundation of their Sense of Self.

As part of the developmental process, a child must be enabled to form an unshakable inner knowing that they are, in fact, separate from their caregivers and/or other authority figures. Mirroring creates a nonverbal, gut-level perception, identification, and recognition of their Self. This Self-image is not innate but is initiated and reinforced by the way the child sees their Self reflected in other people's behavior toward them. Because the primary caregiver is the person to whom the child is most exposed, the mirror he or she presents is of the most significant importance for the development of the child's Sense of Self.

The child will develop the foundational sense of who they are, and what their role is in the life of their parent, based on the way the parent interacts with and relates to them. More specifically, through Mirroring, the caregiver reflects to the child *what he or she means to the caregiver* or what impact his or her presence has on the caregiver's existence, which informs the child what his or her function is in the relationship. This later affects every other relationship in the child's life.

This feedback – the mirrored image – is conveyed very subtly but constantly through gestures, tone of voice, what is said or not said, facial expressions, and actions or inaction. Rarely is it put into direct words, because adults are often unaware they function as a mirror that conveys a message, let alone what the nature of that message is and what it conveys to the child.

Interestingly, the degree to which the caregiver has a healthy or less-than-healthy Sense of Self determines the healthiness of the Mirroring the child receives. As this factor plays a major role in a child's life from birth on, it is crucial in determining the foundation of the child's being and thus the quality of his or her life.

Now let's apply all this to the specific human need for interpersonal (environmental) input that enables the development of a Natural Sense of Self.

Is Mirroring Always Accurate and Neutral?

Primary caregivers are not neutral mirrors. The way they experience their child, as well as the feedback they provide to the child, obviously depends greatly on who they are and on what is at play in their own lives.

Children are unable to distinguish between an accurate reflection and a distorted one. They subconsciously conclude that they *are* who this reflection says they are because they can't see and don't understand what is influencing their caregivers' feedback. Since the child can't perceive the difference between accurate and inaccurate feedback, what is mirrored back to the child forms their nonverbal reality. It is only much later in life that, upon investigation, the truth can be learned about what happened and what was going on for the caregiver back when the child was little. Unfortunately, by then it requires a lot of persistence and hard work to change what has become hardwired in the brain.

Children who receive a reflection that consistently shows they are unique, autonomous human beings with a right to their own natures, needs, and desires develop a healthy, natural sense of being/having a Self – that is, a Natural Sense of Self, or a naturally acquired Healthy Sense of Self.

A number of important caregiver behaviors can facilitate the development of a Natural Sense of Self, including:

- **Acknowledgment of the child**: Acknowledgment of the child happens when the caregiver not only listens to the child but really *hears* what the child has to say. Acknowledgment happens when the caregiver not only watches the child but also really *sees* him or her. In other words, the caregiver needs to be able to see the child as another (separate) human being. Too often the child is considered to be and treated as an extension of the caregiver's own emotional needs.

The specific purposes for a parent to use/direct the child in such a way can vary, but the common denominator is that whatever is supposedly done "for" the child more than likely is self-serving. (Note: **Indirect Motivation**! See page 122.) Here is an example: putting your child in front of the TV under the pretext of allowing the child that privilege when, in reality, you are using that as an excuse to make room for whatever it is you have to do. Allowing your child to work at your side, even if it slows you down, is one way of making room for the child's presence in your life.

- **Allowing a child's Self-expression**: Apart from tolerating early infant behavior, like prolonged crying, without causing them to draw negative conclusions of this natural infant behavior, I mainly want to refer here to children of toddler age and beyond. Giving a child the freedom to express their Self as soon as they are able to – as opposed to being dealt with as an object that only has to comply with the rules of the house – is a positive reinforcement of the child's creativity. When house rules are used to assert a caregiver's hold over the child, the child can experience the rules as a life-or-death matter. To the child, it may seem like the rules are a higher priority than their actual well-being or feelings. The child may feel ignored, which may lead to a strong sense of rebellion against authority, which can later become a harmfully prominent theme in the child's adult life. ("They have a chip on their shoulder.")
- **Personal opinions**: Children are encouraged to form their own opinions, tastes, and preferences, as opposed to being silenced, criticized, or belittled for having any personal opinions, tastes, or preferences that differ from their primary caregiver's.
- **Drawing out potential**: Ideally, a primary caregiver has an eye and an ear open to sense the very essence of the child. The ideal parent considers raising and educating a child as, essentially, drawing out their potential and helping them develop as an independent human being. This is in direct opposition to the caregiver who focuses on whatever pleases him or her about the child, which is usually geared toward either molding the child into a copy or an extension of him- or herself in an effort

to live vicariously through the child, or as a way to use the child to compensate for what is lacking within.

- **"Being there"**: Parents acknowledge their children's presence by consistently being there for them. This means that they are focused on their children and their mind is not elsewhere. The continuous, excessive attention some young parents give to their cellphones (instead of paying attention to their child) is a dramatic example of this. Children can only conclude that these objects are more important than they are. "Being there" means parents engage actively and fully when they interact with their children in whatever they do together. They wholeheartedly provide for their children's multitude of needs and mirror them accurately and compassionately. Actively engaging in verbal communication or being wholeheartedly involved in their new experiences – like sharing in their awe of an animal at the zoo – creates a loving bond and respectful equality.

Using the metaphor of a tree once again, we can paint the picture of parents bending lovingly over their offspring, protecting them and making sure that they grow psychologically "straight" (metaphorically speaking) and well balanced, with a deeply rooted healthy sense of their own Self. They want to make sure their children have a chance of branching out naturally and developing a rich inner fullness that is a tribute to life itself, and which will make the children, when grown, able and eager to express their Self without being undermined by doubts and fears.

As a parent, you need to be equipped to instill in your offspring that crucial sense that the Self they experience is separate from other people's Self, such as their parents, caregivers, siblings, or friends. If you do not have that ability, you need to acquire it – if you already naturally have that ability, even better! Your child's future well-being is at stake.

The Distorted Mirror

Children have a normal, innate need to be acknowledged as unique, distinct human beings. They need to be accurately mirrored by their primary caregiver so they can develop a Natural Sense of Self.

When the caregiver is too wrapped up in their own problems and emotional neediness to be able to do the right thing and effectively acknowledge their child, the child inherits the same problem.

In that case, the (generally nonverbal) mirror conveys a different and very harmful message to the child. The message should be: "You are a unique being who has every right to exist and grow up independent of and equal to anyone else." It can end up being distorted into: "You are allowed to be and to exist insofar as you please me and meet my needs. Who and what you are is inconsequential and your existence is essentially dependent on this conditional relationship with me. You matter only when you do what I want you to do, or when you are the way I want you to be." In the latter case, the child subconsciously learns that they must live up to or fulfill certain conditions imposed by the caregiver to feel even remotely as if they are being treated as a real, existing person who matters.

The message becomes distorted, like a funhouse mirror, but the child inevitably and naturally concludes that they are the reflection they received from the **Distorted Mirror**. Especially during the period from infancy through puberty, the child considers their parent to be a supernatural human being who is always right and assumes (subconsciously) that the parent's reflections are accurate.

Distorted Mirror

The process by which the primary caregiver is unable to effectively acknowledge their child(ren) as a separate being(s), as the caregiver is too wrapped up in their own problems and emotional neediness. The child inevitably and naturally concludes that he IS the way he sees himself reflected by the caregiver, which is, in the light of the child's mind, an understandable but incorrect conclusion that can have far-reaching negative implications.

What causes even the most well-intentioned parents to become Distorted Mirrors? That is a question that deserves more attention.

Becoming a Distorted Mirror

The development of a Substitute Sense of Self results from having a primary caregiver who is unable to provide the child with the building blocks of a Natural Sense of Self during the critical stages of development. Although there may be several causes for such a condition, the SoS Method focuses on one particular reason: the parent is self-absorbed.

I do not believe caregivers behave in egocentric ways because they are innately bad. Rather, they only behave this way because their own needs as children were not met! This is how the eternal cycle of this seemingly subtle but highly toxic inability to acknowledge other people is passed on from generation to generation. Self-absorbed people are likely always operating from, and therefore dependent on, a Substitute Sense of Self because of their own childhood deprivation and the Distorted Mirroring *they* received from *their* parents.

Why are some people more prone to becoming a victim of this situation? I really cannot say. Perhaps it is part of their specific genetic makeup. Maybe it's purely environmental. It could be any combination of both.

Real Self/Authentic Self

The totality of one's body, mind, and emotions and what comes with being a person is experienced in the healthiest, most integrated way as an independent and autonomous being; actions and awareness are based on living experience, not contaminated by pathological motives.*

*Not so much meant in a spiritual sense but more as a reference to the whole person you really are.

Self-absorbed people have an excessive and unhealthy focus on themselves and are unable to focus on others. They think of themselves as the center of the universe and believe that everything revolves around them and is about them. Most self-absorbed people are not aware that this applies to them as these characteristics are born from subconscious reasons. Also, the characteristics are not necessarily easily visible to others, especially not to their children (at least not when their children are still young). Here are a few characteristics that can help you identify whether you or someone you know is self-absorbed:

- Not recognizing that, to a healthy extent, other people experience themselves as the center of their own existence.
- Considering it a given that things happen or should happen to meet their personal (Substitute Sense of Self–oriented) needs, regardless of anybody else's needs.
- Dependent as they are on their Substitute Sense of Self, they are unable to be present to their own **Real Self/Authentic Self**. Because of that, others are also experienced as being "unreal" and not as separate, autonomous people with their own rights, needs, and characteristics.
- Only acknowledging and approving of people, things, and situations if they are perceived as having potential to serve (overtly or covertly) the self-absorbed person's own (Substitute Sense of Self–oriented) needs.
- Other people are seen as objects to be used or manipulated as a means to a (Substitute Sense of Self–oriented) end.
- Seemingly very generous, kind, or giving on the surface, but in reality they have (Substitute Sense of Self–oriented) motives. (Hidden Agenda! See page 125.)
- No genuine interest in other people's (their children's!) stories and experiences: interest can be faked, but there is always a (Substitute Sense of Self–oriented) Hidden Agenda. Anything that cannot be used for this agenda is ignored or rejected.
- Any problem that arises from outside their self-absorbed world is experienced as a **Hindrance** (see page 192) or a nuisance and is brushed off. There is no consideration for the effects of this behavior on other people (their children, their spouse, etc.).
- Based on extreme fear (to lose or not gain their Substitute Sense of Self), temper tantrums occur when they feel out of control or things don't go according to plan.

- When in a position of power, their sudden outbursts of anger create an atmosphere where others have to tiptoe around them.
- They often blame others (their children, their spouse, etc.) if things go wrong. They often anticipate what could go wrong and act on those anticipations, laying blame and causing great emotional upheaval.

As you will see, all these characteristics arise, subconsciously, from fear.

The Challenges of Being a Parent

The moment a person becomes a parent, a lot of attention and focus needs to go to the newborn. For a self-absorbed person, this is quite challenging and nearly impossible to do.

In the beginning, being a parent is something the self-absorbed caregiver can handle as they are often able **To Score** with the baby's cuteness, receiving vicarious attention that satisfies their unhealthy, subconscious emotional goals. However, as the child grows and becomes a person with his or her own many needs and demands, the child's presence becomes more noticeable. The growing child requires more and more attention for personal development beyond the initial daily care.

To Score

Being successful in using a Vehicle to improve on an Ego-Reference; a success that feels like gaining points toward the Hidden Goal, which results in a "Feel-good-about-self" as a placeholder for the real-self experience.

A self-absorbed parent is unable to allow or encourage the child's presence to grow. The parent is fundamentally unable to see the reality of the child as being their own person, equal to the parent in their right to exist. This type of parent has a difficult time attending to the child and investing energy, time, and good intentions. The parent's patience is short lived because the process does nothing to contribute to his or her own (Substitute Sense of Self–oriented) needs and all the caregiver wants (and is able to do) is to focus on fulfilling these needs. Even if something is done seemingly "for" the child, often a subconscious self-absorbed (Substitute Sense of Self–oriented) agenda still exists.

No one in the world can make the self-absorbed parent see how harmful their agenda is because their life is only about them and satisfying their own emotional cravings. There is no real love for others, only self-preoccupation. However, there is no self-love either, as the parent is not present to their own Self. So how can this parent possibly love their child?

Let me give you an example of such a possible Hidden Agenda from my own life: As a young child, I frequently had ear infections. At some point, the mastoid bone was affected and the doctor advised surgery to remove it. My father was opposed to the procedure, but my mother had the last say, so I was operated on. It was a nasty operation that had to be repeated a few times; I ended up having a big part of that bone behind my ear cut away. Looking back, I find it debatable whether my having surgery was even meant for my own good. I know that my mother had a hard time dealing with people being ill, including herself, and the surgery was supposed to stop me from being sick all the time. I highly suspect that my well-being was not taken into account in that situation, as I have come to conclude that it never really was in any other situation.

Self-absorbed parents can never foster the development of a Natural Sense of Self in their children because they do not have one. They not only feel themselves to be the center of their own world but also see themselves as being the center of other people's worlds, including their children's. They subconsciously play their emotional games based on their need to live up to the requirements that they validate themselves through, induced by the demands of their own parents. The tragedy is, however, that this type of parent causes their children to bend over backward to get their need for acknowledgment met, which sets them up to become self-absorbed as well.

For a better overall understanding of the problems involved, refer to the layers of the Self, as explained in Part IV of this book on page 326.

An Eternal Vicious Cycle

When parents lack a Sense of Self and are compulsively driven to fulfill their own perceived survival conditions, their children grow up having to facilitate the parents' Hidden Agenda. Consequently, the children have little to no room to express themselves or have their needs met. The effects of this unhealthy situation reverberate throughout the whole of a childhood, whether that refers, for example, to wanting to play with friends, engaging in activities that the parent has no interest in, or when a child is sick or demanding attention in any way.

These patterns are likely to develop into a vicious cycle of behavior that extends over generations: parents who, in their turn, are not able to focus on their children and acknowledge them as individuals who truly exist. The dependency on a Substitute Sense of Self is passed down in this way, from one generation to the next.

Usually, there is absolutely no harmful intention or even willful neglect. The whole Substitute Sense of Self–oriented system is kept in place by a compulsion that places the parents' needs above their children's. This mindset automatically leads (again) to the lack of acknowledgment for the next generation!

Summary and Looking Ahead

In this chapter, we discussed Mirroring: the way your parents saw, experienced, and related to you-as-a-child. What is reflected back in that parental mirror strongly influences how your self-image is going to be and directly affects your ability to develop a Natural Sense of Self. The next chapter addresses the experience of children whose mirrors reflect a distorted image, and we will shed light on the coping mechanisms these children subconsciously adopt.

Chapter 4 Fear of Annihilation – Approval versus Acknowledgment

When a parent is unable to acknowledge their child as a "real," autonomously existing person, that parent fails to provide the foundation on which their child can build a Sense of Self. Without being aware of its origin, the child experiences the resulting Lack of Sense of Self as a painful void on a primordial level of consciousness. Then, as time moves on, the child develops a desperate need to fill this void with something. This can be anything that leads to approval because of the unfortunate mix-up between approval and acknowledgment in the child's mind.

The SoS Theory refers to this void as a **Black Hole**. A black hole is a region of space that has a gravitational field so intense that nothing can escape. So it is with our void here, sucking up anything that qualifies as approval. Any positive result gained by your effort to do or achieve something immediately disappears into the Black Hole. In that void, it is subconsciously put in the service of your ultimate goal (to be accepted by your parent) and transformed into a potential point to Score with It provides you with a "Feel-good-about-self" that functions as a Substitute Sense of Self. At the same time, though, it generates a tremendous fear of losing that state and feeling empty again.

Substitute Sense of Self

A psycho-emotional structure that develops as the artificial backbone of the psyche of those children/adults whose caregivers relate to their children as an extension of themselves, and that leads them to develop a compulsive drive for achievement-based approval.

Because of the immediacy and the urgency of this process, the child (and later the adult as well) ends up working toward the successful outcomes of their actions and behaviors to get approval, which is interpreted as a sort of existential justification. For a person with a Lack of Sense of Self, getting a positive outcome from an action or behavior fills the void of the Black Hole, thus creating, if you will, a sort of balance in their internal system. At the same time, though, fear of failure is the steady companion of any success. Success is wanted, not for the sake of itself, but for the sake of gaining a Substitute Sense of Self.

Black Hole

Metaphor for an intolerably terrifying emptiness or invisibility as experienced by a person with a Lack of Sense of Self who doesn't feel like (they are considered) a "real" person. Like a force of nature, the Black Hole sucks in behavior and achievements that can potentially lead to approval. It fills itself with anything that serves as a Substitute Sense of Self, which immediately leads to anxiety about losing the Substitute Sense of Self.

"How does a Healthy Sense of Self fail to develop?" you might wonder. "How can I fully grasp this powerful pull of unhealthy motivations that developed from receiving Distorted Mirroring?" To that purpose, we need to take a closer look at the child's inner experience of the Black Hole. The SoS Theory labels that experience as Annihilation. We also need to study the fear that develops from having experienced this void: the **Fear of Annihilation**.

Fear of Annihilation

Terror of being unheard by and invisible to others.

Experiencing Annihilation

Annihilation refers to an inner, typically subconscious, perception or feeling that you are alive but others do not acknowledge your existence. It comes down to feeling like a person without a voice or face. You feel invisible because you sense that you are not being seen. You are not being heard, or taken into account, and you feel essentially reduced to quasi nonexistence.

This type of Annihilation has nothing to do with physical death. The ultimate terror of Annihilation arises from the gut-level experience of feeling invisible; even though you are physically present as a body, you do not feel acknowledged by your community. It is as if your authentic essence/spirit is not able or allowed to manifest itself in your environment.

It is very likely that you don't even recognize you are experiencing Annihilation. A Lack of Sense of Self merely manifests as a rising awareness of something being off in some way. As a result, you feel you are being discounted. It all comes down to a deep feeling of rejection, of being denied access to the world of the others.

Healthy and Unhealthy Aspects of Your Self

There are always certain fundamental aspects of your Self[1] that develop and exist in a relatively healthy way regardless of childhood environment, even when the top layers turn out deformed (see Figure

[1] The word *self* is spelled with a lower case *s* when it refers to the self-experience by means of "Feeling-good-about-self." It is not the same as *Self* with a capital *S*, which, in the SoS Theory, refers to the authentic Self.

15.1 on page 316). However, any Substitute Sense of Self structure you subconsciously managed to build in childhood is always unhealthy. It is formed by a number of conditions you force yourself to live up to that are not based on your own judgment. These conditions are inherited from your caregivers, your family of origin. That's dependency to the max, I would say! You are in a situation where getting or not getting to "Feel-good-about-self" is completely dependent on receiving (or internally perceiving) your caregiver's vibes of approval. That means you depend on others for your own well-being!

Annihilation can feel like a type of death as it creates an intense sense of "not being part of" that can be compared to nonexistence. The physical body dies only once, but Annihilation, as described here, happens repeatedly. This subconscious sense of not existing is experienced as terror, which keeps a person anxiously trying to live up to the conditions that promise approval. In other words, avoiding Annihilation compels a person to seek approval at all costs.

Ideally, the relationship between a child and their primary caregiver(s) confirms the child's need of being acknowledged as an autonomous individual. This then contributes to the development of a Natural Sense of Self. This sense of being (or having) a Self is the opposite of the experience of Annihilation. If a child's primary caregiver fails to provide an adequate Mirror that reflects to the child: "I see you as a (potentially) independent person, no matter what you do or don't," the child is likely to develop a warped (Substitute) Sense of Self.

So, what happens if, as a child, your needs and nature are *not* recognized and respected by others? Well, you may conclude that you aren't good enough to be counted, that you don't really matter. You try to better yourself so you can get a different result; all the while, being overlooked and ignored makes you feel like a ghost with a body – alive but living in the hell of invisibility. An eerie suspicion of "I am not real; I have no real power" may emerge in your mind. This vague uncertainty may lead you to develop childhood strategies to try to overcome or compensate for this situation.

The feelings of dread you experienced in the past when putting these strategies into action can still greatly determine your present quality of life.

Your early childhood conclusions stay with you for the whole of your adult life, ingrained as they are in your system. Only by actively reconditioning yourself and recovering your Sense of Self can you break this vicious inner cycle.

Over the course of many years, I tried to mingle with certain groups of people, but I had no sense of when to enter a conversation or when to speak up in a group. I felt so unimportant to others, yet inside I knew I did have value. I was unable to express myself because I simply wasn't in touch with the part of my being that generates those impulses and that, if trusted, would have made those decisions for me.

Because I had no Sense of Self, I was not aligned with my intuition, and there was no way for me to rely on it. So, instead, I convinced myself I had to work hard, better myself, and excel in something in order to eliminate the chances of being overlooked and unaddressed in the future.

Fearing Annihilation

The feeling of Annihilation is first experienced in early childhood – then on a regular basis throughout adolescence and adulthood. We know now that it stems from not being acknowledged as an independent and autonomous person. Even though there is this intense fear, it is likely that you do not have any conscious memory of this first experience of Annihilation, as it wasn't labeled as such at the time. Therefore, it is extremely difficult to recognize or confirm its role in your current psychological and emotional makeup, but it may be the root cause of your anxiety.

When your parent feeds and clothes you, it looks like he or she cares for you. A child, though, is able to recognize, albeit subconsciously, that the parent merely tolerates them and only lets the child come closer when they comply with the parent's wishes. If the truth of the situation is not visible to outsiders, it doesn't mean that this situation of emotional neglect is less real.

I remember getting into a bicycle accident when I was twelve years old. I had somehow lost my balance and smashed my ribcage hard against the handlebars. I was in pain, but I do not remember a single word of comfort from my mother, and the subsequent trip to the doctor's office lives in my memory as being nothing but a nuisance to her: "How could you do that to me?" was her nonverbal message. She really didn't see *me*.

If the relationship between you and your parent was similar, it may be a challenge to believe in yourself later in life. There is always an uncanny sense that something is at stake: the fear of feeling annihilated, rejected for who you are. If this is a fear that lingers throughout your life, you can consider it the living proof of the defects in your childhood relationship with your caregiver. It can be difficult to put your finger on it, though, as this early stage of your relationship is now only a memory.

You'll always dread not being seen by others as the unique being you are, despite being bodily present. The unarticulated belief is "I am unable to participate in life because nobody sees or hears me." Obviously, this negative inner conviction leads to deep feelings of inadequacy and inferiority, reinforcing the Fear of Annihilation. Trying to stay out of its claws by performing better becomes a constant reality.

Having to battle this fear constantly is what makes getting a Substitute Sense of Self the dominant motive in your life. Gaining and keeping your caregiver's real or virtual approval is the one and only thing that supposedly brings you to the "Feel-good-about-self" (Fgas) state, which then soothes your troubled state of mind.

The ongoing need is the seed for compulsions and addictions later in life, as this fear can be severe and overwhelming. The only possible reaction is to do whatever is perceived to be necessary in your state of dependency: behave and/or act in ways that lead to approval. This agonizing fear rarely reaches conscious awareness and many people experience some milder form of it (anxiety!) and never fully realize what they are afraid of.

The Fear of Annihilation Generates Many Other Fears

Feeling annihilated goes far beyond the feeling of being rejected – especially because you were still a kid the first times you experienced that feeling. You had no access to any reasoning that could have undone the feeling because there was no Sense of Self that you could consult to verify whether this feeling made any sense. It all took place in a period of your life when you rightfully depended on your parent's attitude toward you for finding out whether or not you are okay as you are. Experiencing Annihilation is terrifying for a child, and what is more, it stays terrifying for an adult as well.

That is why experiencing this feeling of deep insecurity becomes the prime motive for interpreting approval as a substitute way of sensing your self. Living this way on a daily basis is comparable to a battle of life and death, which explains why rage, sometimes even murderous rage, can be the result when the drive to avoid Annihilation is thwarted.

Thus, the Fear of Annihilation is the fountainhead for many other fears. Since getting approval is the goal, the fear of not being able to perform well enough is sky-high. Each specific way in which you are trying to get that approval has its own fear related to it. For example, "I am afraid I am not good enough at cooking to satisfy my caregiver's criteria." Whenever the Fgas state (which then functions as a Substitute Sense of Self) seems out of reach, there is fear. In short, the Fear of Annihilation is comparable to – and in some ways possibly even worse than – the fear of death.

In a person with the above mentioned early childhood deprivations, fearing Annihilation never stops. This fear keeps you in suspense (and in a trance) during your whole life. It is a constant threat and a constant, albeit fictional, and unrecognized reality. The attempt to prevent Annihilation becomes a dominant (yet completely subconscious) operating motif in life. The need to avoid the feelings of being annihilated generates an entire system of unhealthy and detrimental habits, beliefs, needs, desires, compulsions, addictions, and motives. This system will enslave you until you die, unless you become aware of it and do something that prevents that from happening.

Fearing the Fear of Annihilation

Then there is a whole other layer to this Fear of Annihilation. It is the fear of experiencing the Fear of Annihilation, which pops up when things seem to be going well for you. This fear does not reflect a concern you have with a potential loss of your well-being. It is the fear of being so undermined by the fear itself that reaching the much-desired state of "Feel-good-about-self" (that functions as your deadly needed Substitute Sense of Self) will be out of reach. It is the anticipation of the dreadful anxiety of not being able to satisfy your need to experience your Substitute Sense of Self, because you feel incompetent or not in control (e.g., in the case of insomnia). This self-doubt can lead to a vicious cycle spiraling rapidly downward, and it can result in severe insomnia, depression, or possibly even suicide[2].

When you fear the Fear of Annihilation, your sense of urgency to be able to function in such a way that your Substitute Sense of Self is within reach intensifies greatly. It adds even more pressure on how you perform or even the sense that you will *be able* to perform. This stressful state leads to behaviors that aim at avoiding this primordial fear. That fear may be generating behaviors you normally would not engage in (e.g., agreeing to have sex when you don't want to or drinking alcohol to feel like you fit in). Just thinking about that fear evokes the fear of experiencing it and kicks your emergency system into gear, which includes an adrenaline rush that can prevent you from sleeping, among other things.

The emotions experienced in such a state are intense, and the situation is highly complex. There is the need to exert total control over your own feelings and behavior, your environment, and your circumstances as well as controlling others' feelings and behavior. And, in the desperate attempt to avoid the (fictional) doom scenario of Annihilation, emotions skyrocket. They are hard to contain.

On top of that, you have to deal with all these self-imposed conditions, like "I should not be angry"; e.g., an inner warning sign that says, "I can't allow myself to experience those emotions!" But the powerful urge to express these feelings may battle the need to suppress them. Fear of your own behavior and your very own emotions comes into the game here: your (own) feelings and behavior clash with your self-imposed criteria.

[2] If you're experiencing suicidal thoughts, please seek immediate help.

Approval and Acknowledgment: An Unfortunate Mix-Up

Gaining approval reduces the Fear of Annihilation, based on early childhood conclusions. In a healthy parent/child relationship, *approval* simply means that the parent appreciates what the child has done (or has not done), and this approval does not affect the child on a deeper, existential level. However, if you lack a Sense of Self, approval stands for much more, both in your childhood and throughout your adult life.

Getting approval through achieving a desired outcome is tied directly to your sense of feeling "allowed to be." Having done well enough to deserve the much-desired approval allows you to imagine that you have been acknowledged. Please note that in the child's mind there is a mix-up between the much-desired *approval* and the ultimate underlying issue: a lack of *acknowledgment*. It is understandable that a child would confuse one with the other. In the present, though, it is crucial to understand the difference between approval and acknowledgment.

Acknowledgment means that you, as a child, were truly *seen* by your parent or caregiver and that they intrinsically agreed and accepted that you are the king or queen of your own universe (as an adult). It means that your parent needed to allow you to discover your own opinions, tastes, and preferences, even if they were not congruent with your parent's wishes. Acknowledgment means that your parent fully accepted that you, as a child, were your very own person.

When there was a mix-up between approval and acknowledgment, though, you (as a child) mistook what was simply your parent's approval for acknowledgment. It looked like your parent really "saw" you when you were able to please him or her.

The real problem was that your caregiver was, fundamentally, not able to connect with you as they were too absorbed in their own world. Because of the absence of a true sense of your Self, you needed that approval, and not getting it hit you almost on an existential level. After all, it substituted an authentic sense of your Self. This fundamental, but fatal, misunderstanding took place over and over again. Whether or not you received your parent's (narcissistically oriented) approval became the determining factor in your experience of feeling alive or feeling annihilated. Getting approval became your condition for feeling seen and heard and temporarily experiencing the right to exist

Not being able to get that approval made you feel the terror of the approaching Annihilation. However, you did get relief from the terror of the Fear of Annihilation by means of approval, although it did *not* give you what you actually needed: being related to as a separate and autonomous human being. All you truly got were positive vibes from a Distorted Mirror: "You are okay because you are pleasing me right now." A healthy mirror would have expressed acknowledgment: "You are [always] okay because of the mere fact that you exist. Sometimes you do things right and sometimes you do things wrong, but that doesn't affect your being allowed to be." So (in case of a LoSoS), despite receiving approval, the Black Hole and the terror associated with it still exist. When you evoke approval and thus temporarily experience the "Feel-good-about-self" state, the Fear of Annihilation morphs into fear of losing this feel-good state.

When you read this as a parent, acknowledgment means that you have the privilege and duty to accompany your children on their way to adulthood while preparing them for that moment when they have to begin taking care of themselves and, later, of their own children. The best way to do that is by addressing the issues your inner child may still have with your parents and restoring your Sense of Self.

Becoming Hooked on Approval

Being pleased by getting approval is one thing, but how do you get addicted to approval? How does approval become the one and only thing that you live for? Below, you will find a potential order of things that can take place and lead to this addiction. Keep in mind that this process happens during the developmental stages of childhood and takes a good many years to develop.

First, *there is the lack of acknowledgment,* which forces the child to get this need met in another way.

Second, *the child perceives that they are at fault*: "If I was different, I would have gotten what I needed: I would have been acknowledged by my caregiver." There is no doubt in the child's mind that the parent is there for them and cares for them like all caregivers (are supposed to) care for their children.

Third, *the Fear of Annihilation is relieved by the child's ongoing attempts to improve on specific behaviors and outcomes of their actions*. These were selected in early childhood because they had proven to lead to approval, which resulted in reducing the child's terror.

Even though this third process consists of seemingly small and hard-to-measure conclusions and actions, it is quite powerful, and we can see the following scenarios occur:

- The child will perform whatever behavior brings relief from the Fear of Annihilation, which is learned through trial and error.
- These actions provide relief from the Fear of Annihilation, but since the respite they provide is only temporary, the child has to *repeat* these actions continuously.
- As the child grows up and the matter never resolves, they keep living in the past. That makes the whole endeavor fictional, as there is a time warp at work: the acknowledgment was needed in the past and the attempt to get it realized is continued in the present. There is a disconnect with reality here – the person's mind and emotions are still focused on the past. No matter how much energy they put into trying to live up to the (self-) imposed conditions, they will fail because they cannot change the past.
- The child can't give up, though! It is a matter of life and death! The now young adult tries harder to obtain the desired outcome. There is no real outcome, though, so the person's (child's) damaging belief of being at fault is continuously reinforced. The need to try harder increases over time and the ability to obtain the desired result seems to recede as if it is slowly disappearing behind the horizon. Depression is lurking.
- The child identifies with the survival patterns. These patterns eventually lead to the **Early Childhood Survival Strategies (ECSS)**. Activities and behaviors that are endlessly repeated

because they obviously lead to a (relatively) positive result become ingrained in the child's system, and they become set in their ways of coping with what is missing. Ultimately, they don't know any better because these subconscious habits have always been a part of their lives. But the initial quest for the Holy Grail stays at work as their fundamental motivator: the child's goal of feeling acknowledged by the parent by way of getting approval

Early Childhood Survival Strategy (ECSS)

Conclusion to take refuge in gaining approval, drawn instinctively by infants/toddlers/children when their needs of feeling acknowledged as separate (unique) individuals by their caretakers are not met. This process becomes the foundation for an unhealthy way of experiencing the Self.

To reiterate, if you received true acknowledgment from your caregiver in childhood, your Natural Sense of Self should have developed. If you experienced a deficiency in receiving the message that you were being seen as a "real" person, though, your Sense of Self might not have developed, leading you to become governed by the need for a Substitute Sense of Self.

This can show up in the conclusions children draw from their attempts to get the acknowledgment they are missing by way of approval. Here is an example:

> *One day my mother was listening to our neighbor, George, play an improvisational piece on the piano in our living room. When he finished, she sighed with pleasure and said, "That was beautiful. You always create the loveliest music."*
>
> *George turned around on the piano bench and looked at her fondly as he said, "It's because you always inspire me."*
>
> *I watched from the doorway as my mother blushed and giggled at his flattery like the schoolgirl I was at the time. His*

visits seemed to make her feel special in a way that nothing else did. My mother was enamored with the attention George paid her and his skill at playing the piano. I thought that if I could learn to play the piano for my mother, I could make her happy, too.

She seemed pleased when I told her I had decided to study music, but she banished me from the piano every time I practiced at home. I was surprised that my music didn't have the same effect on my mother as George's did. Why doesn't she give me the same attention? *I wondered.* I know I'm not as skillful as George yet, but I thought she would encourage me more. Maybe I can get my mother's attention if I practice harder and become a better musician. *I decided that music was the best way to gain my mother's approval, but I was not aware of that motivation.*

This process of seeking approval as a substitute for acknowledgment starts close to the moment of the missed developmental window or critical period of opportunity, but if not detected and addressed, it can last a lifetime. Then your fate seems to revolve around an eternal need to repair the damage done by a missed opportunity, and it becomes your only goal in life; it may never dawn on you that, in the process, you're skipping your own life altogether.

Thoughts on Workaholism

I think that all of what you just read has a lot to do with why people develop the compulsion to work continuously. At the end of the day, it is really all about seeking approval and reaching that "Feel-good-about-self" state. This need functions as a Substitute Sense of Self and is ultimately rooted in *a lack of acknowledgment*. It is tragic when a person, regardless of age, is not equipped to identify the distinction between the concepts of acknowledgment and approval.

Thoughts on Alcoholism

My brother, for whom the use of alcohol would become a major problem later in his life, had this hope that one day he and our father would go for a drink in the pub together. Our father, though, either did not recognize or know how to respond to my brother's deep need to feel acknowledged as a valued son. Once my father was gone, my brother's drinking problems escalated and led to his untimely death. I often wondered how easily that relationship could have gone in a more positive direction if my father had not been so blind to my brother's need to be truly "seen" and accepted for who he was. If only my father had been able to acknowledge my brother as his own person and value him as his son, my brother might even be alive and happy today. Instead, both men died without respect for each other and with a lot of resentment.

Thoughts on My Insomnia

My insomnia was rooted in the fear of not being able to "Feel-good-about-myself" and thus experience Annihilation the next day. The problem of not sleeping showed up in various patterns: Sometimes I was unable to fall asleep. Other times I would wake up in the middle of the night and be unable to fall asleep again. I would also wake up far too early in the morning. In all of these instances, I needed a lot more sleep than I had been able to get.

Anxiety about whether or not I would be able to live up to my self-imposed conditions and "Feel-good-about-myself" would keep me awake. How my subconscious reacted to each fear varied just a little, which brought about a few patterns of insomnia:

- **Pattern 1**: Not being able *to fall asleep* was caused by not being able to let go of certain achievements from the day. It was like this: when I had done some things to satisfaction, my subconscious wanted to hang on to the points I had scored and prolong the state of "Feel-good-about-self" as long as possible, preferably into the next day. The fear of Annihilation made it seem that there was a lot at stake.

- **Pattern 2**: Then there was the apprehension about whether or not I would be able to function well enough to get through the next day. This was the fear that used *to wake me up* in the middle of the night or prevent me from getting back to sleep. As usual, nothing would stir in my conscious mind, as the call to stay awake must have come from a much deeper part of my brain, where flight-or-fight reactions are generated.

The first pattern would have me fall asleep around six or seven in the morning. By then, I had to realize that I had not had any sleep at all and that any hope of being able to function well enough and drag my Substitute Sense of Self into the next day would be in vain. Once the mechanism of holding on to that hope loosened its grip, I would tumble into a deep sleep.

Of course, I also became scared of my own inability to sleep because I was terrified of being so exhausted that I couldn't function well enough to "earn" my Substitute Sense of Self. This way, I had become trapped in a vicious circle that had a strong tendency to lead to depression. In fact, I believe the problematic condition of having a Lack of Sense of Self could very well be a leading cause of depression.

Thoughts on Suicide

With dread, I mention what can be a particularly painful symptom of a Lack of Sense of Self and the resulting stage of depression. Though I am not a medical doctor nor a psychologist, I feel it is my duty to express my gut feeling that these things could be related as I have experienced these inclinations myself. By mentioning the possible correlation between a Lack of Sense of Self (with its accompanying dependency on a Substitute Sense of Self) and suicide, it could potentially put others on the right track.

In my opinion, there is a link between the need to gain a Substitute Sense of Self, the impossibility to live up to the specific conditions that would provide it, and the choice to end one's life. There might be an increased chance for others to avoid this ultimate act of self-destruction if this link were more widely understood and accepted.

I hereby invite experts and scientists in the field to take this connection seriously. Gaining insight into the mindset of people who feel they are unable to realize their Substitute Sense of Self can shed a light on the impulse of some people to commit suicide: it can indicate that these people are at their wits' end, that they feel profoundly inadequate to perform the requirements of their inner mandates.

Depression lurks when you find yourself in situations in which you perceive there is no way you will ever achieve your Substitute Sense of Self. You now know that for people with a Lack of Sense of Self, reaching that goal is their one and only purpose in life. However, it can happen that your circumstances change and the person who is the target of your attempts to get approval disappears from your life. What are you to do then? Is it even surprising that the thought of ending your life would arise when reaching that one and only goal has ceased to be a possibility?

Summary and Looking Ahead

Experiencing Annihilation in early childhood, as well as the fear of experiencing it again, keeps a person prisoner and enslaved to conditions that aim at avoiding this feeling. A lot seems to be at stake when acknowledgment has to make way for its meager substitute, approval. We can possibly explain common problems, such as anxiety, workaholic behaviors, as well as various symptoms of depression, by their likely connection to a Lack of Sense of Self and its resulting compelling dependency on realizing a Substitute Sense of Self.

In the following chapter, we will take a closer look at how the Early Childhood Survival Strategy generates the compulsion to work till the "Feel-good-about-self" state is reached, as it functions as a safe haven against the Fear of Annihilation.

Chapter 5

Early Childhood Survival Strategy and the "Feel-good-about-self" State

In this chapter, you will get more insight into two crucial concepts of the SoS Theory: the Early Childhood Survival Strategy (ECSS) and the "Feel-good-about-self" state (the Fgas state). It will become clear that the "Feel-good-about-self" state is closely connected to the (survival) strategy of trying to fill in the need for acknowledgment that has not been provided, by gaining approval.

You also will see how your ECSS stays alive within the confines of your own person by means of the Internalized Parental Voice (IPV) and how that can result in becoming addicted to the Fgas state. It even brings up the question: Can it be considered borderline abuse to raise a child without providing the building blocks for a Sense of Self?

Early Childhood Survival Strategy

The Early Childhood Survival Strategy is a coping mechanism that develops gradually and unintentionally in babies and very young children. Infants, toddlers, and children are hungry for their parents' sincere attention, and rightly so. By really being seen and treated as their own little person, they are able to grow their virtual spine. When a young girl, for example, finds herself unable to get the attention she needs, she instinctively deduces that she'll have to be content with something that *looks* like real attention: approval. A strategy develops within the child that makes her feel, on a very basic level, that she is in control of getting her needs met and filling the painful emptiness inside. However, the moment she is forced to behave in certain ways solely to gain approval, the development of an unhealthy, substitute way of sensing herself begins.

Over time, as with the child in the example above, these unhealthy behaviors may have been ingrained in your psychological and emotional makeup, influencing many of your motives, choices, preferences, desires, feelings, beliefs, needs, and wants. It is almost as if you grew an artificial spine or used a copy of your parents' spine by being (and staying!) dependent on their approval. This focus stopped you from developing your own spine. (Imagine the facial expression of a child looking at their parent as they await instruction or approval for their actions.) During that crucial window of time in which you needed, but did not receive, adequate Mirroring from your caregiver about who you are and what you mean to them, you surrendered the privilege to discover and create your own (Sense of) Self.

When you had parents who were busy with their own story, you were most likely inclined to lean more and more toward gaining their approval instead of expecting any acknowledgment from them for the person you are. If your parents had a lot to deal with within their own person, they may have been unable to really "see" you, which made you believe that you had to perform to get their attention. You started to sense that something crucial was at stake with whatever you undertook or wanted to achieve. This way you were able to make sure that you would at least "Feel-good-about-self" based on their criteria. This turned into an obsessive-compulsive behavior because it functioned as a substitute for truly being in touch with yourself. It became the compelling target of all of your actions and behavior.

The knowledge and skills you gathered during this early trial-and-error period ended up being consolidated into your ECSS. You became dependent on your caregiver's judgment of whether or not you did well enough to deserve a smile, a hug, or encouragement. Your parent's reaction to you determined the degree to which you experienced "Feel-good-about-self." It was the closest you could get to the absence of that sense of Annihilation. The state of relaxation and relative safety you felt gave you a sense of being at home. You mistook that sense of "Feel-good-about-self" for your self-hood, and from then on tried to reach that state at all costs, even though it was only a substitute self-experience. You internalized the preferences of how your caregiver liked to see you, through a long-term conditioning process. That voice became the medium with which you would be constantly reminded of what to do or avoid.

This inclination is detrimental to your own quality of life because it means that the urge *to achieve approval* overrules everything else. *Any inclination that would have sprung from your own Self is abandoned and will never come to fruition.* You essentially start skipping your own life. This continues even after you become a parent yourself.

If this is what happened to you, you lacked the input to develop a Healthy Sense of Self and, instead, developed a sense of your parent's self! You became an expert in knowing – and sensing – what soothed your parent's mood. Maybe you became a parent yourself and you are still dealing with these issues, which is what happened to me.

In that case, your children, too, developed a sixth sense for how to make Mother and/or Father feel better during bad moments. Maybe they've even learned how to intervene in quarrels between you and your spouse to get you to stop lashing out at each other.

If nothing is actively undertaken to help your children develop their own Sense of Self, they will be just like you – the way you are like your mother or father – because this Substitute Sense of Self–oriented behavior continues into adulthood and parenthood. And, as we know by now, this relationship model is likely to transfer to partners, colleagues, bosses, and other authority figures in adult life.

"Feel-good-about-self"

"Feel-good-about-self" (Fgas)

An emotional state (or thought) of relative well-being and safety based on the absence of feeling compelled to produce certain results at all costs, gained from succeeding to comply to the wishes of the caregiver, which leads to approval. It serves as a temporary and unhealthy substitute for a sincere sense of being alive (as a "real" person).

The "Feel-good-about-self" state is what it says: it feels good, and, as such, it functions as a home for lost, struggling, and homeless souls. It is a moment in time that feels safe. Although temporary, it feels like a good place to be. It is a state in which you experience the absence of the pressure to perform and show you can live up to the perceived requirements for getting your caregiver's approval, *because you were just lucky enough to have done so*. It is the momentary absence of that always-present drive to achieve something. The Fgas state reflects the awareness: "I did it; I was able to live up to the conditions. As it is right now, I will receive approval." That means the absence of stress, as well as a sort of sense of satisfaction – a temporary oasis, if you will.

If you live with a Substitute Sense of Self, life consists of moments of "Feeling-good-about-self" alongside much longer periods of time spent getting to that state. The experience of "Feeling-good-about-self" is your only available reference to your self. Because reaching this state is perceived as a matter of life and death, you cannot stop trying for the best possible version of your action or achievement. This leads to overdoing the things that typically lead to approval: you over-practice, over-achieve, over-care, get over-excited, and so on.

Even though the term may sound attractive, "Feeling-good-about-self" is never a stress-free state. Becoming fully aware of the true origins of this state may be a great incentive for moving away from it, rather than compulsively trying to reach it. For your own sake, you need to get to the point where you can tell yourself, "The reason I

'Feel-good-about-myself' right now is based on the fact that I feel safe, having complied with the wishes of my parent. I have to be well aware, though, that this feeling is not at all of service to my own person." If you were able to see and identify the unhealthy origins of this Fgas state clearly, no doubt you'd be quick to abandon that path.

But the urge to comply with the wishes of your caregiver has to be obeyed if you want to have access to your Substitute Sense of Self and feel like you are allowed to exist. So when you do get to experience the Fgas state, it is always accompanied by two stress factors: the fear of losing it and the need to extend it. When you lack a Healthy Sense of Self, experiencing the Fgas state gives you the illusion of being allowed to exist.

"Feel-good-about-self" is written in this particular way to indicate it it is an SoS term that has the additional meaning of *experiencing the right to exist.* It reflects that a person feels like they are being seen as a "real" person.

For a long time, I thought that "Feel-good-about-self" was a real feeling that was normal to aim for because it was desirable. I did not understand how others could feel so well-balanced and were clearly able to achieve that state as a default while I was always struggling. Eventually I realized it wasn't really a "feeling" in the sense of an emotion.

When I first set out to identify what this "Feeling-good-about-self" meant in my life, I was still far from seeing that the only "feelings" I experienced at the time were those related to living up to conditions and realizing my Substitute Sense of Self. I was terrorized every day by the anxiety of not being able to realize my ultimate goal: being allowed access to the Enmeshment (see Glossary page 373) and being positively acknowledged as a valuable person in my mother's life. I experienced extreme anger and desperation whenever this process was thwarted or disabled. These emotions were so violent and overpowering that there was no room left for anything that truly might have stirred my heart.

Even working on fulfilling the conditions to gain approval made me sort of feel good simply by anticipating it. I was only truly at ease when actively working on these conditions. Anything else – yes, even anything else *that was meant to be fun* – was anxiety-provoking because I felt it as something that interfered with what I needed most: to get to "Feel-good-about-myself." The only way to get there was through living up to the conditions that I had distilled during the development of my ECSS.

The word *about* already indicates the true nature of this term: it suggests self-judgment. In fact, the moments in which I did not consciously or subconsciously engage in self-judgment were rare. It is one reason why I was (and still am) highly uncomfortable with receiving a compliment. Hearing someone say that I did something well used to quickly turn into a Fgas state, which was immediately followed by anxiety. It was as if I already feared that I would be unable to keep up that standard and that I was bound to lose my just-gained Substitute Sense of Self.

If you lack a Sense of Self – when you are dependent on a Substitute Sense of Self for your self-experience – you are continuously monitoring yourself. You (subconsciously) perceive that your right to exist depends on the outcome of your actions or behavior. A continuous self-validation process keeps track of how you perform in light of your ultimate goal. This is an **Indirect Relationship with Self** and precisely the problem that needs to be healed.

Indirect Relationship with Self

Sensing yourself as a "self" through achievements or the responses of others, which gives you a temporary good feeling instead of a healthy abiding sense of being who you are.

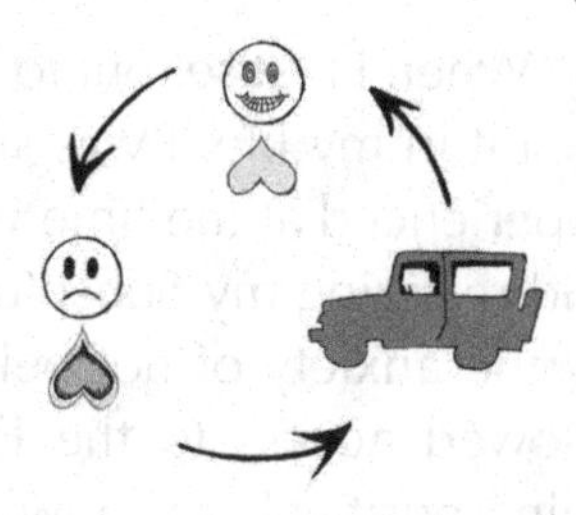

How "Feel-good-about-self" Relates to Early Childhood Survival Strategy

The "Feel-good-about-self" state plays a crucial role in the Early Childhood Survival Strategy. You want to feel good about yourself when the significant people in your life ignore you or your needs. The obvious way to do that is to make them notice you by doing what they want you to do and getting their appreciation. You adopt this strategy for your own survival. As an infant, this is instinctive, but it eventually becomes a learned behavior. Later, when trying to analyze what is off with you, it is hard to identify the difference between the two and conclude you are on the wrong track since a true Natural Sense of Self is missing: it is the only way you know how to be.

Because the opposite seems the norm for you, you also have this need to make yourself reach the Fgas state. Maybe you feel something is off with you, which makes you feel separated from all the other ("normal") kids. That sense of being different or "off" makes your default feeling about yourself "bad." Children think, "Parents can't be wrong. If they don't really (unconditionally) love me, it must be my fault." Almost instinctively, the process of earning approval begins. The Early Childhood Survival Strategy is fully geared toward obtaining that "Feel-good-about-self" state.

As mentioned, people whose Sense of Self failed to develop properly have an excruciating need for their caregiver's approval or that of any person in their adult life with authority over them. These children (or the inner child of the grown-up) naturally feel bad about themselves, so gaining that approval – through living up to the conditions their caregiver set for them – is the only way to experience the "Feel-good-about-self" state that then functions as a Substitute Sense of Self. Reaching this state needs to be repeated continuously, lest the lurking Fear of Annihilation rears its ugly head.

Please factor in that people with a Lack of Sense of Self are not just dependent, but utterly dependent on their caregiver's approval. In fact, it is this high degree of dependency that makes the situation so toxic. Please note that *it is not* the negativity in your caregiver's behavior toward you that causes the problem. In no way does the parent have to like everything the child does or says. It is the constellation in which the parent does not truly "see" the child – does not sincerely connect with the child – and treats the child as if he or she were an object rather than a human being.

If the child/young adult had developed a Healthy Sense of Self, the caregiver's behavior would have no impact on the child beyond a **Quality-of-Life Level** disagreement. For example, the child wouldn't overreact to their parents criticizing their housekeeping or choice of car. A Lack of Sense of Self, though, causes that absence of approval to be experienced as highly threatening. In the child's mind, lack of approval has the potential to destroy their chance of earning their Fgas state, and with that their Substitute Sense of Self, which is experienced as a life-threatening situation. Hence the urgency.

Here is an example: Let's say the mother is a musician. She is dependent on the quality of her performance for her Substitute Sense of Self. That is who she is and how she relates to her child. Her child may be in her life, and the mother may do the very best she can to be good to the child, but the child is not really within her immediate scope of concern or even awareness. Her music performances are. When she is not busy practicing, the first thing on her mind is, "How can I organize my household, my child, and myself so I can practice my music for an extra hour?"

Mind you that a person who depends on a Substitute Sense of Self is always anticipating how to best achieve their goals. Remember that for this musician/parent, the quality of her performance is a matter of life and death because her Substitute Sense of Self depends on it. She relates to the child on a physical level, but more as a living object. The parent is barely aware that this little being has emotions, needs (other than food and shelter), and wants. For this mother, her child is almost an obstacle she needs to get under control. That control takes place by partly giving in to, as well as anticipating (but not wholeheartedly), the needs and wants that require her attention. There is no spontaneous action or reaction – her actions toward the child are all planned to facilitate her ability to dedicate time to her own quest.

What happens if the child is hungry and has to interrupt his mother while she is practicing? Upon being interrupted, his mother would likely scold him, telling him to be quiet and to wait until she is done practicing. If that mother and child have a Healthy Sense of Self, he feels seen and acknowledged and has no problem with being put aside for a moment, or possibly he is not afraid to act up.

However, if the child has been raised in a way that leads to a Lack of Sense of Self, he may conclude that he needs to protect his mother from his own demanding behavior lest she scold him and he would feel bad about himself. He would do that by ignoring his own needs and letting his mother's needs prevail. The fear of not having the right to exist is lurking, so he will squirm and wiggle his way out of the situation or he will duly comply with waiting silently until his mother is finished: he needs his mother's smile to "Feel-good-about-himself" at all costs!

When the child learns that the impulses based on his own spontaneous desires lead to rejection, he may learn to convert to merely wanting to please the parent to get that reassuring pat on the head: "You're such a good boy for not interrupting Mommy again."

Next time, the child will not interrupt the mother's practice and will put aside his own needs for the sake of not having to suffer the Fear of Annihilation. "Feeling-good-about-self" is the only way out, and he has to behave according to his mother's desire to get it. This approach makes the child obedient, but it kills his spirit.

> *Note: We have to be careful when drawing conclusions about how a parent/child relationship is portrayed to the outside world. Caregivers are not always as caring as they seem – sometimes they have their own agenda. Alone with the parent, when there are no outside onlookers, the child may very well be at the mercy of the caregiver's random behavior and mood swings. The moment such a child thwarts the caregiver's purposes, the caregiver may throw a temper tantrum and the child will sense rejection. Experiencing rejection causes feelings of humiliation and Annihilation.*

The Internalized Parental Voice (IPV)

After reaching adulthood, the good vibes from your caregiver are no longer directly necessary. By then, you should have developed your own opinions and criteria. But not so for the person with a Lack of Sense of Self! Even as a grown-up, you still judge yourself by your caregiver's criteria, which you mistake for your own. The need for approval has become a part of you.

After all, you have been dependent on this approval since early childhood, and the message is strongly present in you. The criteria that were once used by your parent(s) reverberate through your whole system, even long after that parent has passed or you moved away. Your parent's criteria fill the areas where you never really developed your own thoughts and opinions.

When the presence of your caregiver's opinions, tastes, and judgments have gotten this strong a foothold in your being – when you do not even realize that they are not your own – we speak of an Internalized Parental Voice. This voice is as strong as the voice of your parent in real life, and, if you do not take action to recognize it and stop it, chances are you will be dominated by it throughout your life!

In fact, the IPV then becomes your captain, and your Fgas state is dependent on living up to its command. You mistake this state for your true Sense of Self and you need to reach this state at the risk of Annihilation! Obeying its commands becomes a matter of life and death.

The presence of a voice – other than your own – contained within your Self may sound strange or far-fetched. Truly, it took me quite a while to discover this aspect, but whenever I looked more deeply into myself, it felt as if my mother was still asserting her presence through my own voice. Then I finally realized *it wasn't my own voice*. The voice that was supposedly mine presented criteria copied from my parent. Those criteria and opinions were not generated by my own little gray cells or through my own emotional intelligence.

Yes, even when you no longer live with your caregiver, you unknowingly and automatically continue the dependency. You keep making yourself "Feel-good-about-self" by working hard to fulfill the conditions or expectations that brought you approval in the past. For example, every time I carry coffee cups neatly on a tray to my guests, I hear my mother's approval; I am almost seventy. Should this really still cause me to beam a little inside? It's hard to believe this small action still makes me "Feel-good-about-(my)self"!

Life in a Substitute Sense of Self–oriented Way

Living life in a Substitute Sense of Self–oriented way is living a life based on a fiction because it involves a fictional Sense of Self. It means being haunted by the fiction that approval is necessary to experience some sort of Sense of Self: "I won't exist unless I get approval." Once a false belief has settled in the subconscious mind, it feels very real. People with a Lack of Sense of Self compulsively seek approval to fill the need for a continuous influx of moments that lead them to "Feel-good-about-self" so they can avoid the feeling of annihilation. Unfortunately, because this ingrained belief feels like an irrefutable truth, the option to disobey these subconscious commands remains outside of their awareness.

The term *substitute* in the SoS Method indicates that a Substitute Sense of Self is unhealthy. When your life is guided by, and anchored in a Substitute Sense of Self, you go through life in an inauthentic way. You are neither in touch with nor able to express the core of your own being, nor are you in touch with your repressed natural, authentic needs, feelings, motives, and desires.

We can say that the Substitute Sense of Self has taken the place of a Natural Sense of Self, filling the empty space where one ought to be but was never developed. That means that on a subconscious level you never feel that you fully exist. An uncanny and ongoing deep sense of longing for something you can't define can be the result, accompanied by feelings of anger and sadness. This vague sense of longing has everything to do with your Self: you are longing to find your Self. I would like to acknowledge that this is a complex idea to grasp, but once you understand it, you can do something about it!

People with a Substitute Sense of Self suffer from an inability to experience joy or pleasure in normally pleasurable acts, because they lack an awareness of an **Real Self (Authentic Self)**, and because of the overbearing dominance of fear and anger that blocks their feelings and that they try to suppress.

Your daily preoccupation is how to best get to your goal of achieving the Fgas state. With that goal in mind, you may engage in activities that are not really of your own choosing. You may study music not for the joy of music but to fulfill the desire of a caregiver. You may wash dishes not because you enjoy a tidy kitchen but to satisfy the compulsion of needing to have your kitchen clean, perhaps based on your parents' insistence that the kitchen always be spotless.

Although your body is not destroyed in the process, as is the case when real death occurs, this way of living eventually leads to a near extinction of a person's spirit and psyche. In relating to other people, this type of self-sensation translates to feeling as if you have to hide something. It can feel like the well-known imposter syndrome: "Oh, this person is nice to me now, but if they knew how I really am, they would think twice." It feels like you are always conforming to something external, never free to know and express your real nature; the real Self never develops because there is no **Direct Relationship** with it. Once your behavior has become totally oriented toward your Substitute Sense of Self (see page 175), this version of self-experience becomes your identity.

Direct Relationship with Self

A way of relating to your own being that includes body awareness, which means that you sense your Self without having to refer to achievements or other people's opinions about you.

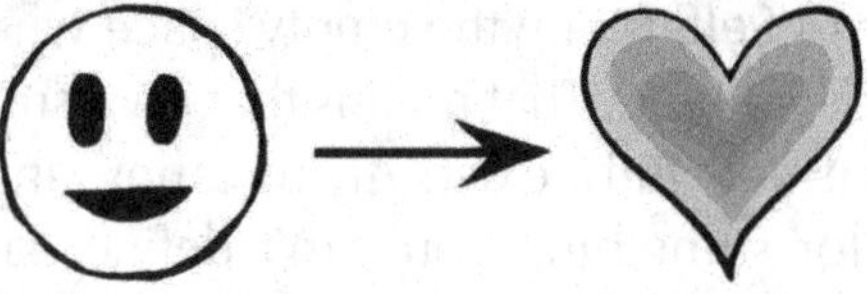

Every Child has the Right to Develop a Healthy Sense of Self

Can you imagine how stressful and sad it is to have to live life without a Healthy Sense of Self? Not to mention the collateral damage due to stress and exhaustion that show up as problems such as insomnia, temper tantrums, divorce, (mental) health issues, substance abuse, learning problems in children, fear of failure, anxiety, depression, and suicide, just to name a few.

If this psycho-emotional pattern goes unnoticed, you are bound to repeat it. The poignant drama here is that you are skipping your own life altogether in the process. You aren't growing and maturing. You are *not* the master of your own life; you are merely a slave to a force of nature that pushes you to live up to the self-imposed conditions that once gave you the illusion that you were being seen and heard. Your life is not about you but about juggling the many aspects you feel you have to improve on to get your fix of approval. In a way, we could even say that your worst fear is realized: *You don't really exist!* In the long run, that can cause disease and depression.

When living in this state of mind, there is no room and no ability to really see others and relate to them. Other people are merely pawns in the game of fulfilling conditions, which is not perceived as a game at all, but as a deadly serious necessity. However, through your actions and behaviors, others sense your inauthenticity because, subliminally, they perceive you as being uncaring, insincere, and distant – which, indeed in that case, you are! (In a different way than they think, though.)

Suppose a person was threatened with being locked up in a hidden shed and physically abused; fulfilling conditions to avoid that would be totally understood and accepted. The person would comply with the wishes of the abuser and hide any personal feelings or expression of them for the obvious reason of stopping more abuse. Anyone would immediately understand that the person was being manipulated into doing things against his or her own will – that person was complying for fear of being hurt or deprived of basic needs. (Compare this scenario with the movie *Room*, based on a 2010 best-selling novel by Emma Donoghue.)

The comparison between physical abuse and emotional abuse needs to be considered. Up until the twentieth century, foot binding was a popular custom among the wealthy in Chinese culture. Mothers would bind the feet of their daughters to keep them from growing normally – having small feet was a symbol of beauty and wealth. While this is obviously physical abuse by today's standards, it was an accepted practice for many centuries. However, would it have been a crime if the mothers who bound their daughters' feet then beat them when they couldn't run a marathon later in life?

Not providing the building blocks for a Healthy Sense of Self could be considered an emotional or mental form of foot binding. Although it is likely not intentional in many cases, and it is not done to meet a standard of beauty, parents of these children bind their own needs and wants around the Self of their child, causing it to become as withered and distorted as a bound foot. Asking a person who lacks a Sense of Self to function as if they have one is like asking a girl with bound feet to run a marathon – it might be possible, but it will be difficult and painful, and the risk of failure is high.

In some cases, we could even consider that not enabling one's child to develop a Sense of Self might be looked at as neglect, or even abuse, in that it makes one's child dependent on the parent for approval for the rest of his or her life. Intentionally withholding from the child what they need to be happier and more self-content – to provide the child with the development of a Sense of Self that they really need – should be considered a severe infraction on humanity.

For centuries, society supported the corporal punishment of children as a common educational tool, but we have come to see how this can damage children for life. Psychological and emotional abuse causes similar or even greater invisible damage, and I believe that over time society will start to address this in the same way physical abuse is addressed now.

I have personally experienced the consequences of this involuntary act of mutilation, albeit of my spirit rather than of my body. However, these effects have lasted throughout my life; in fact, they have determined the course of my life. It is why I have dedicated so many years to writing this book instead of making music. The fact that there was no ill will or purposeful neglect at play didn't attenuate the effects in any way.

So far, it may have been considered normal for a parent to not be well informed enough to be able to provide their children with what is needed to thrive: a Healthy Sense of Self, a virtual backbone, a basic sense that "I am allowed to be." Now the time has come that I want to question this behavior. I want to raise awareness of its consequences that can result in a lifetime of struggle for children who have been exposed to it.

I fully realize that things are not so clear-cut. Consider it a step in the evolution of humanity that, in our day and age, we are invited to rethink these behaviors. Let us pull ourselves together and have the courage to face the facts. You were born a blank slate, and you looked at your caregivers with eyes full of trust and hope. There was an expectation of endless love and care, and your caregiver meant the world to you. Being forced to meet the caregiver's requirements to make them "Feel-good-about-self" is an alarming mingling of two worlds and it is extremely confusing for a child.

On the one hand, there are the newborn's expectations of being loved and sincerely cared for; on the other hand, there is the reality of being emotionally blackmailed, which means you must behave in ways that are unnatural to you. This setup is not only uncomfortable, but it also prevents you from developing your Sense of Self.

If you feel this was valid for you as a child, you may be very motivated to do things differently once you are on the other side of the equation. If, as a parent, you want to do a good job of raising the next generation, you need to become aware that there is a fine line between providing inadequate Mirroring to your child and being guilty of emotional blackmail through withholding approval and/or acknowledgment, even though done without ill intention.

Summary and Looking Ahead

In this chapter, you saw that countering the perception of feeling nonexistent and overlooked (Annihilated) is learned at a very young age and later develops into a habit. Our Early Childhood Survival Strategy makes us prone to searching out approval in lieu of the acknowledgment we didn't get. The notion of complying with the caregiver's demands and trying to live up to their conditions brings the only moment of relative relaxation, which is experienced as a "Feel-good-about-self" state. Reaching that state becomes an obsessive goal for Fear of Annihilation. All of that is stored in the deeper layers of daily motivations.

In the next chapter, we are going to take a closer look at motivations in general and specifically within the person who has a Lack of Sense of Self. The following chapter will go into detail about Direct and Indirect Motivation and the different effects these types of motivation have on your life.

Chapter 6
Motivation & Substitute Sense of Self

The title of the book *Healthy Sense of Self: The Secret to Being Your Best Self* suggests that, on a regular basis, you could be running into things that are preventing you from being your best Self. You know these things should cause you less trouble and shouldn't be so difficult to bring to a good ending. Subconsciously preserved motivations from your early childhood may lie at the root of this issue. Creating clarity and awareness around these motivations will enable you to zoom in on them, examine them from every angle, and investigate whether or not they are still relevant to you in your current life. This is a powerful way to heal yourself of the dependency on an unhealthy Indirect Motivation that you may not even be aware of. You will see that your productivity and your ability to deal with things will increase, and you'll feel much healthier and happier as well.

Insight into your motivations is the key to understanding yourself. In this chapter we point out that there are two types of motivations: healthy and unhealthy. It is of extreme importance to be able to identify unhealthy motivation and replace it with a healthy version.

Introduction to Motivation

From time to time, we need to revisit our motivation and clean it up. Part of sustaining a pleasant living environment is cleaning up on a regular basis. Clothing that you have outgrown needs to be discarded to make room for new attire that suits you now. These days even CDs are old-fashioned, and, unless you are a collector, they just take up precious space. Anything you no longer use or want has to go!

You are the maintenance person of your own system, of your own Self. For your (Self-) system to be healthy, it needs attention and care, just as your living environment does. It requires you to take action and evaluate whether certain goals, ideas, visions, and guidelines are still working for you. Especially if your motivation is sensitive to aging! What you did as a kid needs to be adjusted when you grow up. More than anything, motivation can become outdated, convoluted, or improper, instead of being clear and serving you well in the present time. Understanding and purifying your motivation is the key to developing and maintaining overall health and happiness. What can be more misleading in your life than to keep repeating the same things for the wrong reason?

Cleaning up your motivation is the crucial first step in healing yourself from the dependency on a Substitute Sense of Self and moving toward a Restored Sense of Self – that is, a Healthy Sense of Self. This chapter will show you why and how that works.

If you understand your motivations, you have a key – possibly *the* master key – to understanding yourself. For starters, ask yourself the following question:

WHY do I do WHAT I do,
or
WHY do I avoid doing certain things, often at all costs?

Understanding what you are actually after brings clarity to the picture you have of your Self. By figuring out what your *ultimate* goals are, you learn what you are all about. Self-knowledge is power! Knowing your Self fully enables you to make smarter decisions, which often is also of benefit to others.

Discovering Your Motivations Is Not Easy

If you want to be in charge of your own life, investigating your motivations will lead to discovering the truth about what ultimately drives you. Be advised that it will require total honesty with your Self. It may *seem* easy – it isn't, though! You may find out that the truth about your deepest motivations is not as obvious as you thought and that we humans are masters at denial.

You may be ready to admit that you sometimes deceive others by pretending you are more connected to your Self than you really are. But the fact that, perhaps, you have been going out of your way to deceive yourself – possibly for your entire lifetime – would be a shocking confession to make! Yet, that is what many of us have to be ready to admit!

If you choose to move from a life of self-deception into the truth of who you really are, getting insight into your ultimate motivations is the way to go. This section of the SoS Method contains a great deal of practical information to help you dig deep into your Self and draw a clear picture of WHY you do WHAT you do. It is a crucial step on your way to becoming healthier, happier, and more successful.

How Do Your Motivations Develop?

Body, mind, and emotions are continuously in communication with one another, which results in the way you act and react in the world around you.

Each person is born with certain qualities and characteristics that form the foundation of who he or she is. If you are able to develop a healthy Sense of Self in childhood, then chances are that your life circumstances allow you to live up to your potential.

But what happens if you encounter obstacles at an early age? What if your natural development is blocked or distorted by unfortunate life circumstances? Chapter 2 describes how a toddler, just like a sapling, finds ways (Early Childhood Survival Strategies) by which body, mind, and emotions can compensate for what was lacking.

How does motivation develop differently in different circumstances? In a healthy situation, your motivations are directly connected to an obvious and straightforward reason for why you do (or avoid) something. When a Sense of Self is absent, your patterns of subconscious motivation become more convoluted: you develop complex patterns of subconscious motivations in a natural attempt to compensate for your thwarted development.

Labeling Motivation as Direct and Indirect

A person's motivation is based on their own temperament and character; it is also influenced by circumstances and environment. From the SoS Theory's point of view, motivations can be *Direct* (healthy) and *Indirect* (unhealthy). Normal, everyday motivation should be Direct. Indirect Motivation is the result of a thwarted development of a Sense of Self.

Indirect Motivation

The motive for doing or avoiding something is not what it appears to be; instead, the motive is to accomplish your Hidden Agenda and ultimately your Hidden Goal, which leads to a temporary emotional state that is the substitute for a lasting sense of being a "real" person.

It is important to see the link between a Healthy Sense of Self and **Direct Motivation** and how Indirect Motivation points to a Substitute Sense of Self. Once you have gotten that clear, you have found the starting point for your own healing process and the secret to becoming your best Self!

What Is Motivation?

Your motivation is generated through your reasoning for doing or avoiding things, whether it is conscious or subconscious, verbal or nonverbal. With reasoning, I would like to include the active form of investigating something and drawing conclusions, as well as the passive ways of functioning on automatic pilot. In the latter case, motivation is based on conclusions that were already made in an earlier stage of life.

Motivation is the force that drives you to act (or react); it is the incentive for your behavior. When motives are very strong because perceived needs for survival are at stake, we speak of *drive*. Motivation creates agendas with specific goals to accomplish.

Motivation

In general, motivation is what creates an incentive or urge to do or avoid something. Motivation is the drive that determines behavior.

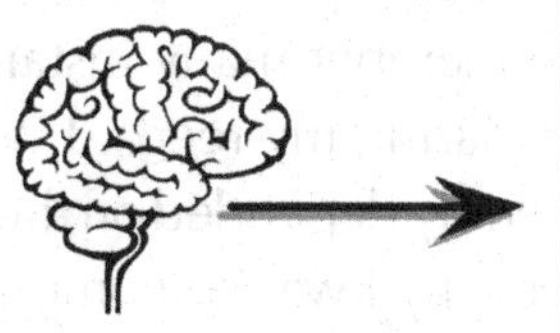

Why Is Knowing the Root of Your Motivation Important?

For me personally, questioning my *motivations* and coming up with true, sincere answers was the key to finding a way out of my predicament, my insomnia, as well as the ongoing emotional upheaval I found myself in. In short, it gave me back my life. By deepening my self-knowledge and getting insight into what was really driving me, I was able to adjust my motivation and restore my Sense of Self. By doing so, I had essentially created the potential to heal my Self from all the symptoms that come with a Lack of Sense of Self.

"WHAT exactly drives me to do WHAT I do or avoid certain things so desperately? What are the *real* reasons for my choices and behaviors?" I asked myself. The moment I was able to see how my *drive* was based on WHAT my true needs were, I was ready to question WHY those needs were there in the first place and *what I could do about it.*

Specifying Motivation

For the sake of clarity I want to mention that, rather than focusing on the obvious universal needs of food, shelter, warmth, and the like, we'll be looking at other kinds of motives: those that are deeply rooted beneath the surface.

"Am I really in touch with what drives me?"

"Are my motives congruent with what I *believe* they are?"

"Are the choices I make truly of service to my Real Self?"

"Do I sometimes feel as if I'm being driven by an invisible power?"

During the period I worked as a professional bassoonist, I remember many instances when I was unable to stop practicing or preparing my reeds. I was extremely anxious, and it felt as if my life literally depended on the quality of my performance. In hindsight, I can see why I was so compulsive in my preparations. Since my Substitute Sense of Self depended on living up to certain conditions, I could not afford to feel like a mediocre musician. I could not go home with that devastating feeling of having failed to perform well. Whenever that happened (it sometimes did), I would feel totally deflated, as if my spirit had evaporated. All I would do was wait for the next chance to do well and divert that lingering sense of Annihilation.

Knowing your true motives is important. Not only does your health and well-being depend on *which* motives are operating, but it helps you to get a clear view of why things don't work out as well as you expected them to.

The distinction between Direct and Indirect Motivation will help you discover the invisible power behind your motives and where that power comes from. That power has everything to do with conclusions you have drawn in the past. You will find that you will have to update these conclusions, which will result in what we are after here, an updated healthier motivation. Only when you know your *true* motives can you clearly see that they really do not serve you anymore. Then you can develop successful strategies for improving your quality of life.

"Things Are Seldom What They Seem"

Consider these examples of differing motivations:

> *Two mothers take their children to music school. Even though these two people appear to be doing the same thing, their motives may be very different. One mother may be motivated to develop her child's talent and interest in music because it increases her child's happiness and quality of life. The other may be motivated to have a child who is a good musician because it reflects well on her as a parent and because she has a great desire to be part of the music scene.*

The outcome of the experience would therefore be different for each person in this scenario. The first mother and child would probably find satisfaction and mutual enjoyment. The second mother and child would probably struggle with stress, fights, tension, and mutual dislike. The second child might not only rebel against the activities, but also feel disempowered, manipulated, resentful, and inauthentic. There is a big chance the second child will want to quit, in spite of having talent.

Here is another example:

> *Two mothers are complimenting their children on their test scores. Based on the differing motives behind the compliments, the effect they have on each child will vary.*
>
> *The first mother is motivated by unconditional love and recognition of the child's intrinsic worth. She is supporting her child's self-image by acknowledging the accomplishment and praising the child's hard work and abilities. The child knows she is loved no matter what her test results are. The effect of the compliment is a genuine smile, a reinforced bond, and better mental health for the child.*
>
> *The second mother is giving the child approval. The child, raised by a self-absorbed parent, has learned to live for approval and is eager to receive it. She is already worried about future failures, though. This mother is being vocal about having her child appear intelligent or talented because she thinks it reflects well on her own intelligence or talent. This mother possibly has some issues with her own level of intelligence, which she isn't sure is high enough to get her own mother's approval. Her motive is to have her child do well on future tests so she can "Feel-good-about-self" as a Substitute Sense of Self.*
>
> *For the second mother, it isn't really about the child; it's about getting her own need for approval met through the child's achievements. For the child, it means that she is in a situation in which she is unable to develop her own Sense of Self and will end up staying desperately in need of her mother's approval for a long time. This vicious cycle of dependence on performance-based self-evaluation leads to a nagging fear of failure that is passed down from mother to child. The child is used as a pawn in her mother's game of life. For her, there is the need to perform well to get good*

vibes from the mother, while the mother depends on the child for her "Feel-good-about-self" state. Stress is lurking around every corner, not to say what it does to the nature of the relationship!

Now consider this example from my life:

The following incident happened one day when my family was still very young. I was visiting my parents, and my mother was preparing lunch for everyone. The weather was gorgeous so my husband and I decided to go for a short bicycle ride through the lowlands with our youngest seated in front of my bicycle. The ride went on a bit longer than planned and our little one fell asleep. Upon arriving home a little late for lunch, my mother threw a temper tantrum, accusing me of being irresponsible and selfish for having taken my child on this ride that took far too long.

She went on and on and acted as if she had been personally insulted. She blamed me for not respecting the lunch hour and not validating the effort she had put into preparing the meal. At least, that is what it looked like.

What my mother was really anxious about was that she feared we would be late and spoil her "Feel-good-about-self" state. Because, in reality, that was why she had gone out of her way to prepare lunch in the first place. Of course, she was not consciously aware of her Indirect Motivation. Subconsciously, she was scared that something would interfere with the outcome she had envisioned for the lunch. Any potential Hindrance to the ideal progression of the meal caused irritation and a need to control the situation. Ironically, it ended up being her own upset that ruined the atmosphere, which just made her blow up even more.

The fact of the matter was that it was neither about the lunch nor about the people involved. It was not about the child who had fallen asleep on the bicycle. These were all pawns in her emotional world that consisted only of satisfying her need to bring this little event to a good ending so she could "Feel-good-about-self." It goes without saying that her temper tantrum did not create a pleasant experience and ultimately was the thing that sabotaged her Hidden Agenda of creating a Substitute SoS.

Indirect Motivation Aims at a Hidden Agenda

The root of your Indirect Motivation can be the real reason you are doing something. That real reason isn't only hidden from outside observers; your true motivations are often hidden from your own conscious mind, too. They can be very hard to uncover. And we are masters at finding excuses! Usually, in any given situation, you can come up with a plausible reason for *why* you have chosen to do or avoid something. That gives you the comfortable illusion that your behavior is justified and that your plausible reason is the *real* incentive for your actions.

In reality, however, your motives and choices are often far more complicated than what you notice. What is really at play when you feel motivated, when you choose to do or not do something or display certain behavior, is generally not as transparent as you would like to believe. Many of us have Hidden Agendas operating behind the guise of our plausible reasons – hidden even from ourselves! These Hidden Agendas are our deeper reasons for doing or avoiding things.

The idea of a potential Hidden Agenda generating our motivation is a key concept in the SoS Theory. However, unlike in politics, where many have a consciously formed hidden agenda or ulterior motive, in this case it is not a conscious process. The reasons that make us decide to do something or behave a specific way have often been with us since we were very young. These reasons have grown with us so – even if there is a slight awareness of them – we never consider questioning them.

"If I dress neatly, my father will actually 'see' me and respect me."

"If I act sexy, my boyfriend will not abandon me."

"If I play volleyball, my classmates will like me."

"If I get this degree, my mother will really appreciate me."

In case of Indirect Motivation, it is not about liking to dress up because it is part of your personality, nor about being sexy because you feel like it. It is not about liking to play volleyball or being any good at it, nor about being interested in a specific field of study. It is all about relieving the Fear of Annihilation by getting validation and "Feel-good-about-self."

The Hidden Agenda is to behave in such a way that there is an emotional payoff, and that payoff is the most important factor of the behavior.

Hidden Agenda

A subconscious purpose that drives your actions or behavior, which is not the obvious, ordinary, expected purpose but the demonstration of the ability to perform an Ego-Reference to perfection, as a path to feel safe and on your way to achieving your Hidden Goal.

Questioning Your Behavior

When I questioned my own motivations, I learned that there was *a deeper layer of motivation* to a lot of my seemingly normal everyday behavior. You could say that my choices and actions were not geared toward getting an apparent result, but that they were subconsciously driven by the desire to accomplish something else. Through many years of introspection and exploration, I was able to consciously examine the part of my motivation that usually stays below the surface of awareness. To my astonishment, there was a strong correlation between what was playing out in my subconscious mind and my overt choices, actions, and behavior.

Over time, I came to understand that these subconscious motivators were the immediate cause of many aspects of my suffering.

Once I began looking more deeply into the causes and consequences of my "unhealthy" motivation, I was able to begin my healing process. Let me introduce you, now in more detail, to the concepts used to describe the various aspects of Motivation: Direct Motivation, Indirect Motivation, the Hidden Agenda, and lastly the **Hidden Goal**.

Direct Motivation

Direct Motivation is the most normal, natural, and healthy kind of incentive for our actions and behavior. Our motives are straightforward and overt; they are not necessarily visible or out in the open, but there is always a straight line from our motivation to our actions or behaviors and to our goals.

Direct Motivation

Motivation that is ordinary, simple, and based in the present.

To the outside world, there is transparency in Direct Motivation because the goal of the activity has a logical and healthy relationship with the performance of the activity or behavior. When your motivation is direct, you have no sneaky, secret agenda.

With Direct Motivation, you do something for the enjoyment it provides or for a practical purpose. There is a direct connection between what you do and your intention behind what you do: You wash the dishes to get the dishes clean. You go to the grocery store to get food in order to be able to eat and live. Period. The appearance of what you do and the goal of your actions are the same.

Contrary to Indirect Motivation, Direct Motivation has nothing to do with proving something or trying to "Feel-good-about-self." Direct Motivation implies that you already have a Healthy Sense of Self and therefore have a Direct Relationship with your Self, as well as with the people and things around you. There is no need for a Substitute Sense of Self.

Figure 6.1 highlights the healthy inner flow of focus and nervous system activity associated with Direct Motivation. This person shows a healthy (inner) activity in playing his guitar and singing his song. No other reason is involved than the fact that he enjoys what he is doing or perhaps wants to convey a message with his song.

Figure 6.1: Playing music inspired by Direct Motivation.

Indirect Motivation

Indirect Motivation comes forth from a perceived need to fulfill a subconscious Hidden Agenda. Indirect Motivation is perceived as a need, not a want; it is experienced as a *must*. You can think of it as a compulsion. It has only one goal: fulfilling conditions that gain approval. The conditions are those that have developed from your Early Childhood Survival Strategy and that you have internalized because they used to lead to approval. Since approval leads to a "Feel-good-about-self" state, it is the Holy Grail of a person who is governed by the need to earn a Substitute Sense of Self.

When driven by Indirect Motivation, you may outwardly appear to be focused on the action or activity, but inside, subconsciously hidden from yourself as well as from others, something else is going on. You are using your actions or activities to get you to your Hidden Goal.

Hidden Goal

Your subconscious ultimate objective of getting the approval of your caregiver as an unhealthy substitute for feeling valued and related to (acknowledged) as a "real" person.

Figure 6.2 (see page 124) shows the inner flow of a person's focus and nervous tension that is associated with Indirect Motivation. This person is playing and singing just like the one in Figure 6.1, but it all happens from a different point of departure. He is dependent on the outcome of his performance for gaining the approval of his father for "being a good musician." This perception would then lead him to feeling accepted by his father as a "real" person (son).

In a later stage of life, living up to his father's conditions and obeying his Internalized Parental Voice would lead the guitar player to the Fgas state that then functions as a Substitute Sense of Self. There is a lot perceived to be at stake for him: avoiding Annihilation! Does this take away from or affect the performance in any way? Most definitely.

Figure 6.2: Playing music driven by Indirect Motivation.

Transference

Without a Healthy Sense of Self, you stay subconsciously motivated to aim for approval, which has been the closest you could get to what you missed out on: acknowledgment as the independent and unique person you really are.

Over time, your caregiver's function as the giver or withholder of approval is transferred onto other people who have characteristics similar to those of your caregiver. For example, they have an authoritarian vibe, just like your father; or they have a strong will, just like your mother.

Unfortunately, unknowingly, you are giving those people the power to either make you feel accepted (and alive) or rejected (and annihilated). As soon as they appear on the stage of your life, they already automatically have that control over you. This means that you, now as an adult, stay in the same position of dependency toward others as you were toward your caregiver. Here is the drama. You are still doing two things:

1. Obeying your subconscious belief that the conditions from childhood need to be fulfilled to achieve the sense of being okay and safe.
2. Giving in to your addiction to reaching the Fgas state through approval.

If this does not change, you will never be your own master.

An example of this is being a workaholic. The sad part is that you are *not* directing these long hours or hard work toward achieving the actual (directly motivated) goal of finishing the work. It is *not* about the fact that it is important for the work to get done right now in a specific way. It is all about your Hidden Agenda, which can range from pleasing your boss or showing off – to your colleagues or even to yourself – that you can do it. Ultimately, though, it is about reaching your Hidden Goal (Fgas as a Substitute Sense of Self).

The Hidden Agenda

A Hidden Agenda that operates within you works pretty much the same as ulterior motives encountered in politics. A specific thing is said or done to create a situation that is more favorable for achieving another (secret) goal.

Thus, a Hidden Agenda in the SoS Theory is an ulterior motive. It is an action or a behavior that is not openly admitted, known, or visible on the surface. Your conscious mind may not even permit you to realize that you are subconsciously operating with a Hidden Agenda, if self-deception is perceived to be in your best interest.

The following story serves as an example:

> *Erica's Hidden Goal was to please her father because she never felt truly acknowledged by him. She knew that her father wanted nothing more than to have his offspring follow in his footsteps. He was a respected medical doctor so Erica decided to study medicine as well. She convinced herself that it was what she wanted to do. It would have been devastating for her to admit that she was only pursuing a medical career to please her father in the hope that he would finally truly "see" her and let her know he valued her as his daughter and as the person she was. That knowledge would have immediately defeated her subconscious plan to win her father's approval. So, her conscious mind preferred to be left in the dark about her real motivation*

A Hidden Agenda refers typically to the desired positive outcome of self-imposed conditions that are based on the Early Childhood Survival Strategy. Hidden Agendas are stepping-stones to the one and only Hidden Goal. By means of realizing Hidden Agendas, a person who needs approval from their parent/caregiver attempts to get to their Hidden Goal. An indirectly motivated action or activity that is used as a carrier for the Hidden Agenda is called a **Vehicle**.

Vehicles

A Vehicle is usually an everyday activity or behavior that is initiated explicitly with an eye on a specific Hidden Agenda. It can be a task that needs to be done anyway (partly directly motivated) as well as something that is done specially to create an opportunity to work on a Hidden Agenda. In the preceding story, Erica's Hidden Goal was to be respected by her father. The Vehicle she chose was "to become a doctor." On her journey to becoming that doctor, there were many conditions she had to live up to with as many Hidden Agendas:

- She had to be smart (to impress her father).
- She had to learn quickly (to impress her father).
- She had to choose specific fields (to impress her father).

Hidden Agendas, therefore, are usually indicators of parental influence. You don't strive to fulfill those agendas based on what you think of things yourself. You fulfill them to the best of your ability to get closer to your one sacred Hidden Goal: acknowledgment. Because certain qualities are valued by your parent/caregiver, they are key in getting their approval.

Vehicle

An action, activity, or behavior used to display the performance of specific skills or character traits rather than the obvious, ordinary goal. The performance is ultimately aimed at getting approval (Fgas).

If you are addicted to approval, your daily activities may not be what they seem. Often the activities are actually Vehicles that serve a Hidden Agenda and show your caregiver that you are better than you believe he or she thinks.

The degree to which the Hidden Agenda is *fulfilled* depends on *the level of perfection* to which the task has been performed. That degree is responsible for getting the approval-related "Feel-good-about-self" state that functions as the needed Substitute Sense of Self. Failing to get there means that Annihilation is waiting

Thus, living up to a specific level of perfection with an action or behavior, fulfilling a Hidden Agenda, opens up a possibility for you to experience a Substitute Sense of Self. If you depend on a Substitute Sense of Self for your self-experience, your motivations for doing your everyday activities, including job-related things, are mostly indirect as they are aimed at realizing this Hidden Agenda. Now, your overt agenda is just a Vehicle to do that.

Note that your Hidden Agenda is not based on what you think of things yourself. It is based on a quality your parent appreciates! However, it is *your* ultimate motivator. That means it is not at all your own well-being that you pursue. It isn't hard to see how, once caught in this dilemma, you end up skipping your very own life altogether.

What I realized after many years of introspection was that nearly everything I did was focused on *getting approval*, either from myself (through my Internalized Parental Voice) or from others – or more precisely, nearly everything I did was to get to that "Feel-good-about-self" state.

Here are a few examples of the Vehicles of my Hidden Agenda and their root cause:

My motives for cleaning my house were not to have a clean house but to counter what I perceived my mother thought of me: "Don't be selfish, clean up after yourself."

My motives for sleeping well were not for myself or to be well rested but to avoid glances of reproach when coming to breakfast with a pale complexion and bags under my eyes. To counter the spoken or unspoken blame: "Don't ruin the atmosphere because of your sleeping problems."

My motives to be a musician were not to enjoy playing music while becoming an expert player, but to compete with the neighbor who got my mother's undivided attention when he played piano: "I need to be just as good a musician as my neighbor because my mother would love that and would adore me as well."

Even my motives to feel happy had nothing to do with my quality of life. I wanted to dismantle my mother's repoach: "Don't always have problems." And live up to her unspoken demand: "Be happy or I'll reject you!"

Those were all Vehicles of my Hidden Agenda to get vibes of approval, which then would help me reach my Hidden Goal!

My ultimate goal was to feel acknowledged by my parents as a cherished and well-respected daughter. However, that goal was hidden even from me!

The Hidden Goal versus the Hidden Agenda

Using the two terms Hidden Goal and Hidden Agenda next to each other may be somewhat confusing. Here is some clarification: Both concepts represent objectives. Both have to do with the objectives of a person who is on a mission to repair the damage of not having felt acknowledged by their caregiver. The difference lies in the scope. The Hidden Agenda refers to objectives a person envisions on the basis of a single instance. The Hidden Goal is the large ultimate goal: to get closer to the person whose acknowledgment they should have had in the first place. The Hidden Goal is the overarching goal, and the Hidden Agendas are the little objectives on the journey to reach that goal.

The reason a person decides to go this route is that unacknowledged children think it is their fault – they think that if they could have pleased their parent more, they would have been acknowledged. Through Hidden Agendas, these children (during childhood and later as adults) try to prove they can do better in a specific aspect or behavior, so their parent might think: "Maybe my child is not as bad as I thought. Now I am able to love her. Now she is worthy of being my child. Now I can finally appreciate her for who she is." The Hidden Agenda, with each action, is one small step on the long road to the Hidden Goal. The Hidden Goal is always an equivalent of being considered worthy of being taken into account.

Ultimately, the Hidden Goal is an attempt to turn back the clock toward that window in time when the parent missed the chance to be an adequate mirror for their child. What it tries to achieve is to make the parent change their mind about the child and shift from negative to positive. "But this time around let me make sure I succeed in being acknowledged as a real and definite human being with the right to exist the way I am," would be the subconscious reasoning of the desperate child upon trying once again to reach the desired perfect standard in their action or behavior.

Reaching the Hidden Goal, unfortunately, is an illusion. It can rarely take place, as the culprit is not the (former) child but *the caregiver*. It would be up to the caregiver to work out their own issues and overcome their own dependency on a Substitute Sense of Self before being able to truly "see" any other person, even their own children. If the caregiver had a Healthy Sense of Self, the child would not have been in this situation in the first place.

Aspects of Indirect Motivation

To better understand the process of Indirect Motivation, we can identify an order of things:

1. There is a task to be accomplished.
2. There is the Hidden Agenda to be completed. It is tied to that task.
   - reaching the "Feel-good-about-self" state
   - realizing the Substitute Sense of Self
3. There is the (ultimate) Hidden Goal to be reached:
   - acceptance and validation from the parents

Emphasis on Proving You Can and its Result

An aspect of Hidden Agendas that needs attention is the fact that the emphasis is on *proving that you can*. This greatly affects the ultimate outcome and is possibly one reason that any activity done with Indirect Motivation is less successful. Here are a few examples of a Hidden Agenda where the reason for doing the activity is about:

- Showing you *can* be selfless
- Showing you *can* be normal
- Showing you *can* have a good reputation
- Showing you *can* always be on time
- Showing you *can* sleep well

Why do I say "can" here? Because the main (Indirect) Motivation is *not* related to the content of *what* you are doing or *how* you are behaving.

The focus is entirely on showing (proving) that you can!

The Hidden Goal is to get approval; hence, "showing that you can" is more important than actually achieving the observable result. You are not really busy trying to get a certain result – you could say that the real motivation is to get the parent to change their mind about you. Washing the car or cleaning the kitchen is just a Vehicle to get that done.

This is why, in this case, over half of your efforts go into your Hidden Agenda, which is energy and focus taken away from (the directly motivated part of) your activity. Consequently, you do not get the desired result. You were not really aiming at the obvious result – you were aiming at getting the result your parent would approve of. Your intention was not to "play that sonata well" or "make beautiful music." Your intention was not to "become a doctor." Yet, to the outside world, that is what your intention appears to be. "Isn't it strange?" others may wonder. "They worked so hard, but they didn't get there." Now you know why. Because your heart wasn't in it.

The purpose of it all is to avoid experiencing Annihilation. Instead, you experience ongoing anxiety, stress, and rage, especially when you are hindered in some way. You fear failure in performing whatever tasks you need to perform because underneath there is always this battle to gain someone's approval.

Indirect Motivation and the Sense of Self

So, yes! I have to conclude that during the last twenty-five years, along my inner journey, whenever my mind was playing the Hidden Agenda game, I was (subconsciously) trying to compensate for the missed chances of developing a Healthy Sense of Self in my childhood. However, the window for such development was closed and the only thing I could achieve was the Fgas state. For all those years, I had mistaken that Fgas state for my Sense of Self, but it was, in fact, a Substitute Sense of Self.

If you are starting to resonate with what is being said here, please mind the possibility that you aren't consciously aware of lacking a Sense of Self, but it certainly could explain your current issues. With all the conditions operating to achieve specific Hidden Agendas, you can lead your whole life doing things that appear normal but that are geared toward those specific Hidden Agendas.

Ultimately, it could be that all you want is to reach your Hidden Goal, which serves to let you experience, however vaguely, your Substitute Sense of Self through the "Feel-good-about-self" state. This is the only thing that matters to you when you find yourself in this condition.

The normal results of cleaning the kitchen – for example, having a clean kitchen – may not really matter to you! At any rate, this question is not even within the scope of your consciousness because you are living to fulfill your (self-) imposed conditions. A way to help you assess your own situation is by consulting the SoS Comparison Chart on page 159.

Summary and Looking Ahead

A Lack of Sense of Self means that even the most normal-looking action or behavior turns into a cover-up for an opportunity to realize a Hidden Agenda. When you have a Healthy Sense of Self, your actual actions or behaviors aim at achieving normal, intended, predictable, and obvious outcomes – the outcomes anyone would expect. The behavior (in this case, *not* a Vehicle!) and its desired outcome (the directly motivated goal) are in sensible, ordinary alignment.

In the case of a Lack of Sense of Self, there is a discrepancy between the directly motivated part of the task (which is used as a Vehicle) and the actual goal (the Hidden Agenda) of the action, activity, or behavior. The natural alignment is distorted, or we might even say, perverted. The energy put into the action that serves as the Vehicle is not aimed at the given goal but at the Hidden Agenda. This bolsters the Substitute Sense of Self, which always disappears and continuously needs to be re-earned.

The Hidden Goal is the overarching bigger goal to which the Hidden Agendas are applied.

Each person with a Lack of Sense of Self has their own specific attributes in their Hidden Agenda. There are, in each person, different specifics that they feel should be improved and that come back often on a daily basis. Your Early Childhood Survival Strategy selected certain behaviors or qualities that you are adamant to improve upon, based on what your parents valued and blamed you for not doing well enough. These are your Ego-References, quite a difficult-to-grasp topic, but utterly useful to help you extend your self-knowledge. The next chapter will deal with this topic and explain where and why this behavior was adopted.

Chapter 7

Ego-References and Enmeshment

Because of this extreme dependency on parental approval, when you have a Lack of Sense of Self, you try to find as many ways as possible to be successful in getting that approval. It becomes your ultimate motive, which is what contaminates your overall motivation: Instead of living your life and enjoying things for their own sake, your major concern becomes how to get that approval. You tend to bend whatever it is that needs to be done in such a way that you can use the activity to serve this ultimate motive – that is how Indirect Motivation is born.

Technically, this process takes place, as we have seen, by means of Vehicles and Hidden Agendas. There is a third component in the game, though. Let us start out by calling that a system of personal rules. Each person has a set of specific personal rules that he or she, historically, has been conditioned to live up to. In the SoS Theory, we call these rules Ego-References. This chapter will clarify how these rules or habits play a role in your attempts to realize your Hidden Goal. But let us first zoom in a little more on Indirect Motivation.

The word *indirect* in Indirect Motivation suggests that, instead of a one-on-one connection between you and your goal, there is a third party involved. This aspect is best illustrated by comparing the dynamics that are at play when Indirect Motivation is the incentive of your action, to a strategy in billiards: a long bank. In this game, you do not aim the cue ball directly at the ball you want to send into the pocket; instead, you aim the cue ball at the opposite end of the table so that it bounces off the cushion and travels back down the table to hit your intended ball.

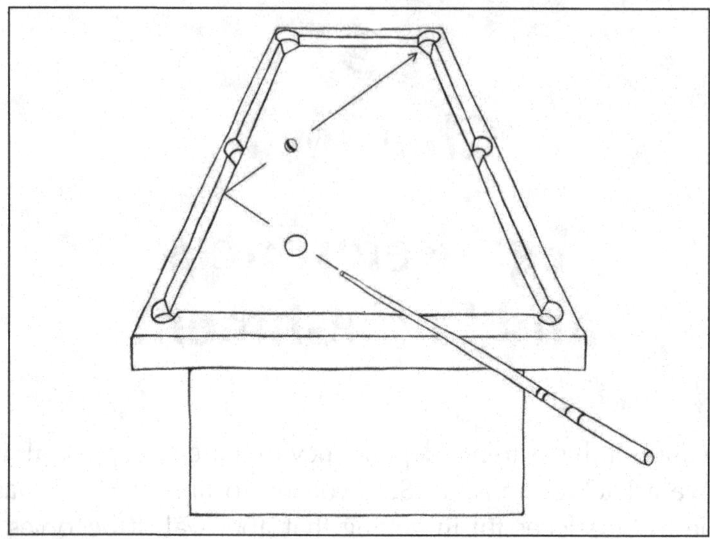

Fig 7.1 Pool table.

When does Indirect Motivation come up? Your motivation becomes indirect when it serves to alleviate your Fear of Annihilation, which comes forth from not feeling acknowledged. Aiming for the next best thing (approval), you learned how to behave or not to behave when (subconsciously) testing the reactions of your caregiver. The behavior that led to the desired result of approval turned into a more permanently attempted behavior, and later it became one of these personal rules.

These actions and/or characteristics have been on your mind so often, and getting them right has meant so much to you, that they have become a part of you. You always feel you need to improve on them, to do better next time. When this is how these actions or behaviors show up for you, you can count on having discovered your Ego-References! They come forth from and are an active part of your Early Childhood Survival Strategy (ECSS). Being able to live up to your Ego-References provides you with a surrogate way of feeling like an accepted person and makes you "Feel-good-about-self."

Ego-References

It is a rather complex concept, but it is central to the SoS Method and therefore to the process of recovering from the addiction to a Substitute Sense of Self. So, it is crucial that you recognize your own Ego-References as clearly as possible.

Ego-References refer to a set of conditions that are required to be performed at a high level of perfection. They include specific behaviors and actions that are valued by your parent, whose approval you need to "Feel-good-about-yourself." They refer to those tasks and/or behaviors that your parent used to regularly criticize you for not performing well enough. Those were the occasions in which your parent clearly showed displeasure with you, and in ways you remember as rather traumatic. You believe that by improving your performance of these tasks or behaviors, you will satisfy your parent and you hope it will get you the approval you crave.

Here is an example: Upon visiting my mother (I was a grown woman in my fifties), we planned to go to a concert. However, on the hour that we had agreed to leave for the concert, my daughter and I were a little late. My mother was so upset that she ignored both of us, demonstratively went by herself, and stayed silent for the rest of the evening. My heart sank low – what should have been a fun outing was ruined, not only for her, but for me as well as for my daughter. I will never forget the amount of effort I had to make to sooth myself and my daughter and make the situation somewhat manageable. "I should not be late. I should not be late." That is how an Ego-Reference is reinforced.

Ego-References

Subconsciously accepted requirements to feel and behave in certain ways and achieve certain results in order to feel approved of, as a substitute for a healthy way of experiencing the Self.

Origin of the Term *Ego-References*

During my years of introspection, I discovered that there was a strategy operating in my psyche that functioned below the surface of my conscious mind. In studying my own motivation, I observed that this strategy urged me to improve on certain behaviors that I felt were never good enough. On a daily basis, I needed to live up to these high standards to sooth the anxiety of not qualifying for the approval I craved. Anticipating my mother's rejection, I was my own worst critic. Not being able to live up to these standards caused me to fiercely hate myself. Trying to do certain things better the next time around would then give me the opportunity to "Feel-good-about-myself" again, and this cycle of trying harder the next time had become a compulsive urge. When I started to see what was happening and what kept me hostage, I realized that I needed to anchor that in my mind. I needed a name for this phenomenon so I would be able to identify this strategic behavior and keep track of it.

I remember the absolute necessity for me to find a word that would do the trick, and intuitively the term Ego-Reference came to mind. Understand that the examination of my own mind and emotions was not planned ahead. It was not a labor of love or leisure, but a job I had to do in the moment the need presented itself. Usually, the urge would come up in moments I actually planned to do something else. So, I wasn't exactly prepared to create names for the concepts I wanted to label in such a way that they would be commonly understood or even accepted in traditional psychology.

Ego-Reference seemed to cover the content of the concept as it formed in my mind. The word *Ego* referred to "what was *not* the 'I' with a Healthy Sense of Self." *Ego* was that part of my self that I had mistaken for my Sense of Self, but that, in reality, was NOT my Real Self; it was my Substitute Sense of Self. My feeling of existence relied on obeying the commands of that fake Sense of Self; that is why that fake Sense of Self always needed all those references, all those conditions to perform well in order for me to be considered allowed to exist.

So, I used *reference* because it referred to the desired behavior or specific action I had to perform in an optimal way to "Feel-good-about-myself." If I could have put it into words, I might have said, "My (Substitute) Sense of Self exists only when I am successful in meeting these conditions and requirements." Successfully performing my Ego-References made me feel like a person and avoided Annihilation.

"Working on an Ego-Reference" is short for trying to win approval while soothing the ever-present Fear of Annihilation. This is done by attempting to perform an action or a behavior to the point where you can win your parent's approval. As stated earlier, Ego-References are formed based on the conclusions you drew in early childhood, which then grew into solid, unchangeable strategies. Later in life, these childhood strategies turn into compulsions you are unable to free yourself from because they have become so much a part of who you are that you identify with your specific set of conclusions:

"Oh, I am always late." (My parent used to complain about it a lot.)

"Oh, I am always taking things too lightly." (My parent wants me to be more serious.)

"Oh, I never clean up after myself." (My parent complains about my being messy.)

In general, the term Ego-Reference is used to describe the behaviors and strategies of adults that have roots in more or less traumatic childhood experiences.

Perfecting specific behaviors is meant to result in receiving the right vibes from your caregiver/boss. For example, you may think: "I have to finish this work today," not so much because the work needs to be finished today (Direct Motivation) but because by finishing it early, you anticipate a sense of approval that will lead to "Feeling-good-about-self," which is the real motive for finishing the work early.

To reiterate, Ego-References are the specific self-imposed conditions that are used to get the approval that will lead to "Feeling-good-about-self." In other words, what started out as a strategic way for you to get your needs met in childhood has now grown into a full-blown, extremely unhealthy, self-defeating way of *being* in adulthood.

As you grew from an unacknowledged child into a young adult, you subconsciously started to identify with this way of being.

Ego-References developed in response to your earlier childhood observations and strivings, and led you in a constant pursuit to improve upon them. Please bear in mind that your Sense of Self never developed, so there is no way to consult your Self, and you feel you are only able to exist through fulfilling those conditions. You are filled with an exhausting, debilitating, and stressful need to achieve. You have no inner place to rest, which can lead to exhaustion, burnout, disease, and a lifetime of frustration.

Conditions That Become Ego-References

Which characteristics or behaviors become Ego-References later in life depend on an individual's specific circumstances. As a young child you were interpreting your caregiver's responses to your behavior and adjusting. Their positive reaction to your adjustments determined what Ego-References you developed. Each individual child discovers different behaviors (to do or refrain from) that evoke approval from his or her primary caregiver. Thus, you developed actions and behaviors unique to you and to your situation.

Chosen Ego-References may also have to do with your own specific temperament and inclinations. They can be colored by particular conditions and requirements your caregiver imposed on you. They can be, but are not necessarily, your caregiver's own Ego-References. Here is an example:

> *Erica had a hard time falling asleep at night, so she had a tendency to oversleep in the morning. She hated oversleeping because she knew it made Aunt Alma angry. Not that she would yell at Erica, but her eyes would be accusing; she would be curt and withhold the affection that Erica so needed. Aunt Alma was the closest thing to a mother Erica would ever have since her mother had died in an accident several years before. Even though Aunt Alma and her mother hadn't been very close, Erica would always be grateful that Aunt Alma had taken her in. She was desperate for her aunt's approval – and Aunt Alma did not approve of oversleeping.*
>
> *Neither did she approve of Erica staying home from school, even if she wasn't feeling well. Erica took what comfort she could in knowing that Aunt Alma had no*

patience for anyone being sick – including herself. Just like her grandparents, who were the same way, it was as if they believed even coming down with the flu was a weakness more rooted in the spirit than in the body.

A sharp rap at the door had Erica flinging off the covers and leaping to her feet. She felt a little dizzy, feverish. But she couldn't be sick; she just couldn't. And she didn't have a second to waste getting dressed while Aunt Alma briskly snapped from the door's other side, "Erica, your breakfast is getting cold! Do I have to come in there and get you dressed myself? The bus will be here in fifteen minutes, and if you miss it again, I'll be late for work. Hurry up, girl, hurry!"

"Sorry, Aunt Alma," Erica called back, trying hard to sound wide awake and livelier than she was actually feeling. "I'll be right there. Don't worry, I won't be a hindrance today and make you late. In fact, I'll make you proud! I'm ready for my test in English and promise to bring home an A!" Even as she said it, Erica silently prayed for her head to clear so she could do as well as she promised. She prayed even harder that Aunt Alma might give her a rare hug at the end of the day. Maybe then she would sleep so well she'd even have sweet dreams and wake up on time tomorrow morning, feeling "fit as a fiddle" as her mother used to say. Yes, that would be wonderful. It might even make Aunt Alma glad to have her there instead of wondering how much better her own life would be without the nuisance of a niece who might make her late for work. Erica felt like a stray dog begrudgingly taken in by a cat lady who didn't mind cleaning a litter box but would rather mop floors than pick up puppy poop in the yard.

There was one way to fix that. Erica just had to become a cat – a very healthy cat that did not oversleep.

This is a prime example of Ego-Reference. Erica is motivated, even desperate, to win her aunt's stingily imparted approval and affections, and with guilt fueling Erica's internal engines, "sleeping well" becomes her Ego-Reference. Having a good night's sleep and waking up on time becomes her imagined keys to the castle. (This is a metaphor for being allowed to get close to the parent while feeling included and accepted by them. See "The Castle of Enmeshment: An Analogy" on page 154.)

Similarly, Aunt Alma's dysfunctional view of sickness – passed on from her own parents – is her Ego-Reference. This is a trickle-down, intergenerational effect on par with shared DNA to meet a desired Fgas state. No wonder Erica, at an early age, is developing a serious need to be fit and well at all times, to pretend she is fine when nothing could be further from the truth.

Reactionary Ego-References

Reactionary Ego-References differ from regular Ego-References in that you use them for the opposite goal: to rebel. You are compelled to behave in the opposite manner you know your parent would like.

> *Let's say Erica is now in high school and has a friend named Peter. Peter likes to engage in reckless driving. This is particularly true when he peels out of his parents' driveway and burns rubber down the block. He especially gets a kick out of scaring his parents senseless whenever one of them is in the car with him.*
>
> *Instead of taking away the keys from their dangerous son or investigating the reason behind this senseless behavior, Peter's parents covered up his behavior with so-called understanding: "He is still young. He'll make sure not to get into an accident. He is a smart boy!" Peter's parents told themselves there was no problem, because accusing their son would lead to conflict in the family. Keeping the atmosphere in the family pleasant at all costs was their own Ego-Reference, so they had to obey this unspoken rule for fear of Annihilation. This of course had to do with their own dependency of the approval of their own parents that was still active in their system. But it made them allow Peter's dangerous driving style to go unaddressed.*
>
> *Unaware of his parents' quest, Peter felt empowered, sensing he could get away with what he thought was "cool." The slightest thought of his parents made him drive in an even more irresponsible and potentially self-destructive way. The more they asked him to be careful, the more careless he became. It was as if he was not really present in his own body, as if he was taken over by a demon. Otherwise, he might have thought about what could truly be at stake. If he could have thought for himself, he would have immediately become aware that he could get into a serious accident and hurt himself or someone else.*

Even as a grown man, he still felt belittled by his parents' nagging reminders to be careful. Behind the steering wheel of his car, all he felt was the reaction against what he intuitively recognized as an insincere and self-centered form of parental "caring." They did not even really see him. "Be careful – don't drive too fast!" they constantly repeated. Often they would even add, "We say it for your own good!"

Subconsciously, Peter sensed that they were not really concerned about him. He always felt his parents didn't relate to him as to a real person but more as an extension of themselves and one that didn't serve their goals. He had noticed that his parents were always sucking up to authority figures – to his teachers or even to neighbors – and put him down in front of them, excusing themselves for his behavior. He had never experienced them standing up for him in conflicts with his childhood friends. "You have to stand up for yourself," is all they would say, blaming him for making them feel ashamed of him. No, in Peter's mind, there was no doubt that his parents were more concerned about their precious car or about their need to be in control so nothing unexpected would interfere with their lives.

He was used to feeling that his presence in his parents' lives was more of a roadblock in their desire to live a life without ripples. He did not really matter to them as the person he was. Driving wildly was his way of rebelling against not really being seen as a separate and independent human being by his parents. Because of his Lack of Sense of Self, every day, again and again, Peter risked ending up in the hospital, not to mention the risk of hurting or killing innocent third parties that might be unfortunate enough to cross his path.

This is what I call a Reactionary Ego-Reference, which does just as much of a disservice to you and your environment as a regular Ego-Reference.

Ego-References and Vehicles

As discussed in the preceding chapter, the term Vehicle is used to indicate an action, activity, or behavior that serves as a carrier for, and as an opportunity to work on an Ego-Reference. The action that serves as a Vehicle has two functions: It brings about an overt result (Direct Motivation), and it serves to realize your Hidden Agenda (the positive outcome of an Ego-Reference). Your focus is only indirectly on the overt goal though; your real intent is to attain the Hidden Goal, or at least reach the Fgas state, feeding your Substitute Sense of Self.

Here are some examples of behaviors that can be used as Vehicles:

- Household- or job-related activities.
- Visiting someone.
- Sending a card.
- Helping someone in any way.
- Pursuing a certain level or area of education.
- Educating children a certain way.
- Going to specific places; e.g., church services, vacation destinations.
- Washing your car.
- Being on time.
- Having specific relationships with specific types of people; for example, from higher or lower social levels, people with a specific political or religious belief.

You can do or be all of these things, not because of what they are, but to get approval, even from yourself: "Look how good I am."

Examples of Ego-References

Remember that Ego-References are subconscious rules concerning perceived flaws that need to be bettered. You can think of Ego-References as self-imposed conditions, but you need to soften this judgment by keeping in mind that it was the best you could do at the time. It was a second best option.

Even though holding on to Ego-References degrades your quality of life and makes you the slave of fulfilling these (self-imposed) conditions, considerable introspection may be required to discover that you hold the belief – accepted in early childhood – that you desperately need to fulfill these requirements.

Ego-References are compulsive by nature; they form the cornerstones in your battle to gain a Substitute Sense of Self. There's no use trying to discard them right away, as you need to find out the truth about them, which lies deeply hidden under the surface of your daily life.

To get a better feel for what aspects of your life are susceptible to becoming Ego-References, you'll find below a list of the ones I had. Based on my observations as a child (my ECSS), these were my main character and behavior issues that I felt compelled to continuously improve on to "Feel-good-about-myself." Even if you do not immediately recognize any of these as yours, Ego-References could still be ruling your life.

- As a mother, I must make sure that the atmosphere in my family is positive at all times.
- As a daughter, I need to be in shape physically, emotionally, and psychologically, and always seem to be okay.
- I have to sleep well, be fit, be in a good mood, and look well rested.
- I have to know what I want.
- I have to be on time.
- I have to have my act together.
- I need to achieve something in life so others recognize my success and make me feel respected.
- I need to avoid getting angry, upset, irritated, or even annoyed.
- I need to avoid conflicts at all costs.
- I should not have problems or create problems for myself or for anyone else.
- I have to make sure I do not become sick or feel unwell.
- I need to do things differently from other people and find ways to be special.
- I need to be different from what and who I naturally am; who I am is not good enough.
- I have to stand out from the crowd.
- I must not complain.
- I should not be selfish.
- I should always be truly interested in what others do.

Of course, your list may be different, though some of these are quite generic and undoubtedly universal among people with a Lack of Sense of Self. Most likely, you are not consciously aware of all your "rules," but by becoming aware of them, you will start to see that you are forcing yourself to be careful all the time: that you are walking on eggshells.

The need for a good outcome to your Ego-References increases with age. As both child and parent grow older, there seems to be a subconscious awareness that the time to convince the parent that "I am a valuable human being" is running out. So not only do you try harder, but also the now-elderly parent may become increasingly more difficult to please.

When I visited my mother in the last decade of her life (I was in my fifties), I would not enter her house without bringing flowers or a little gift. I never thought of actually making her happy; I did it to get approval. (Ego-Reference: "not being selfish.") In my battle to feel appreciated, I felt I had to keep up with my sister, who gave her even more presents and flowers. In hindsight, I felt I had to keep up with so much that there was no room left for any spontaneity.

Other times, I felt I had to take my mother on trips to change her impression of me. She had concluded that I was leading a selfish life. My sister took her out, so I also had to do it if I did not want to lose points. But I was unable to offer that option as generously as I wished, tied as it was to that other Ego-Reference I had: "Make sure I sleep well." No use promising to take somebody out and having to blow it off, yet again, because I didn't sleep. A drama in a nutshell, maybe, but for me, still quite a bit of a drama.

Ego-References and Inner Conflict

Inner Conflict

Two or more competing and incompatible inner mandates to work toward experiencing a Substitute Sense of Self. This leads to high anxiety because the competition causes a no-win outcome.

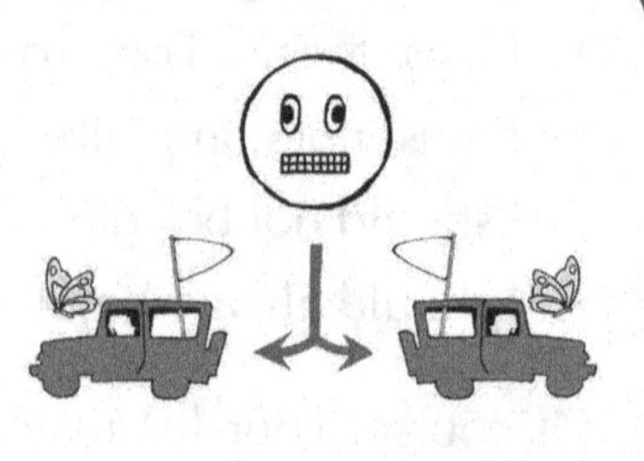

It is relatively easy to strive to fulfill one Ego-Reference. What do you do, though, if two or more have to be fulfilled and they contradict one another? This complication leads to an **Inner Conflict** – a battle already lost, because a choice has to be made to fulfill one and ignore the other one. Because so much is perceived to be at stake in the fulfillment of an Ego-Reference (to avoid Annihilation), tremendous fear comes up.

Figure 7.2: Inner Conflict.

If you have an Inner Conflict, you may experience the following physical sensation: A collision of nervous currents going in different directions, resulting in a noticeable buzz throughout your body. There is not necessarily tension in the muscles. You feel as if your nervous network is under stress. Imagine a place in the sea where the waves roll ashore from various directions. It leads to a point where those streams meet and collide. That is how your nervous system feels in moments of Inner Conflict.

My problem (the Inner Conflict) usually emerged during the night and prevented me from sleeping. My nervous system would be under stress, because the impulses to take action were heading in opposing directions. Ironically, I noticed that my mind wasn't really worried about anything. It seemed as though nothing was on my mind, and therefore trying to trace *what worried me* wasn't of any help in finding relief from my Inner Conflict.

Eventually, I figured out that the conflict was playing on a deeper level. Being able to label my behavioral strategies as Ego-References has been a blessing because, each time, it helped me to identify a Hidden Agenda that obviously was at play. Often, it was still hard enough, though, to identify which Ego-Reference was being executed and what exactly my Hidden Agenda was, but when I did, I would fall asleep like a baby.

When Inner Conflict occurs there is no "good" choice because the Ego-References are incompatible or contradictory and you can only focus on one Ego-Reference at the time. Consequently, only one Ego-Reference has the potential to be fulfilled, which means that the other(s) will be ignored at the cost of (perceived) Annihilation. The practical result of this situation is that, due to lack of sleep and stress, it is impossible to bring any of the Ego-References to a good end. This again increases anxiety and generates a greater Fear of Annihilation, which can manifest as a panic attack.

In short, we are talking about a tangled knot of perceived threats to the Substitute Sense of Self, and the body experiences this particular knot accordingly. This situation can lead to a "blank night": a night of total insomnia, plus the unpleasant and exhausting buzzing sensation.

Erica's Situation: An Example of an Inner Conflict

To see how some of the elements discussed in this chapter can affect a person, let us visit with Erica again.

7 Ego-References and Enmeshment

Remember Erica and her aunt Alma? Aunt Alma had stepped up to take care of her niece when Erica's mother had died in a car accident. It wasn't for reasons of compassion though, but more to impress her own mother. Even at her age, Alma still wanted to show her mother that she could be a caring person. So she came into this story from her own angle, thinking, "I know my mother dispproves of me for not being married, but if I take in little Erica, I can show her that it is not because I am an uncaring person. She always reproaches me for being all about myself and says that is the reason no man wants to stay with me." Her mother's negativity hurt Alma more than she could say, and this was her chance to prove the opposite! It was Alma's focus in life, and she was so preoccupied with her Substitute Sense of Self that she passed that way of being on to her niece.

We now encounter Erica as a married woman, at a moment in the evening when her husband is not yet home. She has to get up early the next day because there will be an important meeting first thing in the morning. She wants to go to bed early so she can get a good night's sleep, but Paul, her husband, is not home yet. At first, Erica tries to calm herself down by finding all sorts of little tasks that need to be done anyway. "If I do this now, it just feels like I am not planning to go to bed yet and I won't be so upset," she tries to fool herself. Being upset is the last thing she wants now. It will only make her lie awake for long hours, and she needs to be well rested tomorrow morning.

As it gets later, she loses her temper. And when her husband comes home, happy from an enjoyable night spent with friends, she blows up at him: "I don't understand. You know I have a hard time sleeping if you're not here, and you know I have an important meeting tomorrow. How could you do this to me?" she screams, smashing the trash bag she's holding on the floor, scattering the contents. Then she hurries to pick it all up and starts squirming: "Oh, I am so sorry I yelled at you. Of course you didn't do it on purpose. I know you always think about what's good for me. I'm just so nervous about tomorrow. Please don't be mad at me. Please don't abandon me!"

So what is going on in this relationship drama?

Erica has to get up early the next day, and we know she is dependent on a Substitute Sense of Self for her self-experience. To make sure she

"Feels-good-about-self" and feels safe, she has to accomplish all the following Ego-References:

- Have peace of mind
- Sleep well
- Look fresh and fit in the morning and be in a good mood
- Be productive and deliver good-quality work
- Be flexible about her husband's behaviors

During Erica's upbringing, Aunt Alma had warned Erica on a regular basis that she'd better live up to those conditions; otherwise, her relationship with a significant other would be at risk. Erica failed to see, of course, that her aunt was just passing on her own Ego-References to her niece so Erica would help Alma realize her Hidden Goal. Erica's behaving properly and staying married would reflect well on the education Alma gave her – Alma's mother would value her for that – and Alma would have her hands free to continue cultivating her own Fgas state. For Erica, it meant that on top of having to live up to the Ego-References she had developed to get her aunt's approval, she also had to make sure to be forgiving toward her husband, for fear he would walk out on her.

Erica's Ego-References are in conflict: Going to bed before her husband comes home is not an option because she needs him to be home before she can sleep. She needs things to be "just so," to ensure she doesn't encounter challenges that could throw her off.

Erica is caught between several incompatible needs:

She needs to not cause Paul any problems, make any demands on him, or create any drama by asking him to be home by her bedtime, and she can't be upset when he is late. (Fear of Abandonment = Fear of Annihilation.)

But she also needs to sleep well in order to get up early and be in good shape to do well at work the next day.

She can't sleep until he gets home and she knows "everything is all right" (Fgas).

In other words, a complex Inner Conflict is going on. Note that Erica is not focused on the content of the conflict but solely on what is at stake for her, which is to make sure she is able to realize her Hidden Agenda in order to feel safe. But the two Ego-References are demanding opposite behaviors from her.

1. "I must sleep well so I need to go to bed now, but I can't," is an Ego-Reference fed by the fear of not being able to function ("and I MUST function; otherwise, I won't get to my Substitute Sense of Self").
2. "I must not speak up and cause quarrels" reflects fear of abandonment, in conflict with the need to create circumstances that allow her to get a good night's sleep.

You might say these issues look like ordinary, everyday issues between a husband and wife. Yet there is a significant difference. Because of the Ego-References and the Substitute Sense of Self–oriented behavior of at least one of the two people (Erica), these games are (perceived to be) playing out on an existential level.

> *On nights like this, and on many other nights, Erica lies in bed stressed, with a buzzing nervous system, unable to understand what is going on within her own body or in her mind. She is being pulled in many different directions by her feelings, and she doesn't even really know what it is all about. If she could express all those feelings in words, here's what she might say:*
>
> *"I don't agree with his coming home so late, but he doesn't listen to me. So my needs are not being taken into account. To me that feels like Annihilation, it leaves me with the sensation that I don't really exist. I feel bad about myself, and I know I can't sleep when I feel bad about myself. I need to 'Feel-good-about-self.' So I have to do everything in my power to change that." (Read: I really need that Substitute Sense of Self!)*
>
> *"It's late and I need to go to bed. I have to get up early. I can't sleep when he is not home – I need to feel safe. But if I start arguing right now, if I openly disagree with him when he comes home, he'll disapprove of me and then I won't sleep because I won't feel safe." (Ego-References: sleep well, behave normally, feel safe, avoid abandonment.)*

> *"I should not create drama because I can't afford to lose this guy. I depend on his approval. Without him, I wouldn't be able to feel safe because my aunt will despise me." (Ego-Reference: create no drama, problems, or quarrels; feel safe; avoid abandonment.)*
>
> *"I'll feel unworthy if I can't do good work tomorrow. If I don't do good work, I feel terrible. If I can't sleep, I will be unable to function." (Ego-Reference: deliver good-quality work.)*
>
> *"I feel dirty and ashamed if I don't sleep well. Everybody can see it in my face and then I feel like I don't belong in the workforce, and that I'm not a 'real' person." (Ego-Reference: Look fresh and fit in the morning and be in a good mood.)*

It's important to understand that the actual content of these issues is not what really matters to Erica. None of this is really about sleeping well or about arguing with her husband. These issues are Vehicles for achieving the Hidden Agenda of her Ego-References.

In a situation like this, the outcome for Erica is a total crash, a feeling-bad-about-self state, possibly depression for a number of days, and insomnia due to fearing the inability to gain a Substitute Sense of Self. In the best-case scenario, she will start her Sisyphus labor over again and try even harder to make it work this time.

The situation appears even more painful when we realize that Erica's life isn't about her own life at all – nor is it even about her husband's life, for that matter. The eternal pursuit of her Substitute Sense of Self is what her life is all about. This is the way Erica has become a slave to her own Early Childhood Survival Strategy.

However, with enough time and help in understanding what is going on inside herself, Erica could become conscious of her Hidden Goal and her conflicting expectations and feelings. She would have to do the tough inner work to uncover the true nature of these Ego-References. But, as a result, they could be laid to rest, thus putting an end to the feelings of being unsafe and the disruptive quarrels that ruin Erica and her husband's quality of life.

That is exactly the insight and understanding the SoS Method aims to offer those who need it.

Enmeshment and the Addiction to Approval

Now that we have an idea of what Ego-References are and the role they play in the life of a person with a Lack of Sense of Self, it becomes clear that the presence of Ego-References suggest a unnaturally strong tie to the parent. How this tie came about has everything to do with the unhealthy dependency on approval that developed instead of being your own independent person. It is almost as if the parent and the child are one and the same person. Maybe, with that concept in mind, the child using the parent's criteria is a little more understandable. Below, you will find a more extensive clarification of this hard-to-imagine concept.

Enmeshment is a SoS term that refers to an extreme emotional and psychological entanglement with your caregiver. The umbilical cord was never really cut, and your caregiver still has an overbearing influence on you and a strong demand to have you adjust to their needs and wants. There is no room in your caregiver's mind or heart to allow you to be true to your nature. Your caregiver merely experiences you as an extension of their self and (involuntarily) manipulates your approval-seeking behavior in ways that best serves their own goals.

In this situation, it is very likely that your caregiver has no clear Sense of Self either. Your caregiver needs you to be just so, so they have time and energy left to work on fulfilling their own Ego-References.

If you grow up in this invisible network of tension, you learn in an early stage to cooperate with your caregiver's need to live up to the Ego-References *they* depend on to reach the Fgas state, and most likely, you become enmeshed with your caregiver in the process. You learn to focus on the needs of your caregiver and fail to develop your own criteria, and that has its price. It costs you your authenticity. What develops instead is the skill to read your caregiver's state of mind (facial expressions and tones of voice). This results in a lack of development of personal values, criteria, tastes, opinions, motives, and goals – all aspects that make a person unique.

As a child – with no way of knowing what a normal or healthy relationship with a parent is – you become overly dependent on receiving approval from your caregiver. Getting attention or even a smile from your caregiver makes you feel (momentarily) allowed "into" the Enmeshment. Outside of the Enmeshment, you were/are unable to function properly because you did not develop the virtual backbone necessary to support yourself as an independent person. There is a continuous hankering for good vibes and for feeling included in your caregiver's world.

Later, getting approval functions as a reminder of this feeling of being allowed into the highly desired state of Enmeshment. It is within the confines of Enmeshment that the need to earn a Substitute Sense of Self can be suspended for a moment. It is as if, for that brief moment, you are back to being a part of your parent, and the absence of your own backbone is not so painfully felt when you are able to lean on theirs. It feels like being close to the fire that warms the heart. It is a treacherous feeling, though; in that moment, you don't consciously realize that your caregiver's approval is temporary. One wrong move and you are kicked out of the warm embrace of Enmeshment and thrown back into the cold reality of having to work hard to comply with your caregiver's wishes to get a Substitute Sense of Self and avoid Annihilation.

What you learned as a child does not change when you grow up. So, after being raised this way, your situation stays exactly the same. In other words, you and your caregiver are enmeshed for life, whether or not your caregiver is still alive.[1]

Here is an example of the way such an Enmeshment plays out in life:

> *Erica, now a grown woman, had moved away from her aunt Alma's house to live on another continent. Intuitively, she felt a drive to free herself from what she didn't know existed: an Enmeshment with her aunt to whom she was tied by a guilty sense of gratitude. She now had two children of her own and was determined to be a good parent.*
>
> *After the move, Erica and Aunt Alma would call each other on a daily basis. These conversations were usually quite animated, but toward the end, there was always*

[1] After a caregiver's passing, this dependency on the caregiver can be transferred onto other connections: spouses, children, etc.

this funny situation. Erica would start to feel increasingly uneasy and walk on eggshells to make sure to stop the conversation at a point where they both would "Feel-good-about-self." In her mind, she would replay the conversation to convince herself she hadn't said anything wrong and that there wasn't anything that could be held against her before hanging up. Frantically, she would search for signs and symptoms of something that would have left her aunt unsatisfied with the way the conversation went, and she felt an almost obsessive need to end the conversation on an upbeat note. She would go on talking, sometimes extending the call endlessly with small talk until it was clear that everything was okay. Only then would she feel safe enough to end the call.

Throughout her life, Erica had felt responsible for her aunt's "Feel-good-about-self" state, and this was still true, even while she lived far away. Sometimes, she would call her back to ask if everything was okay; they would laugh about it, but then something was said that made her doubtful again, so she would call her back five minutes later: "Everything is okay, right?"

When Aunt Alma didn't call her for a few days, she would panic and feel deeply troubled. She would be unable to sleep at night because her aunt had sounded a little annoyed in the last call. "Perhaps she's taken offense at something I did or said," she worried. What Erica wasn't aware of was that she was not really interested in the effect of her words on Aunt Alma for her aunt's sake, but that it was only because she desperately needed her "Feel-good-about-self" state as proof that she'd been allowed into the Enmeshment. She and her aunt shared one spine, so to speak. Any sense of being rejected made Erica feel as if she did not exist – she felt Annihilated.

Being granted access to the Enmeshment is your ultimate Hidden Goal when you are without a Sense of Self. There you can experience the missing part of your virtual spine and feel the illusion of being whole, if only for a moment. You feel allowed to be, that you exist, that you are being seen and heard as a real person, that you are just like "other people." Feeling *bad* about yourself is your default state and a powerful motivator to keep working toward achieving your Ego-References.

When Erica moved into her new house, far away from her aunt, she planted tomatoes and pepper plants in her big backyard because her aunt would have liked that. She never thought of what she, Erica, might have liked.

Being brought up in an Enmeshment causes you to be driven to please your caregiver based on the earliest conclusions that developed into your Early Childhood Survival Strategies. It is as if you not only crave your caregiver's approval, but you also almost need a part of his or her identity, because your own, as a person without a Sense of Self, is missing.

The Castle of Enmeshment: An Analogy

The following tale explores the difficulties and pressures experienced by someone who exists in an Enmeshed relationship with their caregiver.

Far away, in a country hidden in a valley covered by fog, lay a village called Struggletown. It was a village like any other, and most villagers lived a reasonably happy life: they worked, did what needed to be done, and on the weekends, they usually found small pockets of time to do what they truly enjoyed.

A number of inhabitants, however, were under a lot of stress and felt restless and unhappy. They were naked and seemed to have no access to clothing – everyday shirts and pants like the other villagers wore – but they didn't have the faintest idea why. As a result, they hardly ever came out of their hiding places, keeping themselves compulsively busy with soul-searching in the hope of getting to the root of this problem.

Since birth, these unhappy individuals heard people whisper about the Queen of MOD, who lived in the Castle of Enmeshment at the top of a very steep and rocky mountain. It was said that this queen had a factory in the basement of her castle that produced plain, flesh-colored bodysuits. With artistic skill, the bodysuits were painted in such a way that they looked like normal clothes, but in reality, the jackets, pants, skirts, and cardigans were like the faux-finish furniture and chandeliers in the castle: only painted on.

Nevertheless, the naked people would do anything to obtain a suit like that so they could go down to the village and mingle with the other villagers. They could almost look like them ... though not quite. From afar, there was no visible difference between the clothes of the normal villagers and the fake suits from the castle. Up close, though, the naked villagers feared the imitation would be visible.

The Queen of MOD had put specific requirements in place for the villagers to qualify for these suits. The applicants for the suits had to create and maintain a good atmosphere while making sure that the queen was continuously the center of attention and the recipient of an ongoing flow of feel-good energy, something she particularly needed to feel like a real person herself. The queen made sure that everyone who entered the castle felt the responsibility of meeting her needs to the extent of manipulating their own feelings in favor of generating these feel-good vibes for the queen. The villagers traditionally accepted the deal as they felt that so much was at stake for them.

Halfway to the castle was the House of Ego-References, where the naked villagers had to register, pick a task, and carry it out to perfection. These tasks had to be accomplished while displaying certain behaviors: avoid creating or experiencing any tension; be happy at all times; never be late; no conflicts or disagreements with others; no sleeping problems; be able to socialize while completing the tasks to perfection; never get sick; never have money problems; and never complain. The chosen task had to be performed to a high standard, one that was higher than the standard for the normal villagers.

Occasionally, a desperate naked villager was able to fulfill all these conditions and arrive at the castle in good shape. The villager looked fresh and fit, without any problems or lack of money, appearing well fed with rosy cheeks and a smile on his face. Then the Queen of MOD would open the doors to her Castle of Enmeshment and allow the villager to enter. .

This was the moment the villager had been working toward his whole life. It was like a homecoming, and, satisfied, he let his guard down in total happiness. Often, though, this act of vulnerability proved to be a fatal error.

As it would soon turn out, any interference in the flow of feel-good energy was detrimental to the villager's mission, and the moment his task was not performed to perfection, the Queen of MOD would immediately deny him further access to the castle. The door simply remained closed and the poor villager had to crawl back home to his hiding place, recover from the blow, and start all over again, planning and preparing the unavoidable next trip to visit the queen in the castle.

In the case that all had gone to plan, the naked villager was provided with what he came for: the plain bodysuit painted to look like a normal outfit.

The situation was never safe, though, and things could take a turn for the worst at any given moment: a hindrance, an obstacle in the flow of feel-good energy, would be enough to set the queen off and have her explode in a terrible temper tantrum, yelling and screaming at the villager, shattering the windows of the castle with her nasty, shrill voice.

The villager would be kicked out of the castle, his painted bodysuit disappearing into thin air as if by a trick of black magic. The shocked and shaken villager, naked again, would hide as quickly as he could, trying to find his way back home while not being seen by others. After spending some days mourning the loss of his suit, he would embark on the journey to the castle all over again.

Meanwhile, the other inhabitants of Struggletown had no idea what was going on in the lives of the naked ones. They just sensed that these people were different. Most Struggletowners felt there was something off with the naked ones and didn't include them in their daily lives. So, in the end, acquiring their painted bodysuits didn't really help the naked ones; they still felt excluded and lonely.

After the attempt to look normal failed, the unfortunate villagers would break down and be overcome with rage. It caused them to commit crimes and act badly toward others. On occasion, one would even kill himself and his family. Out of desperation, they sometimes burned down their own or other people's houses. Their target should have been The Queen of MOD instead, because she was the holder of the suits. But that never happened. They needed her …

Then one day, after being rejected by the queen one too many times, a naked villager spent an enormous amount of time and energy thinking about his peculiar way of living. He found himself exhausted and at his wits' end when he was struck by a mind-altering thought: "What if I just make my own clothes like the other villagers do?" he pondered. "Isn't it strange how that solution never occurred to me before?"

He recognized that ever since birth, his people had been the naked ones. They were brought up with this unquestioned idea that the only way of getting their clothes required fulfilling tasks and conditions for the Queen of MOD. It was just their tradition to get their clothing in an indirect way instead of directly buying them or making them. "We have focused all our attention and spent all our energy on pleasing the queen. It never occurred to us that we had the option of providing clothes for ourselves, and real ones too! We actually can meet our own needs in a direct way! We can wear whatever clothes we choose."

He pondered this new concept for a long time as he sensed the impact of this insight. Then he concluded, still in awe, "I guess our minds were just not able to generate the concept of that possibility because we were brought up to believe that pleasing the Queen was the one and only way for us. What creatures of habit we are!"

Still, the villager had to collect all his courage to face the fears of going through town with his first self-made clothes. But as he grew more skillful in cutting the fabric and sewing the parts together, his fear lessened and eventually subsided altogether. He had broken free from the prison of his own mind and opened up a path to normal life. He was finally free. He also had found his mission in life: teaching the other naked ones to make their own clothes!

When a child is brought up in an Enmeshment with the primary caregiver, he or she doesn't develop an adeguate sense of being an independent person, fully separate from the caregiver. You can almost say that the child looks with the eyes of the mother or hears with the ears of the father. The child makes choices in life about what to do, based on what he or she believes would be the most successful way to Score points with the parent.

The child never gives up the hope that the parent will look upon him or her with kindness and compassion and open the door to the Castle of Enmeshment. In other words, it is the child's deepest desire to have the caregiver's direct, undivided attention and feel one with him or her.

Being brought up in an Enmeshment produces a craving for the unhealthy, but desperately needed, Substitute Sense of Self.

Summary and Looking Ahead

Throughout the last several chapters, we have covered a lot of information: what happens when developing a Natural Sense of Self is stunted; how the Fear of Annihilation, in its many manifestations, leads to Indirect Motivation; and the way Early Childhood Survival Strategies lead to developing the behaviors that work best to ensure the achievement of some approximation of what we need most – acknowledgment.

The next part of the book ties it all together. You will get a glance into the world of a person who has a Lack of Sense of Self, who operates based on Indirect Motivation because they are addicted to approval and hooked on "Feeling-good-about-self." The devastating reality of living a life that is Substitute Sense of Self oriented will be fully exposed.

The SoS Comparison Chart: Do I Have A Substitute Sense Of Self?

If you begin to suspect that your life is more about compulsively fulfilling conditions instead of actively choosing your dos and don'ts, you might want to check out the SoS Comparison Chart, which aims at giving you some clarity about which group you should place yourself into.

My point of departure for this chart was my hunch that humanity can be split into three basic groups based on their quality of Sense of Self: Group A are people with a Natural Sense of Self that was developed in early childhood. Group B are people with a Lack of Sense of Self that leads to the need for a Substitute Sense of Self. And Group C are people with a *Restored* Sense of Self, which is developed through a recovery and healing process that successfully replaces a person's Lack of Sense of Self with a "learned" Healthy Sense of Self. While Group A and Group C both have a Healthy Sense of Self, this Comparison Chart will illustrate some of the differences between them.

How to Use the SoS Comparison Chart

The first thing you want to look at is the physical, mental, and emotional states experienced by someone who *does* have a Natural Sense of Self. This will allow you to check how you match up. Since I myself never had a Natural Sense of Self, these descriptions are based on research rather than on personal experience. The list here is my best estimation of the attributes associated with a Natural Sense of Self.

Successfully developing a Natural Sense of Self is healthy and normal; therefore, I consider the absence of that development to be abnormal. This abnormality leads to all kinds of pathological signs and symptoms. That is why I chose to use the following description: "*The presence of a Sense of Self is marked by the absence of symptoms of a Lack of Sense of Self.*"

Column B in the SoS Comparison Chart describes the signs and symptoms that manifest when you are not in touch with your Self and are relying on a Substitute Sense of Self. If you identify with Group B, chances are you fall into the category of people who relied on coping mechanisms in early childhood to get their needs met. As it became obvious over time that your need to be acknowledged as a potentially independent person wasn't automatically met by your caretaker, you had to find alternative methods to meet that need for acknowledgment.

Based on your observations, you concluded that various conditions had to be fulfilled to get some sort of a response from your parent. These conditions were based on trial and error, and success meant you felt you were worthy of your caregiver's attention. These conditions shaped how you thought you had to act in order to be considered a "somebody." They determined what you thought you had to do in order to feel you were allowed to "be."

Unfortunately, these are subconscious processes. The decisions you made between birth and six years old seldom come to the surface of your mind. You are totally unaware of the conclusions you drew back then, when they seemed to really help you get specific needs taken care of. But because there really isn't anything in your memory that you can pinpoint as an important decision, you consequently still find yourself fulfilling those same childhood conditions in adulthood.

The conditions you imposed on yourself as a child had something in common: "I cannot be who I naturally am because that doesn't make me a visible, valued contributor to the family." Battling your own nature is a continuous struggle, so you tend to find yourself "enduring life as opposed to living it as the person you actually are."[1]

[1] This expression is borrowed from Melody Beattie, author of *Beyond Codependency,* Hazelden 1989.

If this feels like it could be true for you, it is time you become conscious of those observations and decisions that led to your Early Childhood Survival Strategies (see page 95), which turned into your Ego-References (see page 133). You might find out that instead of living your own life, you are functioning more as a slave to the "Feel-good-about-self" state (see page 95).

In the long run, you too mistake this "Feel-good-about-self" state for a sense of your Self, because it's the only moment you perceive yourself as being allowed to be. In reality, though, this state is nothing more than an altered version of parental approval – a memory of the vibe you got when you behaved in ways your parent liked or, at least, wasn't bothered by.

Now you are doomed to continuously fulfill those conditions that are required to get into that state of "Feel-good-about-self." The sad fact is that it is an unrealistic way of relating to yourself, and it has nothing to do with who you are as your own being.

A person with a Healthy Sense of Self has no need to go out of their own way to "earn" a perceived right to exist by trying to be different from who they are. They don't have to suffer the stress and the consequences that stem from this type of living. That doesn't mean there will only be sunshine in their lives, but whatever problems do arise aren't immediately tied to their Sense of Self because they don't suffer from the deeper issue of dependency on the outcome of achievements and behavior.

So once again, the presence of a Healthy Sense of Self is marked by the absence of the symptoms that are generated by the dependency on a Substitute Substitute Sense of Self, which replaces or fills up the void left by a Lack of Sense of Self.

Assessing your own condition cannot be done by checking on particular feelings or sensations that are typical for a Natural Sense of Self. You have to check yourself for the presence of any signs and symptoms related to a Substitute Sense of Self.

The presence of symptoms related to the dependency on a Substitute Sense of Self is unnatural and unhealthy. It is more natural to not display any of those symptoms. If you don't show any of the symptoms, it probably means you have successfully developed a Natural Sense of Self.

So *how* do you feel if your Natural Sense of Self developed in a healthy way, and *how* do you feel if it didn't? If you put the question that way as opposed to asking, "What are the specific sensations that indicate the presence of a Natural Sense of Self?" you will find an extensive answer in the chart below.

This chart is a list of characteristics that go with each of the three types of Sense of Self. Comparing these characteristics will give you a clear view of how each of the types of Sense of Self manifest in a person's life and can be recognized. It will possibly even allow you to assess which kind of Sense of Self is operating in you.

As you read the descriptions in each column, consider the following questions to do a quick self-assessment: Which do you identify with most? Which describes your experience of each characteristic?

You might highlight or circle the characteristic that is the best match for you and tally up which type of Sense of Self is dominant in your own inventory.

As you continue reading this book, keep the results of this quick self-assessment in mind. Most important, stay curious even when you are presented with Sense of Self concepts in this chart that you have not yet been exposed to. That may be a challenge, but they offer an explanation for *WHY* you do *WHAT* you do and can help you begin to find a way out of the jungle of Indirect Motivation.

You've heard it said that *what we resist, persists*. When we stay curious, though, we create the space for insight and wisdom to be revealed, and that could make all the difference. Let this self-assessment be a benchmark as you progress through Parts II and III of this book.

SoS Comparison Chart: Natural Sense of Self, Substitute Sense of Self, and Restored Sense of Self

Group A Natural Sense of Self	Group B Lack of Sense of Self, compensated for by a Substitute Sense of Self	Group C Restored Sense of Self
ALONE/BELONGING Generally comfortable being alone and being with others, depending on one's authentic nature; potential leaders.	Excessive need for others to provide feelings of belonging or group identity and for feedback on how one should feel about oneself.	In touch with true natural personal inclinations of the balance between being alone and the need for belonging (different for each individual).
ANGER Can be angry, but on a healthy level, in direct response to the current situation. Ability to let things go and move on once anger is released; no constant or recurring anger.	**RAGE AND VIOLENT BEHAVIOR, CURSING** Issues with excessive unreasonable anger, rage, and/or violence. Ever-present undertone of anger.	Feelings of desperation dissolve; anger can be experienced then released, but is no longer ever-present in the background.
ATTAINMENT OF LOVE AND HAPPINESS Normal expectation and ability to attain and experience love and happiness.	**NOT WITHIN REACH** Love and happiness are not within reach; the heart is squashed under the stress of the perceived immediate necessity to achieve Ego-References.	The need to work on EgoRefs has been dismantled. Now there is room for love and happiness.

Natural Sense of Self	Lack of Sense of Self, compensated for by a Substitute Sense of Self	Restored Sense of Self
FOCUS MODE* Healthy ability to focus on real life. The mental freedom to attend to anything relevant to the moment as well as genuine personal well-being and authentic goals. * See glossary.	**SCANNING MODE** Continuously in Scanning Mode: attention is restricted to Substitute Sense of Self-relevant aspects of life; not in touch with Self or actual real life. * See glossary.	**FOCUS MODE** Leaving Scanning Mode behind and replacing it with Focus Mode. Increasing ability to focus on actual real life; developing ability to focus on genuine personal well-being and authentic goals.
AUTHENTIC TASTES AND PREFERENCES Personal preferences and tastes are well developed and are felt as aspects of the Self.	**NO PREFERENCES** Tastes and preferences are borrowed and copied; they are used for unhealthy ulterior motives.	Growing development of authentic personal tastes and preferences, sensed as aspects of the Self.
AWARE OF OWN VALUES Knowing what you want, care about, and value are intrinsic aspects of the Self.	**SUBSTITUTE SENSE OF SELF-ORIENTED** Unable to make up one's own mind about what is important as there is no real Self present. What counts is how things serve the Hidden Goal.	Discovering more and more of what one truly cares about, wants, and values. Ability to set priorities and boundaries and gauge own potential.

Natural Sense of Self	**Lack of Sense of Self, compensated for by a Substitute Sense of Self**	**Restored Sense of Self**
CENTER OF GRAVITY The body's center of gravity is experienced in the lower belly: the traditional "abdominal power house." Life energy is spread evenly throughout the body.	Center of gravity is felt as if it is outside of the body (compare to Enmeshment). Mostly "in one's head" during activities; tension in neck and shoulders blocks energy from going into the head – reduced oxygen in the brain – all kinds of head problems (vision, hearing, head colds, congestion).	Felt sense of location of the Self is more in the body (heart/abdominal area); strain is taken away from eyes and brain; less tension in nervous system and muscles; healthier breathing leads to taking in more oxygen.
DECIDING, COMMITTING Healthy Self-confidence. Leadership. Comfortable making choices and committing. Not compelled to take unnecessary action.	**INDECISIVE** Often in flight-or-fight mode, which makes for erratic behavior and bad decisions. Uncomfortable making choices and committing.	No reason for flight or fight anymore. Growing ability to make adequate decisions and commit. Growing ability to be an efficient part of a team.
DEDICATION AND WELL-BEING Doing what needs to be done or what is desired, taking into realistic account one's own well-being and one's possibilities and/or limitations. Healthy sense of boundaries.	**COMPULSIVENESS AND LACK OF SELF-CARE** Obsessive-compulsive behavior; no room for failure; dependency on reaching a positive outcome. Doing what serves the need to get approval regardless of one's well-being or limitations.	Letting go of controlling behavior. Learning to distinguish dedication from compulsion and taking one's own well-being into account.

Natural Sense of Self	Lack of Sense of Self, compensated for by a Substitute Sense of Self	Restored Sense of Self
NO EATING DISORDERS Less prone to eating disorders.	**EATING DISORDERS** Prone to eating disorders such as anorexia, bulimia, or overeating if eating is used as a Vehicle to feeling grounded.	The function of food normalizes. There is no longer a need for food to feel grounded, numb emotions, or to experience a Sense of Self.
EMOTIONAL STABILITY You stay balanced because things don't affect your core. Emotionally stable with normal highs and lows directly related to life events.	**EMOTIONAL ROLLER COASTER** Easily aggravated, nervous, upset, and offended because everything is perceived as a threat to maintaining the fragile and ever-fleeting Substitute Sense of Self.	Increasingly better balanced emotional life plus overall inner sense of stability.
EMOTIONAL LIFE Normal emotional peaks and valleys; overall not easily hurt or excited. Emotions are integrated and rooted in the Self. Energy is available for happiness and joy.	Emotional roller coaster: deep valleys or depression and the need for (rewarding) highs. Emotions are created by the Substitute Sense of Self–oriented system and are not in any relationship with one's own being.	Emotions, formerly related to the Substitute Sense of Self gradually even out and become Quality-of-Life emotions; milder and much more balanced moods.
ENERGY IN NERVOUS SYSTEM Nervous system energy is balanced; emotions are experienced as being related to one's own personhood.	Experiencing overexcitement in the nervous system upon perceived (Substitute Sense of Self–oriented) success.	Calm nervous system; no overexcitement.

Natural Sense of Self	Lack of Sense of Self, compensated for by a Substitute Sense of Self	Restored Sense of Self
FEAR OF CROWDS Normal relationship to crowds.	Fear of crowds due to experiencing a Lack of Sense of Self. Feeling of "dissolving" when in a crowd.	Normal response to being in crowds.
FEELING GOOD ABOUT SELF "I feel good about myself" is a Quality-of-Life* matter. Everyday life has its ups and downs and that is all there is to it. "I am in agreement with myself and have enough Self-love." * See glossary.	**"FEELING-GOOD-ABOUT-SELF"** Excessive/obsessive need for reaching the state of "Feel-good-about-self" because it is experienced as a Substitute Sense of Self.	**GROWING SELF-LOVE** Ever-decreasing anxiety due to the ever-lessening need to reach the Fgas state. Feeling good about oneself becomes increasingly a Quality-of-Life matter (nothing existential is at stake).
FLOWING Going with the flow of life; ability to improvise; ability to reset when needed after an upset.	**(SUPER-) CONTROLLING** Controlling of self, others, and circumstances; inflexible; no improvisational skills; no sense of flow in life. Thrown off and angered by unanticipated turns of events.	Trusting the process of life more and more; not having attachment to outcomes brings back the flow of life and drops the need for control.
GENETIC FACTORS Possibly stronger genetic predisposition with regard to whatever factors are related to the development of a Sense of Self.	Possibly weaker genetic predisposition with regard to those factors.	No change in original genetic predisposition.

Natural Sense of Self	Lack of Sense of Self, compensated for by a Substitute Sense of Self	Restored Sense of Self
HEALTH AND EMOTIONS		
Normal health and emotions; inner stability. Valuing your own life and that of others.	Prone to accidents, illnesses, disease, panic attacks, migraines, anxiety, depression, suicide. Overlooking your own life and the lives of other people.	Elimination of excessive fear, anxiety, and panic attacks; awareness of the value of one's (own) life.
INNER ENERGY, PRESENCE IN WORLD		
Inner sensations of clarity and balance; steadily sensed presence of the flow of life-energy. Potentially charismatic; "present" in and to the world.	Inner sensations are chaotic and confused; continuous collision and competition of energy molecules upon closing eyes (can be experienced as tinnitus). "Presence" to the outside world is low. Living in a trance.	Inner sensations of energy clear up and become quieter (in the head, behind the eyes when sensed in meditation or upon going to sleep at night). Overall increasingly more connected to the flow of life-energy; learning to be "present" in the world and to others.
MASTER OF ONE'S OWN LIFE	**SLAVE OF FULFILLING CONDITIONS**	
Master of your own life; independent with potential to be interdependent.	Slave of Early Childhood Survival Strategy, dependency-oriented, oriented to Substitute Sense of Self. Self-centered.	Increasingly becoming the master of your own life and thus ready for teamwork and cooperative activity.
MOTION SICKNESS		
Less likely to have car/motion sickness.	Prone to car/motion sickness: nausea and dizziness. Lack of balance.	Reduced car/motion sickness due to being grounded in oneself.

Natural Sense of Self	Lack of Sense of Self, compensated for by a Substitute Sense of Self	Restored Sense of Self
MOTIVATION		
Ability to focus on the content of the action or goal: doing things for their own sake; no Hidden Goal.	Dependent on the outcome of actions, achievements, events, and other people's opinions. Focus on the one and only Hidden Goal through fulfilling Ego-References (Hidden Agendas).	Over time, more ability to focus on things for what they are. Increase in content-oriented focus and therefore achieving much better results.
Naturally Direct Motivation.	Actions and behaviors mostly based in Indirect Motivation.	Motivation gradually becomes more and more direct.
PARENTING BACKGROUND		
Received adequate supportive parenting and Mirroring for growing an independent Natural Sense of Self.	The parent/caretaker was excessively self-absorbed and was unable to adequately mirror a Healthy Sense of Self to the child.	For some, optimal healing and sustained health purposes require limited or no contact with the parent/caretaker.
PRONENESS TO ACCIDENTS	**MORE PRONE TO ACCIDENTS**	
Accidents happen and are experienced as facts of life. Recovery from accidents is generally smooth.	More accident-prone due to erratic and ill-managed behavior. Experienced as devastating to the Substitute Sense of Self and hardly felt as a simple personal misfortune.	With more awareness and presence to Self, you are less prone to accidents due to naturally mastering your behavior. When accidents occur, they are experienced on a Quality-of-Life Level.

HEALTHY SENSE OF SELF

Natural Sense of Self	Lack of Sense of Self, compensated for by a Substitute Sense of Self	Restored Sense of Self
RELATION TO REALITY		
Realist. Living in the reality of the present world and able to focus on the things in it. Very much "present."	Idealist, utopian, not in touch with reality. Living in a trance. Comes up with unrealistic solutions to world problems and is angered when nobody wants to listen. Others seem to be able to read your body language that conveys one is "not present," which leads to exclusion.	"Realist apprentice"; aware of own situation and willing to work on it. Aware of tendency to come up with theoretical dream solutions and starting to understand why that is of no importance in reality. Growing awareness of what the world/life is really like. Increasingly "present."
SEE AND ACCEPT OTHERS	**NOT SEEING OTHERS**	
Others are acknowledged as real people separate from the Self. Able to actually look at others and see them for who they are. Able to listen to others and actually hear them.	Others and self are only seen and heard when it is useful for self-serving (usually hidden) goals; others are used as pawns or Vehicles, or are considered Hindrances to fulfilling Ego-Reference conditions. Transference of key figures from the past onto others in the present.	Others are seen and heard for who they are. Acceptance of Self leads to acceptance of others, which opens many possibilities for healthy interactivity.
SENSE OF TIME	**NEVER ENOUGH TIME**	
Healthy ability to let go and set reasonable limits. "Tomorrow is another day! What I can't get done today I can do tomorrow!"	Perceives achievements to be of the highest importance; no relaxed perspective of time because achieving is always the highest priority at any given moment. No ability to let go. "I must finish this tonight, no matter how long it takes!"	Achievements, actions, and events don't strike on an existential level. There is increasingly more ability to let go and bide one's time. For example, "I would like to finish this task tonight, but it's okay if I don't. It won't affect my Sense of Self if I'm not able to finish until tomorrow!"

Natural Sense of Self	Lack of Sense of Self, compensated for by a Substitute Sense of Self	Restored Sense of Self
SLEEP Normally sleeps well, and reasons for sleeplessness are clear, concrete, and situational (e.g., new baby or puppy, new job, big life event).	**INSOMNIA** Lying awake at night unconsciously obsessing about finding or keeping the state of "Feel-good-about-self" as a Substitute Sense of Self.	Sleeping much better, knowing that you are already and don't depend on fulfilling specific conditions. No Fear of Annihilation; peace of mind and a connection to your own being.
STRESS MANAGEMENT Healthy stress is generally managed well.	**CONTINUOUSLY HIGH PSYCHOLOGICAL STRESS** Chronic and unmanageable high levels of stress.	Healthy stress is generally managed well.
SUCCESS/FAILURE IN LIFE High likelihood of success in most endeavors. When failure occurs, it can be seen as a learning experience and appreciated.	**WRONG FOCUS** Widespread failure in endeavors big and small because of focus on getting approval instead of on the endeavor as itself. Self-sabotage.	Focus on real goal instead of Hidden Goal; absence of self-sabotage; being visible to others because being energetically "present" creates a greater opening to success.
TEMPERAMENT, MOOD Even-tempered and in touch with what outside factors affect your moods.	Never an average mood; unpredictable because you are not in touch with your authentic temperament and mood. Often overexcited, driven for the wrong motivation, over- reactive, frenzied, anxious, sensitive, high-strung. Or feeling nonexistent, wretched, flat, depressed.	Much calmer, more in touch with authentic temperament; rarely moody.

HEALTHY SENSE OF SELF

Natural Sense of Self	Lack of Sense of Self, compensated for by a Substitute Sense of Self	Restored Sense of Self
TENSION VS. RELAXATION Normal body posture and muscle tension. The heart leads!	**FREQUENT INJURIES** Cramped muscles that lead to knots and pain in neck, back, and shoulders (dislocated vertebras). The head leads!	Much more relaxed and improving all the time. Learning to let the heart lead!
USE OF EYES Use of eyes for what they are meant for: observing your environment and ensuring personal safety.	**EYESTRAIN/FATIGUE** Eyestrain and fatigue due to the need for achievement at all costs; vision is always on hyper-alert, constantly vigilant for ways to achieve and experience a Substitute Sense of Self.	More normal need for achievement so less stress on the eyes. Ability to relax, be off-duty, and just use eyes in normal ways.

Disclaimer: The conclusions in this chart represent my own personal findings and are solely based on my own experience and research.

PART II

The Effects of the Dependency on a Substitute Sense of Self

Chapter 8
Substitute Sense of Self–Oriented Behavior

When you have a Lack of Sense of Self, you are in a different mindset compared to people who have a Healthy Sense of Self. Your goals, desires, beliefs, motives, feelings, and perceived needs that are at work in your inner life are all oriented toward gaining this Substitute Sense of Self. Since all of this operates on a subconscious level, it may help to get a clearer mental picture by comparing your mindset to an army.

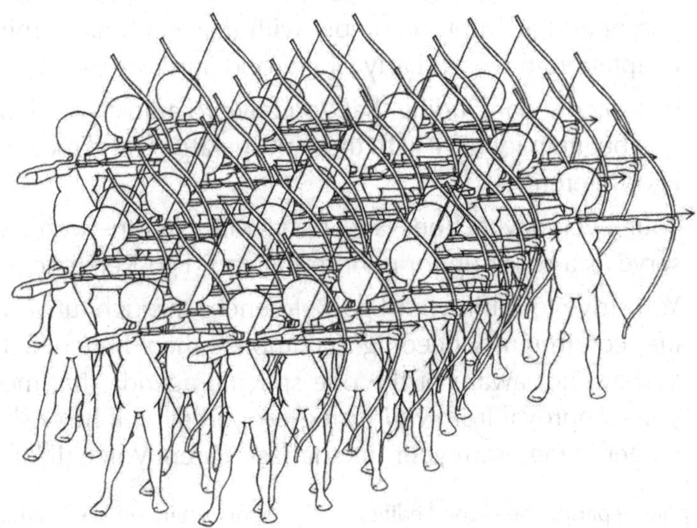

Figure 8.1: The army of your inner processes aiming at gaining a Substitute Sense of Self.

As you can see in Figure 8.1, all the different squadrons are mobilized to attack or capture the enemy, each by means of its own special force and expertise. In a person, it is similar: all of your functions and capabilities are applied to the one goal of repairing, compensating for, or retrieving the acknowledgment missing from your childhood. All these subconscious activities and conclusions leave their traces in your behavior, which becomes primarily Substitute Sense of Self oriented.

Let us review what setup can cause you to develop a dependency on a Substitute Sense of Self:

1. It all begins with you receiving Mirroring from a Distorted Mirror (e.g., a caregiver/parent who is self-absorbed) that states, "You are not unconditionally okay," which causes you to believe that you are not worth being taken into account the way you are.
2. From this Mirroring, you perceive that you are deficient in some way and also that *you* are to blame for not being acknowledged as a unique human being with the right to be the way you are. You experience Annihilation (your spirit is not acknowledged). You don't develop the virtual spine for your psyche – a Healthy Sense of Self. Instead, you develop Fear of Annihilation and become totally absorbed in avoiding Annihilation.
3. To avoid feeling annihilated, you observe what pleases your parent and attempt to comply with these criteria, turning that adaptation into your Early Childhood Survival Strategy.
4. Repeatedly concluding that you have to adjust your behavior, you begin to identify with these observations and they become Ego-References.
5. Your everyday actions and behaviors become Vehicles that serve as a cover-up for performing your Ego-References.
6. You strive to fulfill your Ego-References throughout your daily life; continuously needing to complete them better each time. You are not aware of the one specific agenda that motivates you – approval from your caregiver/parent or, if he or she is no longer living, from your Internalized Parent Voice (IPV).[1]

[1] Upon preparing the second edition of this book, I started to see that approval might not be the only incentive to perform Ego-References. Based on traumas experienced, there may be a Hidden Goal that would not be an issue had the trauma not affected the development of a Healthy Sense of Self.

7. Every time you bring your Ego-Reference to a good ending, you experience the reward: the "Feel-good-about-self" state.
8. Because the Fgas state is a fleeting one, you have to repeat the process over and over again to make sure you can experience it as if it were permanent. Each time, you become more determined to succeed in achieving your Ego-Reference's goal (Hidden Goal). So, what you do or how you behave is actually driven by a goal that is unknown to you. That means you are ruled by an automatic pilot without being aware of it.
9. On top of that, even the remote possibility of experiencing the Fear of Annihilation triggers fear as well: the fear of experiencing the Fear of Annihilation.

You suffer from many other Substitute Sense of Self–oriented fears, which augment your anxiety and stress and lead to exhaustion, physical ailments, and disorders. Your Substitute Sense of Self wants to remain in place within your psyche, hence the constant need to meet conditions, obey Indirect Motivations, realize Hidden Agendas, and perform near-perfect behaviors. All of this, together with the accompanying emotions, ends up forming the reality of a person whose behavior is dominated by the need to gain a Substitute Sense of Self.

Substitute Sense of Self–oriented Behavior

Figure 8.2 below is a graphic representation of the daily ups and downs of moods and behaviors dependent on a Substitute Sense of Self.

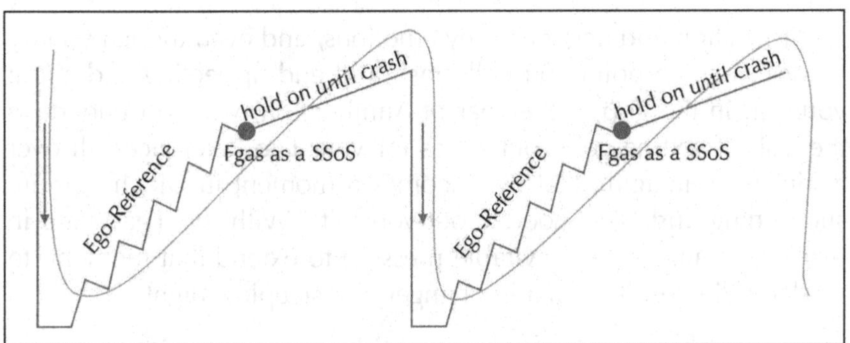

Figure 8.2: The ups and downs of a person's moods and behaviors.

To get an understanding of what the reasons are for so much upheaval, you need to look at the elements that play a role in this behavior.

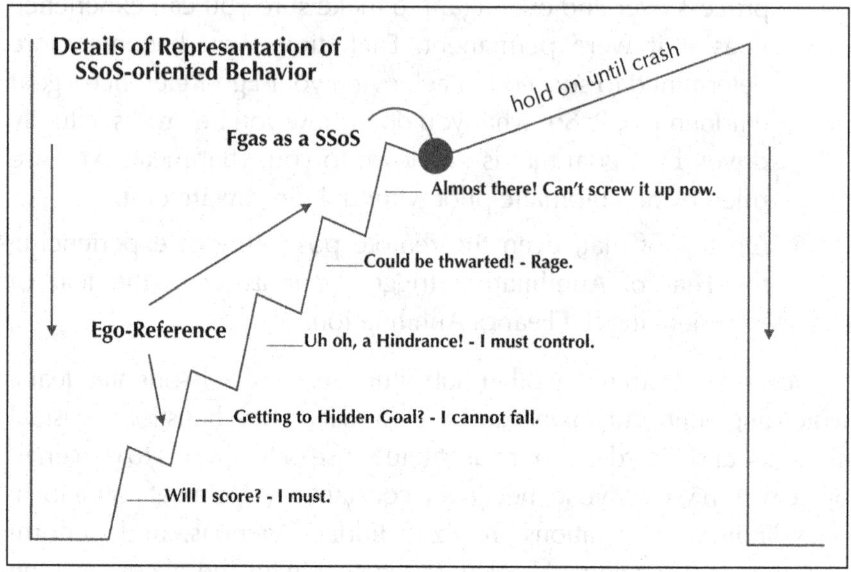

Figure 8.3: Elements affecting a person's moods and behaviors.

Figure 8.3 represents a closer look at the thoughts and feelings you may go through. Here is what raises your stress and anxiety levels: You are continuously aiming to satisfy your Ego-References, but your attempts are constantly being thwarted. The common obstacles life puts in your path can already make it more of a challenge to get good results, and self-sabotage combined with your perception of what is at stake complicates those challenges.

Frustration and anger are key emotions, and even though you try harder, at some point you will crash and end up feeling bad about yourself. In the grip of the Fear of Annihilation, you will undertake the task of getting good outcomes for your Ego-References all over again. Now imagine that there comes a moment in which you are succeeding and "Feel-good-about-yourself." With this Fgas state in place, you attract the inevitable pressure to extend that moment, to not let it die, resulting in a fit of anger or a sleepless night.

Figure 8.4 below is a comparison of the chaotic mood swings with a representation of a healthy, balanced lifestyle. There are the ups and downs at the Quality-of-Life Level, but overall, there is steadiness and a feeling of being rooted in one's life.

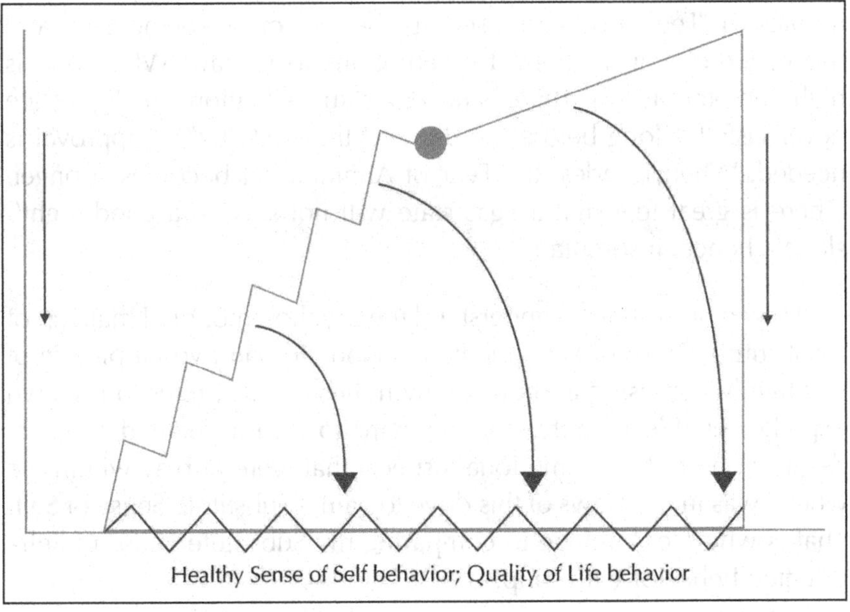

Figure 8.4: The ups and downs in a healthy person's moods and behaviors.

Quality-of-Life Level (QoL Level)

A healthy level of experiencing life's events and interactions with others and responding with emotional reactions that are in sync with the degree of intensity of the actual effect these events or the behavior of others have on your life. It is indicative of a Healthy Sense of Self and distinguished from a (usually unaware) dependency on a Substitute SoS where, for the same type of events, emotions are experienced that strike down to the level of your sense of existence-as-a-self.

Emotional Complexity

There are two predominant emotions in a person who has a Substitute Sense of Self: the Fgas state that reflects a sense of safety and the Fear of Annihilation. The basic motivation for doing whatever it takes to "Feel-good-about-self" is the fear of not being seen and heard, which causes these two emotions to seesaw. When one is high, the other is low. There is never a stable situation. The Fgas state never lasts for long before it fades and the next "fix" of approval is needed. When it fades, the Fear of Annihilation becomes stronger. (There is great fear that a Fgas state will not survive a good night's sleep – hence, insomnia.)

How can we start to understand the psycho-emotional makeup of a Substitute Sense of Self–oriented person? To paint you a picture of this highly confusing and unhealthy mindset, I will refer to my own experiences. Please note that it is hard to give a detailed, "linear" description of all the emotional aspects that were at play within me when I was in the claws of this drive to gain a Substitute Sense of Self. That is why I took refuge in comparing my Substitute Sense of Self–oriented behavior with soup.

The Soup of Substitute Sense of Self-Related Goals and Emotions

The complexity of all the emotions that the dependency on a Substitute Sense of Self generates in a person is best compared to soup: everything is in it, but it is difficult to recognize the individual ingredients. Everybody's soup tastes different, even though many of the ingredients might be the same. All of these psycho-emotional ingredients are interrelated, and they interact with one another until they inevitably escalate. Here is an attempt to list the main ingredients:

- Normal, Quality-of-Life events and emotions (normal events and behavior that is required in everyday living and what comes with it).
- "Holy decisions" such as "I am never going to do this or that; I am always going to be such and such; I'm absolutely going

to do things in a different way compared to my parents; I am going to be different from everybody else."

- The two sides of Ego-References: the normal Quality-of-Life motivation, e.g., "not wanting anger in your house," and the highly emotionally charged Substitute Sense of Self–oriented motivations, e.g., not wanting to be angry for Fear of Annihilation.
- Multiple simultaneously existing but incompatible Ego-References that lead to Inner Conflicts.
- Artificial harmony at home, in which everyone tries to avoid upsetting the other family members. In my family of origin,[2] we shared a Hidden Goal: to "Feel-good-about-self" as each one of us relied on a Substitute Sense of Self. Creating or contributing to this artificial harmony was, and always had been, the thing our parents gave us approval for. Therefore, it was what we desired most, and each family member learned to be very careful to make sure that everyone else would get or preserve their Fgas state. In the end, though, it was purely for the selfish reason that they themselves would be able to end up "Feeling-good-about-self" – in other words, feeling safe.
- Fear of encountering reasons to be angry, and the continuous conscious and subconscious drives to avoid those.
- Fear or one's own feelings and/or behavior.
- Fear of "screwing things up." Within my family of origin, I had an ever-present fear of being the one who would cause a problem and ruin the good vibes in any situation that could potentially lead to a Fgas state for each one of us. On any given day, whenever I had been successful in living up to certain conditions, the stakes seemed to rise. The fear of blowing things at the last minute would skyrocket. The need for control would increase as well as the eagerness to lash out when obstacles showed up. This wasn't only valid for me, but for every member of my family, with the exception of my father. I have to say, he always seemed puzzled by what was

[2] This unspoken rule that one has to help others preserve their "Feel-good-about-self" seems to be a typical "elephant in the room" in my country of origin, the Netherlands. In other cultures, people have different elephants in their rooms: In the U.S., for example, family members seem to have a strong tendency toward being able to feel okay when they can function as a "hero" of sorts, in big or small ways.

going on with the rest of us. A highly explosive situation would develop like a high-pressure field ready to boom, something that indeed never failed to take place.

- The unavoidable crash of the Substitute Sense of Self–oriented activities and behavior as described in the preceding paragraph. (See Figure 8.2 on page 177.)

Remember, we are still talking soup here:

- The need to control your own and other people's behavior; the constant presence of fear, stress, and anger; and the overzealous effort to do things the right way can be seen as the starch that binds the ingredients and thickens this soup.
- Other random ingredients are thrown into this pot of soup as herbs of the season, such as parental expressions like: "Darn you! All my effort to keep things nice is wasted now," which means something like, "We could have had a pleasant evening and all end up feeling good if things had not turned sour in the end!" The effort was wasted since nobody ended up with a Fgas state, which was the only goal.
    - "You are always the one who screws it up."
    - "If you are this or that way, everybody will walk out on you."

Put this pot of soup on the fire of the Hidden Agenda (determination to bring the Ego-Reference to a good end), stir it really well while heating it to a boiling point, and serve it to your loved ones.

Principles at Work in Making Soup

Let's elaborate some more on the soup analogy so you get a clearer sense of the mood and mindset of a Substitute Sense of Self–oriented person. There are a number of principles at work in this process:

- Dependency on the outcome of an Ego-Reference leads to heavy control.
- Ego-Reference versus Ego-Reference equals Inner Conflict.
- Inner Conflict leads to rage, depression, insomnia, and blaming others (to name just a few of the many negative results).

- A person's mood and temper spiral downward and can lead to misbehaving and unfair treatment of others (children!). The need to repair the physical and/or emotional damage done afterward and make up for it can lead to extreme submission or to going overboard in buying presents or allowing boundaries to be crossed. The end of this unfortunate cycle is usually a firm inner decision to never let it happen again. This leads to tighter control of self and of circumstances, which only increases stress and fear.
- Self-sabotage continuously thwarts potentially good outcomes to Ego-References.
- Anger, rage, insomnia, and/or depression when Ego-References are thwarted add more stress.
- Stress plus fear equals more need for control.
- Stress plus need for control equals more stress. Ultimately, there is a point that the body and/or mind can't handle it anymore, and the person falls ill from exhaustion.

Suffering and Stress

The dependency on a Substitute Sense of Self creates constant stress, which increases suffering. The perceived life-or-death situation that underlies Indirect Motivation raises stress levels to absurd heights. Objectively, the stress levels are incongruent with what could be expected when interpreting the external stressors. Therefore, it is clear that internal stressors are at work and need to be dismantled.

Not being able to take refuge in the shelter of your own Self makes you prioritize feeling safe, feeling alive, and achieving a sense of belonging in different ways – all feelings that were missing in your childhood. The attainment of who you believe you have to be requires constant vigilance and continuous manipulation. This produces constant frustrations and constant anxiety – stress. Addressing unhealthy internal stressors is exactly what the SoS Method tackles.

Compulsiveness and Addictive Behaviors

The driving force to create and sustain the Substitute Sense of Self is as strong as any other survival mechanism. The obsession with fulfilling Ego-References leads to compulsive behaviors. And where behaviors such as incessant hand washing are obvious and easy to spot, the behaviors that are tied to the Substitute Sense of Self are attached to, and inseparable from, everyday activities, making them less apparent.

Within the reality of Substitute Sense of Self–oriented behavior, your intentions, actions, and activities are continuously self-sabotaged. It almost seems like life itself interferes with, and drags down, your positive attempts to realize your Ego-References. This means that any Substitute Sense of Self–oriented behavior is accomplished with much more difficulty than the action or behavior itself would justify, if it were directly motivated.

Here is an example: I want to prove to my parent/caregiver (or even to my Internalized Parental Voice) that I can be on time (note: for Substitute Sense of Self–oriented reasons). However, I know I have a hard time getting a good night's sleep, which will make it hard to be on time in the morning. So I'm already scared that I won't be able to sleep. Of course I get upset with things that prevent me from going to bed in a relaxed way, be it a quarrel or an overflowing bathtub. Anything can become a Hindrance to achieving my goal. I become high strung and easily aggravated and can't deal with all the interferences. I blow up, which makes me feel bad about myself and leads to insomnia, etc.

Getting your Substitute Sense of Self in place is a need that doesn't want to be compromised because getting that approval is an absolute requirement for your sense of feeling like a real person. A Substitute Sense of Self functions as an artificial spine; it is something that simply cannot be missing without causing total collapse.

To prevent total collapse and keep the terror at bay, gaining the Fgas state by means of getting approval becomes compulsive. Living this way is not based on conscious decision-making or geared toward your well-being – it is geared toward the relief of emotional pain.

It can lead you to do many things that are detrimental to your quality of life. Your life is lived in emergency mode. To prevent what feels like a potential disaster, priorities are shifted and you become a slave to those priorities.

Nothing is what it looks like in the life of a person who is continuously focused on gaining a Substitute Sense of Self. To the outside world, it looks like you are doing something (an activity or behavior), but in reality, you are aiming to realize something completely different (your Hidden Agenda in service of your Hidden Goal). You are just *performing your Ego-References* instead of really living your life. This performance is meant to lead to a Fgas state, but if you fail, you end up feeling bad about yourself. Then you immediately make sure the next task can serve your Ego-Reference to better yourself by trying harder – or else it plunges you into depression or worse.

Everyday life situations turn into performances, which means that instead of tasks being executed for the sake of an obvious goal, they are being used to Score! Here is an example:

Smooth-Floor Syndrome

When I was a mother of two toddlers, I used to enjoy that moment at night when the house was organized. No toys or clothes on a clean, swept floor. Whenever I managed to achieve that, my husband and I would then (finally!) each sit down with a book and spend a quiet evening reading after the kids were in bed. Oh, what a delight! I can still remember the satisfyingly pleasant feeling of looking at the "smooth" hardwood floor of our living room.

The bad surprise (which eventually became predictable) was that I could never sleep after an evening like that. Somehow that good situation was subconsciously used to Score in my struggle to end the day with a Fgas state. In other words, it was obviously NOT for my (real) Self that I had managed to have the house clean. It was to comply with the demands of my Ego-References and "Feel-good-about-self." It was to feel safe. But how was I to know the difference? There was nothing weighing on my mind, nothing that was worrying me. There was no indication of any problem needing to be solved. I would just lie there wide awake. I would be tired but not sleepy – I could not fall asleep!

It was a challenge to figure it out, but ultimately I got it: the life-and-death Fear of Annihilation was causing me to hang on to that finally achieved "Feel-good-about-self" state. In other words, I would stay awake all night so that my Substitute Sense of Self would not disappear on me. My flight-or-fight response stayed on red-hot alert to "guard" that most important sense of achievement I had gained. I would stay in that mode until about 5:00 or 6:00 in the morning. Then, at daybreak, after an endless, sleepless night, I would finally crash, convinced that further protection of my Substitute Sense of Self would be a lost cause. My ability to function well and prolong it throughout the next day would be undermined by lack of sleep now anyway.

Desperately hanging on to the Fgas state is the subconscious process that I hold accountable for my twenty-five years of insomnia. There was a (subconscious) need to always make sure I had a Vehicle at my disposal to earn a Substitute Sense of Self. Ending my day with a "smooth floor and a clean house" was my Vehicle, and I was unable to sleep because, on a subconscious level, I was unable to let go of the achieved "Feel-good-about-self."

The fear of not being able to function at all the next day worsened my fear of insomnia, as you may well understand. A negative spiral of increasing anxiety was the result. Intercepting the perceived need for a Substitute Sense of Self and concluding that need was fictional enabled me to break free from this cycle.

I would like to point out that, for me, there were two different insomnia patterns caused by two different fears. First, there was the fear/need to make sure I had a Vehicle to earn the Fgas state again the next day, which resulted in my waking up too early (like between 3:00 and 5:00 a.m.). The second was the fear of losing the feeling of success, which resulted in my not falling asleep until I felt completely exhausted. These fears were conceptually different in the SoS Method, but both were generated by the fictional need for a Substitute Sense of Self.

A Personal Example of Self-Sabotage

When visiting my mother, it was hard to balance "mother time" with "personal time." Once, during my adult years, I had been running errands for her, and it took a little longer than I'd hoped, but I was still on time. On my way back home, I went through a lot of psychological stress because I feared *I had blown it* (compare to the soup ingredients). I feared that if I were late, I'd ruin whatever credit I had collected from doing something good for her. Note that I agonized about being late, not about the fact that my mother would have to sit there and wait for me – which is how a Substitute Sense of Self–oriented person works. I worried myself sick about what would be waiting for me: her blaming facial expression; that "hurt" tone of voice; her obvious difficulty to get over herself and speak to me at all. I would have to look her in the eyes and feel annihilated. Of course, I was not aware of all these things at the time!

My mother often criticized me for being late and called me selfish. So being on time was an Ego-Reference for me. When I entered the room, I saw her sitting there relaxed and *not* blaming me. To my surprise and immense relief, I was not greeted by that look of "What are you doing to me?" Then, on the spot, a migraine started, sabotaging my experience of being judged as okay. Obviously, I was just performing my Ego-Reference of being on time and, as a result, was not at all concerned with what was happening in the reality of the moment. Even though I had succeeded in pleasing my mother, my own body ruined my Fgas state.

"I almost made it!" I almost experienced being allowed into my mother's Castle of Enmeshment (see page 154). The stress and fear of a last-minute Hindrance had made me focus on the situation with tunnel vision, which caused the overload in my brain that resulted in the migraine.

On many occasions when I *"almost made it,"* this migraine would pop up. It always occurred when I was about to finish satisfying an Ego-Reference. It all was part of my Substitute Sense of Self–oriented behavior.

Teasing Thoughts/Solo Syndrome

I worked as a professional bassoonist for many years. Whenever my part contained a solo, I would prepare obsessively for it. At the crucial moment of my performance, I would start out well, but then halfway through, it would suddenly feel as if I had stepped outside of myself and had become an observer. I would then "tease" myself involuntarily, actually *against my own will*, with thoughts such as "What if you don't manage to bring this to a good end?" or "What if you didn't count your rests correctly here?"

It took the utmost concentration to effectively bring the solo to a good conclusion. Often, the teasing thoughts caused the quality of my playing to deteriorate. I could have easily done well if such negative, intrusive thoughts had not always been in the way, sabotaging my good performance.

Self-Sabotage: A Sign of Substitute Sense of Self–oriented Activity

Why does this self-sabotage happen? Here is my explanation: One of my Ego-References was to be an excellent musician. When my solo would go very well, my Substitute Sense of Self would seize the performance partway through and try to turn it into a chance to Score. It was pulled into the Black Hole with the force of nature discussed earlier. This would of course activate stress and fear, which interfered with the quality of my performance. It was as if the ground would fall out from under my feet and the enormous degree of concentration required to bring the musical performance to a good end would drain all the fun and joy out of being able to play that solo.

By "ground," I literally mean the ground of my being, because I could not sense a separation between my "being" and what I was "doing." These teasing thoughts were a manifestation of the fear of failing to reach the desired outcome: "Feeling-good-about-self" (*not* making beautiful music!). No Sense of Self was present,[3] so it was as if I were performing while floating on an ocean. My being had no roots in the earth; no steadiness in an inner knowing that *I exist* or that I had the skill to play this solo. I could only perceive that I had *the right to exist* if I did well.

[3] I mean this not in the usually desired state of becoming one with your creation: the dancer becomes one with the dance, which means to express an ultimate ego-less state. Mine was a state of no Sense of Self, which is very different. To reach that "oneness," it is first necessary to experience your Self so that, in the next step of performance, you can let go of it.

Teasing thoughts in general can sabotage your Substitute Sense of Self. Self-sabotage is nature's way of showing you that you are on the wrong track, but you have to be able to understand the hint. It means that nature (or your Higher Self) is trying to tell you that you are aiming to reach your Hidden Goal and that your motivation is Indirect. Self-sabotage gives you the message that you need to investigate your ultimate motivation and wonder if you are being present to yourself or if you are merely functioning on automatic pilot with a warped Hidden Goal in mind.

Teasing thoughts can also sabotage your sleep. For me, they would come up as I was about to drift off into that most-wanted world of calming slumber. Out of the blue, a thought would arise: "What if teasing thoughts come up right now and keep me from falling asleep?" It would startle me as badly as if I had been punched in the stomach. Adrenaline would rush profusely, which would leave me awake for a few hours. Imagine the frustration I felt, being kept awake by the mere stupidity of my own thoughts: "I should not be doing this to myself, now should I?" But I never asked if I was really even in charge of my Self.

However, at some point, it became clear to me. Even sleeping well could turn into a performance. And as desperate as I was, the truth was that I did not want to sleep well *for myself* but to be "okay and normal," whatever the definition of *normal* was – and especially *whose* definition of *normal* that actually was.

Summary and Looking Ahead

As you have seen, repetitive patterns are predominant in Substitute Sense of Self–oriented behavior, and they affect you greatly. An unhealthy dependency on the fulfillment of your Ego-References prevents you from being free to live your own life the way you see fit.

These patterns are bound to be repeated by children whose caregivers are dependent on a Substitute Sense of Self. In turn, these children will develop into the same kind of self-absorbed people they were raised by.

Dependency on a Substitute Sense of Self and the accompanying compulsion to live up to one's Ego-References cause a lot of suffering, upheaval, and unhappiness. In the next chapter, we will zoom in on several of these aspects and discover that the majority of this suffering is due to the predominance of two emotions: anger and fear. Looking at these emotions through the lens of the SoS Theory, you may even discover how to break free of them.

Chapter 9

Harmful Effects of the Addiction to Approval

As we discussed in the previous chapter, being dependent on approval for your (substitute) self-experience means that almost all your behavior is being put in service of getting that approval. It is a very unhealthy, distorted way of living. Remember those trees that are almost falling over because of their crooked trunks? What has happened is that you are actually misguided about what life is all about. You have no idea that you could have a whole lot more say in how your life unfolds, that you could live your life much closer to the way *you* want it. However, to be able to see it that way, you need to be able to hear your own voice and recognize your own face in the mirror.

Instead, you continue to be the slave of fulfilling your Ego-References aiming to realize your Hidden Goal. By living that way, you are not focused on your Self but on the person/people you have unfinished business with. The obstacles you encounter that are blocking your efforts to make your life work will throw you off time and again, which will lead to ongoing frustration.

Where a Natural Sense of Self provides a stable point of departure, a Substitute Sense of Self is a complex and chaotic psycho-emotional-behavioral structure and a very unstable point of reference. There is no authentic Self present to function as a guide. Therefore, in reality, hanging on to a Substitute Sense of Self for your self-experience results in a great array of suffering for yourself, as well as for the people you interact with. In this chapter, we will highlight various side effects of living with a Substitute Sense of Self and end with a story to serve as an example.

Next to high stress levels, the harmful effects of being addicted to a Substitute Sense of Self vary widely throughout your daily life and can range from mild to severe. Experiencing anger and fear is a predominant issue, which we will discuss in depth below.

Anger and Rage

For a Substitute Sense of Self–oriented person, anger and rage come from subconscious thoughts such as "Why can't I get things the way I need them to be?" or "Why can't the world allow me to achieve a good outcome to my Ego-References so I can get the respect and acknowledgment of my caregiver?"

Now think of a young mom who is dependent on things being *just so*, so that her Fgas state is being facilitated. What are the odds that things are working out in her favor? What happens if they don't?

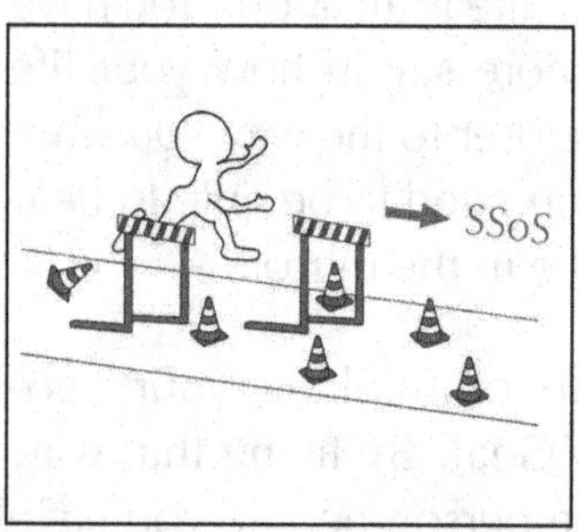

Figure 9.1: Hindrances on our way to a Substitute Sense of Self.

If your Ego-References are your first priority, like they are for that young mother, you perceive a lot to be at stake (Annihilation). That means there is *no room for failure*. Anything in the way is a Hindrance and leads to anger or rage, which can be a gateway to violence or its counterpart, depression. Anger and rage are always lurking and can emerge at any given moment in a person with a Substitute Sense of Self.

Hindrance

Any obstacle on your path to gaining a Substitute Sense of Self that frequently leads to anger or rage, which can be a gateway to violence or its counterpart, depression.

This is the reality of the life of a Substitute Sense of Self–oriented person; once in this state of suppressed anger, sometimes a minor irritation – the infamous "straw that breaks the camel's back" – is enough to make the person snap. Sometimes, ironically, trying to talk out a situation can provoke an unforeseen and unintended eruption of stress and anger. Why? Because it is done for the exact same Indirect Motivation!

Figure 9.2: The straw that breaks the Substitute Sense of Self–oriented camel's back.

Here is an example:

> *Erica and Paul had been married for many years now. They were a seasoned couple and knew each other quite well, but there was a dark side to their relationship. Paul felt criticized by Erica, a lot. Erica had an Ego-Reference of not becoming angry. So for the sake of preserving her Fgas state, Erica dreaded the moment she would detect symptoms of being frustrated with her husband. Whether it was the way he sat or the way he ate or drank too much. The way he didn't say anything or talked too much when they had guests. She knew she had to smooth out her path*

and be vocal about it. Even if she made a vow to herself to not say anything, it would come out sooner or later, and with even more upset. So Erica thought it would be smart to anticipate the situation and reduce the risk of becoming more frustrated (Ego-Reference). She would ask Paul, who didn't suspect anything, to sit down with her and talk it out. But even that didn't work out the way she had planned.

After all these years, Paul's behavior had been shaped by the repeated quarrels. He detested the way Erica made him feel as if he couldn't do anything right when he did his very best to make her happy. So the moment Erica began with: "I need to let you know that your habit of ... really gets on my nerves," he immediately became defensive. So in spite of all Erica's good intentions, the talks usually did not go according to plan. Instead of solving issues, it created new ones. They would start yelling at each other, and their arguments often led to feelings of "I don't want to deal with this any longer! I want a divorce!" She knew she had the best of intentions and he knew he didn't want to break up, so they both felt worn out and at their wits' end.

Erica definitely had good intentions, but her sense of reality was off! She was pursuing her Substitute Sense of Self. She was not looking at her husband with eyes that were able to truly see him. He had no idea of her Hidden Agenda and was therefore unable to help her with it. What Erica ended up achieving was the opposite of what she had envisioned.

Now keep in mind Erica's dependency on her Substitute Sense of Self here. That is where her main focal point was. She was not focused on the reality of the situation. Yes, she was talking to (or screaming at) Paul, but she didn't really see him – let alone his point of view. In this state of panic, all she was able to do was try to get back to a state of Fgas in one way or another. She could not afford to let her Substitute Sense of Self go down the drain. All she needed was her husband to react in a positive way to her quest so she could avoid becoming angrier.

Paul, though, had no clue what was going on in his wife's mind. He felt powerless and at his wit's end about how to accommodate Erica while still staying true to himself.

In moments like this, people can lose control over their words and actions. Even those with good intentions can be driven to commit acts of violence or behave in destructive ways either verbally or physically, or both. In this state, children or spouses can get beaten up or road rage may occur. Luckily for Erica and Paul, the only violence that happened between them was an occasional cup or plate smashed against a wall.

Please note that it cannot be stressed enough that:

Violence often is an expression of the ultimate powerlessness to fulfill that compulsive drive of getting a Substitute Sense of Self.

Of course! The nature of life is such that there are no guarantees for us to find safety or protection when we need it, but we all would benefit from knowing how to reduce negative reactions and emotions in ourselves. Anger that is Quality-of-Life Level is less dangerous and less destructive than anger that comes from the deeply rooted Fear of Annihilation. At times, when we are unable to fulfill our basic needs, our frustration may fully justify those negative emotions and violent reactions, but we still want to eliminate them if we can. Recognizing the true source of anger and violence can be a great way to help yourself and your loved ones – yes, even the world at large – to do just that.

Blind rage can lead to violence. This rage is generated by the false but sincerely perceived life-or-death threat of unfulfilled Ego-References! If we learn to fully understand that, we may be able to get a grip on it. Putting this statement under a microscope and thinking it through is crucial for each one of us. Doesn't every instance that someone is able to make a different choice and avoid destructive behavior count?

Consider the following: In the summer of 1971, at Stanford University, Professor Philip Zimbardo conducted an experiment on the psychological effects of imprisonment. Twenty-four healthy, intelligent, middle-class male students, without any particular psychological problems, were selected to participate. The students were randomly divided into two groups: guards and prisoners. The experiment was to last thirteen days but had to be shut down after only six days due to atrocious behavior, cruelties, and power plays. The explanation was that the prisoners and guards had lost their sense of reality.[1] I dare to question here whether they ever had one in the first place.

A bold statement, maybe; however, I vividly recall the intense experience of my own emotional distress and my fits of rage about seemingly minor, unimportant things. Most fortunately, my husband managed to deal with my unreasonable anger, my need to justify my requests, and my need for control over daily events.

Experiencing any kind of obstacles on the path toward the achievement of any Ego-Reference can lead to irritation, anger, and/or depression. The rage and fury experienced when Ego-References are thwarted is ultimately rooted in *terror*.

Substitute Sense of Self–oriented Fears

There is ordinary, everyday fear that is justified by the nature of existence. Even when you don't have an existential attachment to the outcome of things, you still wish for and need desired outcomes. It is therefore normal to experience apprehension and fear when a situation is anticipated or desired or when facing threats or danger.

However, a person with a Substitute Sense of Self has many more fears, all of which stem from the root Fear of Annihilation. These fears are related in complex ways as one comes forth from, or triggers, another:

- Anxiety
- Fear of your own emotions
- Fear of your own behavior
- Fear of not being able to function
- Fear of change
- Fear of failure
- Stage fright

[1] Visit www.prisonexperiment.org to learn more about this experiment. It should be noted that there were several ethical concerns raised about this experiment, but these should not diminish the results regarding the conclusion that anger and rage lie (hidden) within some of us. The question is in who and why!

Anxiety

Because it is hard for a person to label these fears and get insight into them, they are experienced as vague and undefined and are commonly referred to as *anxiety*. Nevertheless, they are very strong, and the way they manifest is intense because of the life-or-death sense of Annihilation that lies at their root.

It is impossible to overestimate how dominant the role is of the many kinds of Substitute Sense of Self-related fears. Those fears are exhausting due to the continuous high level of stress they cause. They form a heavy psycho-emotional burden for the person with a Lack of Sense of Self, and are likely to be the ultimate cause of many physical, mental, and/or emotional symptoms that, over time, can develop into physical and mental disease and dysfunction.

Imagine the following scenario:

> *Erica is on her way home after a good day at work, and Paul has agreed to have dinner ready for her at a specific time. He can be a bit picky when he is the cook because he values good food and the quality of food is time sensitive.*
>
> *"Oh, I can still pick up my boots," Erica decides. She leaves her office on time but encounters a lot of traffic, which causes her to feel increasingly anxious. She convinces herself that it isn't her fault traffic is heavy and wonders if she should call Paul.*
>
> *Inside, her anxiety-generator starts ticking. She sees flashes of Paul's disappointed face or, worse, his annoyance about her being late. It isn't easy to call while driving, and she is also afraid that she will get a migraine (Ego-Reference "do not have problems") if she attempts to multitask, just when her day was going so well. So she decides not to look at the clock. Her mouth gets dry and her heart starts beating faster.*
>
> *From the outside, an onlooker would not suspect that Erica is experiencing high levels of stress. She hardly pays attention to traffic, and she even ignores the traffic lights, just to be able to speed up.*

Now this story can have two different endings:

A) Erica is not aware of what is at play inside her and acts on her emotional cues:

> *It is a bit late when she finally calls Paul, and he has already started to prepare the meal. Erica squirms and feels bad about herself. She wishes she could make him see that it really wasn't her fault. She apologizes a million times for not being on time.*
>
> *Note: Feeling bad about herself is not because she believed her tardiness would ruin the meal her husband had prepared, nor because she didn't want to disappoint him, but because she failed to live up to her Ego-Reference of being on time! All these intense emotions Erica experiences are not at all justified by the reality of the moment. They are based on Erica's deep Fear of Annihilation, which is what causes her to overreact.*

B) Erica actually deals with the issue that is playing on a deeper level:

> *Slowly, it starts to dawn on her that, once again, she is a victim of her Ego-References. Recognizing the subconscious source of her anxiety, Erica understands her fear and is able to let go of it, after which the fear of getting a migraine vanishes as well. She is able to let reality kick in. It would definitely be better for her husband to know that she will be late so she calls him.*
>
> *Note: This is an example of a much better outcome, which is possible once you gain insight into your deepest motivation.*

Now let's zoom in on the various types of Substitute Sense of Self–oriented fears.

Fear of Your Own Emotions

When, and (especially) why, are you scared of your own emotions? Emotions come and go, and, if they are constructive, it is easy to welcome them. However, if they tend to be destructive – like fear and anger can be – it is easy to imagine why you would prefer not to have them. They can destroy a good situation. They can damage a relationship. They can break a deal. They always ruin the atmosphere.

Therefore, suppressing anger and being expected to do so is quite common in relationships, and where there are kids involved, parents often need to manage their own conflicts. However, when suppressing anger becomes an Ego-Reference, it is different. It feels more like a matter of life and death; you can't afford to ignore the rules you have set for yourself at the risk of Annihilation. That leads to dreading both healthy and unhealthy reasons for being upset.

You may *fear* having to face the fact that you do not like something or somebody because getting upset about it conflicts with one of your Ego-References. And mind you, your Ego-References are supposed to lead you to your most important quest: your Hidden Goal and freedom from the Fear of Annihilation. That means there is a whole lot perceived to be at stake, and getting angry is absolutely not an option.

So, because of your Ego-Reference, you are (subconsciously) driven to be nice to your spouse, not because of who they are but because it calms your fear of abandonment (another Ego-Reference: "don't cause problems"). To be successful at this, you want to make sure that your spouse behaves in ways that will cause you to like them. If your spouse behaves in a way that you do not like, you freak out. Over time, you might even start to anticipate this situation, and fear that you might not like what your spouse is going to do even before they do anything.

In the same manner, you can dread receiving a gift for fear that you will not like it. Or you can avoid making an appointment for fear of being late.

Fear of Your Own Behavior

Emotions lead to behavior, and the fear of your emotions and the fear of your own behavior are related. If you fear your emotions, it is because you fear your behavior. When you feel "forced" (by circumstances) to display a behavior that is in opposition with your Ego-References, you experience fear because you perceive your safety to be in jeopardy.

Say that your (life-giving) Hidden Goal is getting your parent's approval and you associate that with feeling safe. Doing something that puts that approval at risk will cause fear. If you do not recognize the root cause of your agony because you are not consciously aware that you are trying to live up to certain conditions, you are at the mercy of this overwhelmingly strong sense that your safety is under threat. What do you think? Will you be able to identify your emotions in that moment and have the willpower to not allow them to control you? Are you actually in charge of yourself?

Think about it for a moment: Which part of YOU is actually involved in the decision-making process of allowing or not allowing yourself to give in and react to that fear? Are you in touch with *the actual cause* that triggered the fear? Do you even recognize what event or behavior caused you to freak out in the first place?

What would *you* actually think about this if you were able to identify the root cause of your fear?

Here is an example: Suppose your Ego-Reference is to never be angry because your parent has ingrained a need in you to avoid being angry or risk rejection and abandonment. Now your spouse does something that makes you mad, but you are scared she/he will leave you if you show that you are upset. This fear is not really about your spouse's potential reaction of walking out on you. It is only about your Ego-Reference of not wanting to be angry, which is based on your deep fear that you can't please your parents (another Ego-Reference) if your spouse walks out on you because of your anger. It is of great importance to recognize that you are not even dealing with the cause of your upset, but only with your "staying (emotionally) safe."

Note: If you have a Healthy Sense of Self, the initial reason for this upset might not even lead to the type of conflict described above, as you do not perceive any threat to your safety. In other words, you are able to let go of minor annoyances. This is one of the positive effects of having a Healthy Sense of Self.

People who rely on a Substitute Sense of Self do not have an authentic sense of being their own person. They are dependent on an inner structure that provides their criteria and operates on autopilot.

Their will and their best judgment for how to make a decision or how they ought to behave are run by their Ego-References. They are only fulfilling learned conditions that they perceive are necessary, as if their life depends on it.

Here's the irony: a firm decision not to be angry aggravates anger instead.

There is another important aspect to the Ego-Reference of "not wanting to be angry." The moment you feel unable to accept a situation or someone's behavior, the Ego-Reference *"I don't want to get angry"* creates a huge anger against the person or circumstance that causes it, which can culminate in rage. It is upsetting to come across something that will make it extremely difficult for you to be successful in satisfying your Ego-References. You can also end up aggravating your anger by being angry about getting angry. Suppressing your anger is not the solution; it is unhealthy and creates the risk of it exploding in a moment you least expect it. Just as the (Substitute Sense of Self–oriented) emotions are disproportionally intense, for example, when you are late, so it is with being angry – only the effects are usually much more noticeable.

All this plays out at a subconscious level; you sense great apprehension for what life will throw at you, and you try to stay away from conflict. Avoiding conflict is, of course, a challenge for anyone, even for those who have a Healthy Sense of Self. But when avoiding conflict is tied to whether or not you feel you are worth being taken into account, the quest has an almost existential layer to it. In the end, being afraid to show anger creates a ton of unnecessary upheaval for you as well as for others. You become afraid of your own behavior, as if you are *the victim* of your own behavior and emotions, instead of being in control of them.

Fear of Not Being Able to Function

For a person with a Substitute Sense of Self, the resulting high stress and tension put their system in overload, which creates a tendency to become ill and have physical symptoms (e.g., migraines and insomnia) that then sabotage the Substitute Sense of Self. So, even though part of that fear (of failing to function) is not based in reality, there is a legitimate reason for it as well. Because of the heightened vulnerability, symptoms of illness pop up with distressing frequency, which makes *not being able to function* a constantly lurking fear. Achieving a good outcome to Ego-References then becomes even harder.

Fear of Change

Big changes like moving or taking on a new job and even small changes in general are challenging if you depend on a Substitute Sense of Self. You do not want to spend time on anything other than your Ego-References. When change needs to happen, it looms over you because it mostly creates Hindrances.

Therefore, much of your attention is given to *anticipating the perfect setup* for fulfilling your Ego-References. Clearing the path so you *can* spend time working on Ego-References is already a chore and needs to be as efficient as possible. Change causes you to lose control over your circumstances. Rather than embracing change, you compulsively control your environment and yourself to *avoid* change.

Note that we are referring here to strategies that are completely subconsciously driven.

Fear of Failure

When you are dependent on a Substitute Sense of Self, you have a heightened fear of failure. In (almost) whatever you are doing, Annihilation is lurking, and you are concerned about bringing your activity to a good end.

But there is one other, even more potent reason for this high level of fear of failure. You can anticipate the likelihood of being unsuccessful for the following reason: Whatever you do, you are not really present in your own grounded Self. Everything you undertake is geared toward your Hidden Agenda – that is your true goal. Only a small amount of your energy and intent goes to the project at hand. So, you cannot fully function and that is why it takes so much effort. That is why you have to spend so much time on your undertakings.

And, of course, your fear of failure itself affects your body and your mind, and undermines your performance of a task as well.

Here are four reasons why people with a Lack of Sense of Self are much more prone to fearing they are inadequate:

1. The outcome of their activity is experienced as a matter of life and death, which adds a whole other level of stress.
2. They are unable to dedicate themselves fully to their activity because a large part of their attention is focused on the Substitute Sense of Self.
3. The fear in and of itself undermines the ability to focus.
4. There is a history of failure.

Now let's focus on a very specific type of fear of failure: stage fright, or performance anxiety.

Stage Fright

Stage fright is often rooted in the Fear of Annihilation. Let me describe the underlying processes of what happens to some performers. Please bear in mind that you can just as well substitute "presence *on stage*" with any situation in which you have to perform.

Imagine you have an upcoming performance. You are well prepared, but anywhere from a day (or several days) to five minutes before the event begins, your hands become clammy, you start to shake, you are nauseous, and if you are a singer, your throat starts to act up.

The following is an example from my own life: During my years in the orchestra, I made several attempts to develop my voice as a singer. I took that very seriously because I thought I enjoyed singing. But when an opportunity arose to give a small performance, I had no voice. "Was this accidental?" I wondered. I hadn't overused my voice or anything – I just came down with a cold. The Universe works in mysterious ways, but I got the message at some point. In hindsight, I can see my motivation was not pure. Even though I enjoyed singing, a big part of my efforts went into "proving that I could do it" and get away from a sort of family curse that has haunted me forever: "Others can do that – our family just can't!" Those were the words expressed repeatedly during my upbringing. I had no other choice than to prove I could. However, by doing so, I wasn't focused on singing. I was focused on proving that I could sing and get the credit for it. My motivation was Indirect.

As a performer, you may be worried sick that you are going to forget your lines (as an actress or a professional speaker), slip and fall (as a dancer), or have "a frog in your throat" (as a singer). In short, if you are scared out of your wits about not getting the desired outcome, you may want to ask yourself, "Where is this coming from so suddenly?" People around you may even want to try to soothe the pain of the issue with: "Oh, that's normal. Everyone has stage fright."

I do not believe that.

Fear is always rooted in a cause, and with such a strong reaction, there must be a lot that is perceived to be at stake. Now, don't get me wrong – if you are endowed with an intrinsic sense of knowing who you are and you do not depend on the outcome of your activities nor on what others think of you, you can still get a bit tense. However, if you chose to be a performer based on healthy motivation, you would most likely be excited and thrilled as well. You need the adrenaline rush to create that special performance – whatever it is you do.

If you do a job every day for a great number of years, you get used to a certain level of tension. However, if you are a performer who experiences severe symptoms of stage fright, please consider the following: It may be that you are in need of acknowledgment by means of admiration and applause and that your Substitute Sense of Self depends on it. In other words, you use your performance as a Vehicle to get your fix of "Feel-good-about-self." What you may not be aware of is that you perceive your psychological backbone to be at stake, and that is why you are so anxious. Without your knowing, performing well might be a matter of feeling you have the *right to exist*, and you need to be able to reach that goal at all costs. What really is at stake for you is the fear of being discounted as a "real" person.

Some train and study for years, marry specific people, and choose specific jobs, not because of sincere dedication and interest, but to use these things as a Vehicle to get to their Hidden Goal. From the outside, nothing is visibly at stake for these people, but hidden deep down inside is a profound fear that they might not reach that "holy" goal.

"What could be *my* holy Hidden Goal?" you may wonder. "Why would I have that fear of failure?" Look within and ask yourself these questions: "What do I want most in my life? What am I all about?" Make sure you are completely honest with yourself! You might discover that your fear of failure really has nothing to do with the content of your performance or activities, but is related to that buried hope of getting to your Hidden Goal.

The unfortunate thing is that, although the fear is not directly connected to the content of your performance or activity, it still affects it a lot. The result is a double disadvantage: The existing fear contaminates your activity, which makes it hard for you to concentrate on your performance. The bulk of your intention goes toward achieving your Hidden Goal and is not aimed at the actual performance.

So what amount of your energy and effort remains available to actually create your best performance? On top of that, even though the audience likely can't put their finger on it, they may somehow sense that what you are doing on stage isn't about giving them a wonderful experience and they can quickly lose interest. Performing from a place of Indirect Motivation is a struggle of the highest intensity and will yield only a mediocre result.

To rid yourself of the nagging fear of failure or stage fright, you need to ask yourself this most important question: "What is truly at stake for me during a performance?" The answer to this question can only help you if you are completely honest with yourself. It might surprise you how much you do not know about yourself. Addressing that issue and finding the answers are what will ultimately allow you to fully concentrate on your performance. When nothing other than the beauty of the event is at stake, your fear of failure will have dissolved to make space for the thrill of the moment.

Summary and Looking Ahead

Anger and fear are predominantly ruling your life if you are Substitute Sense of Self oriented. Can you imagine what it means to keep your plates spinning, manage your moods, perform your Ego-References to perfection, suffer from lack of acknowledgment and sleep, while trying to earn a living and be happy somewhere along the line?

In the next chapter, you will get a more concise overview of what dependency on a Substitute Sense of Self does to specific areas of your life and body and the overall lack of accomplishment that is the result.

Chapter 10
Impact on Your Life

Dreaming about my Hidden Goal …

I did not know that I was living in a fictional world. I was longing for what would have solved everything: the loving embrace of my mother in acknowledgment and respect for the devoted daughter I was. Her unconditional acceptance of who I was would have wiped out all former misunderstandings, quarrels, and struggles. That would have been my ultimate reward. If only my mother would have come up to me and said, "Wow, you are such a wonderful person! I am so glad that you are my child." If my mother would have done that for me, her child in agony, whose only craving was to be truly seen and heard, it would have meant the permanent elimination of my gnawing sense of inadequacy and my never-ending quest to make my mother happy! Then my deepest need would have been fulfilled, and my Substitute Sense of Self could have changed into a healthy, Restored Sense of Self. It was never meant to be, though …

My need was not met because of the intrinsic inability of my mother to do that. And what about me? I was not even aware that was what I actually wanted. Once I had a Restored Sense of Self, I started to understand that my Hidden Goal was just the dream of an emotionally needy and deeply disturbed child.

Unhealthy Motivations

Unhealthy motivations, like Hidden Agendas, are fairly common, and people using them are not necessarily mentally ill. But Hidden

Agendas that are outside of your awareness are bad for you; once you become aware that you have them, you need to make sure that you do not allow them to take over your life. They are not about you or your present life; they aim at compensating for past traumatic experiences, and they tend to lead to many kinds of suffering. The little everyday actions and activities that function as Vehicles for your Hidden Agendas may seem pretty harmless. Not so!

The following overview gives you a sense of which areas in your life need to be investigated and tested for possible contamination by a Substitute Sense of Self. It describes, in a nutshell, how your behavior and functioning can be affected when you are addicted to fulfilling Substitute Sense of Self–oriented conditions so you get the approval necessary to alleviate your Fear of Annihilation:

> ***Compulsive Task-Fulfilling Behavior***: When behaviors are linked to a Hidden Agenda, they become compulsive. If the achievement of this agenda feels at risk, you can erupt in uncontrollable rage and violence, become overwhelmed by your emotions, and not know why! Or you can become chronically depressed and suffer from insomnia or many other types of mental, physical, or emotional distress. It can lead to family fights, broken friendships, and even divorce. All of these can be tracked to one root cause: being motivated by a Hidden Agenda to get your fix of approval. We now know that it is more than just approval because it provides you with your artificial spine. By revisiting and decontaminating your motivation, you not only improve your own quality of life but also help make the world of those in your immediate environment a better place.
>
> ***Physical Symptoms***: I am not a medical doctor, so I cannot go into the medical background of specific physical symptoms. However, it seems to me that much physical distress may be the direct result of the dependency on a Substitute Sense of Self, including seemingly unrelated problems: a lowered immune system or possibly even an autoimmune disorder. It is quite likely that there is a whole array of diseases that could be included here. I strongly feel that research in this direction would help solve the root cause of many symptoms of ill health. For more suggestions, i refer to my first website (1997), www.holispsych.com.

Mental and Emotional Symptoms: Various types of fears are related to the presence of a Substitute Sense of Self (Fear of Annihilation). These may include, but are not limited to, anxiety; fear of failure; certain phobias; common depression with its many symptoms; suicidal thoughts; certain cases of post-traumatic stress disorder; a lack of ability to focus, which may include memory problems (possibly even Alzheimer's disease or dementia) in adults, or learning problems (e.g., math or reading) in children; and emotional numbness or the inability to experience feelings.

Social and Interpersonal Problems: Interpersonal and social problems related to a Substitute Sense of Self are perhaps the easiest to identify as the consequences are often obvious, including, but not limited to, a heightened sensitivity to criticism, an unstoppable urge to hurry in everything you do, problems relating to other people, and loneliness.

General Dysfunction: The negative effects from being dependent on a Substitute Sense of Self can be encountered on a daily basis. They range from major to minor difficulties in complying with rules and regulations that are common in society: an inability to function in the morning due to sleeping issues, an inability to drive for the same reason, anger issues, problems with violent behavior, child-rearing problems, divorce, greed, bullying, frequent family fights, possibly even specific cases of war and the performance of atrocities, and many more ...

A Lack of Integrity – Body Language

As much as the processes described in this book happen on a subconscious level, there *are* clues that others notice. Your body gives information about your motivations. Then, within a split second, others react to the vibes they detect, sometimes even before you speak. Interpreting body language is part of the human survival system.

You know that people are straightforward with their goals and intentions when they look you straight in the eye and you get a sense of solidity. When people are operating from Indirect Motivation, they tend to look away, or sometimes they have a look that gives off a vibe you might label as *dishonest* or *insecure*. Their pupils are larger than normal, and their eye color might change slightly. Overall, they seem very subtly evasive and nervous. When they speak about an activity that is indirectly motivated, their message does not ring true, nor does it come through clearly. It seems like these people don't have much to say or, as a compensation, they are too loud when trying to be convincing.

Isn't it interesting to notice that, even though nothing seems visibly unusual, you can pick up on the lack of integrity in their motivation? You might not get a clear sense of what is going on, but somehow you feel uninterested and are inclined to ignore what the person is doing or saying, or ignore the person altogether.

Indirect Motivation and a Career in Classical Music

Imagine listening to a singer. A number of things may happen: You are captivated by what you experience; you feel engaged with the performance. Or you may think there is nothing special going on or that it is an "interesting" experience at best, but you are not touched by it. In the first case, the singer is fully present and gives his all to the performance. He is able to get out of his own way in order to perform the music. He facilitates the piece and does not use it for his own (needy) purposes.

When there is "nothing special going on," the singer produces the notes but is unable to put his whole Self into the performance. As a listener, you don't sense any emotion in what is expressed; the singer stays in total control. It is almost as if he has a safety valve in place that monitors his performance and filters out what needs to be altered as he goes. There is no joy or emotion because reaching his Hidden Agenda at all costs is what subconsciously motivates him. He doesn't know it, but he can't afford to let the music lead him, so all he can do is give a flat interpretation of the melody. His focus is divided between the technical aspects of giving a quality performance and his subconscious concern about whether or not he will end up in a Fgas state.

Limited Access to Achieving Success

A split focus affects the results of your actions. The amount of intention that goes into any goal (be it directly or indirectly motivated) is responsible for the amount of success in getting the desired result. It is no wonder that the result of an indirectly motivated action is not optimal; the majority of focus goes to achieving the Hidden Agenda and not to the overt (directly motivated) ordinary result of such an action because it merely functions as a Vehicle. That doesn't imply that Direct Motivation always leads to success, but accepting failure is not encumbered by an existential burden

Here is an example from my own life: Once I was taking care of my parents' home while they were on vacation for a few days. I wanted to surprise them by repairing the broken laundry machine. I was so eager to get the thing working that I didn't thoroughly study how to put the filter back into the machine – it broke. What I got from my mother was: "Stay away from my washing machine. You always mess things up! Why don't you just leave things be if you don't know how they work?" Once again, I had proven to be unable to direct my mind to the actual thing at hand – in this case, the repair. It was as if there was emotional white noise blurring my ability to think clearly. And a reaction like my mother's, even though somewhat understandable, only reinforced my feeling of worthlessness.

The whole story would certainly have gone differently if I had been directly motivated. In other words, if my motivation would have truly been to help them, I would have taken the time to read the manual or understood that my technical knowledge wasn't sufficient and I would have left it alone. Most likely, the thought to repair the machine wouldn't even have occurred to me.

Here are two more examples:

A husband wants to reach a "Feel-good-about-self" state by doing the grocery shopping for his wife. He roughly anticipates what she usually buys, but the shopping list is not his major concern because his trip to the store is not really about helping out his wife. His focus is mainly on anticipating how his wife will appreciate what he did.

He forgets some crucial items and does not do a good job overall, and his wife has to return to the store anyway. Instead of reaching the Fgas state, he feels like a failure, which reinforces his belief that "I can't do anything right."

A person at work is very smart and capable but never meets his deadlines. He keeps on tweaking and adding and removing materials because his work needs to be "perfect." But, in the process, he completely loses track of time and commitments, to the point that his colleagues go on without him. Eventually he loses his job. Why did this happen, even though he was the most capable person in the office?

Anticipating the shame of having to face a negative mirror and being subconsciously dependent on "Feeling-good-about-self," he needs to achieve perfection. Because of the paramount importance of his quest, he not only doesn't deliver but also completely loses sight of the collaboration he is supposed to be part of.

If you find that all too often your own efforts do not produce the desired outcome, it is worthwhile to check your motivation.

Because the Hidden Agenda's goal is based on the experience of a fictional self ("Feeling-good-about-self"), you could say that *all of the effort* put into that part of the action *goes to waste*. It is fictional, right? For the sake of argument, let us say that 100% of the effort should have gone into the overt goal (Direct Motivation), but the fictional one used 60% of it (Indirect Motivation). That means that only 40% of the intention went into the overt goal, and that was not enough for it to be successful. The other 60% that went into serving the fictional self did not lead to any tangible result either.

Here is another scenario: Giving a concert for the sake of celebrating the beauty of the music is what should be the norm. You are one with your audience, and everybody (yourself included) enjoys the music. However, performing can be a Vehicle for a musician to achieve approval from a caregiver. On top of that, it can work as a Vehicle for the parent of the same musician, in an attempt to Score with their own parents! For example, "Look, Dad, my daughter is a wonderful concert pianist! Aren't you proud of me now?"

Or maybe the attempt is geared toward the inner approval of your Internalized Parental Voice: "I worked so hard to get into good shape for this concert. I think I didn't do too bad. Maybe I can consider myself a good musician now. Maybe now my mother/colleagues will give me the attention and respect I crave."

The 40/60 rule applies in all these cases, as the main goal is to make your caregiver proud. That leaves 40% for the music. The fear of not being able to succeed while the stakes seem so high undermines attention and focus and increases compulsive practicing. Add a dose of self-sabotage to that, and you will understand how I got to these otherwise randomly chosen numbers. This is how a concert can become a purely technical, lackluster performance. You may have worked hard, but if your hard work is underscored with a great fear of failing to earn your Substitute Sense of Self, you won't be ready to let go and give an inspired performance.

Here is one more example: Imagine you are fourteen years old and your father has never really been present, so you are in desperate need of his acknowledgment. He likes to play computer games, so you pretend to be interested, too. You play them all the time, with his virtual approval in your subconscious mind, but you don't truly enjoy them. Your mind is scattered, you aren't focused on actually playing the game, and you never reach the higher levels. What you are focused on, deep down inside, is the anticipation of receiving your father's approval that then soothes your need to "Feel-good-about-self."

Know *WHY* you do what you do!

It took me a great number of years of practicing my bassoon like mad while playing in top-class orchestras before it dawned on me: "I play the way I am. I practice the way I am."

If you keep convincing yourself that you have to practice all the time because "practice makes perfect," you may end up disappointed. The truth is that no amount of practice hours will enable you to surpass your crooked motivation that causes at least half of your efforts to go to waste. WHY you do WHAT you do greatly determines your skill level, your musical know-how, and success. The musician you are – or the one you're going to be – depends totally on the person you are and that includes the degree of healthiness/directness of your motivation. To take your playing to the next level, you have to work on yourself and clean up your motivation.

Have you reached a certain level of expertise that you are trying unsuccessfully to surpass? Are you grappling with ever-receding success in some endeavor or other? Inspect your motivation! What is really at stake without you knowing it or wanting to admit it? No amount of effort will help you overcome the handicap of having a Hidden Goal that you are unaware of. Do you do what you do with Direct or Indirect Motivation? The answer to that question has a major influence on how high your level of success is going to be.

Pleading for Compassion and Early Understanding

The unspeakable pain of not having been acknowledged by a caregiver may very well underlie a troubled performance as described above. Chances are the person is in distress and trying to accomplish something that others take for granted – being seen and heard – only because he or she did not have a chance to develop a Healthy Sense of Self.

Sometimes we can be so off in judging a person as egocentric. Most of the time, egocentric behavior is trying to compensate for a bigger need or a greater fear. Awareness of this apparent contradiction can lead to more compassion, both for ourselves as well as for our fellow human beings.

How useful would it be if teachers and professional institutions were educated in recognizing students with a Healthy Sense of Self versus those with a Lack of Sense of Self? Attempts could be made to help the student restore their Sense of Self, and career advice could be tailored to helping students avoid choosing a profession that feeds into their Ego-References.

When considering all these harmful effects of Indirect Motivation, we may wonder if there could be a relationship of causation between motivation and those who make it in the world and those who don't.

Could this have something to do with what we tend to call natural selection? Maybe each of us can positively influence the number of people who make it in this world by cleaning up our motivation.

By now, you know that by doing so, you will finally be ready to provide your children with the building blocks for a Healthy Sense of Self. Studying the SoS Theory and Method and applying the concepts to your own life might do exactly that for you!

Summary and Looking Ahead

When you perceive that you have to live up to conditions – whether self-imposed or deduced from childhood trial and error – you may not be aware of the life-altering effects it forces you to accept, simply because you don't know any better. You have never experienced what it is to have a Healthy Sense of Self and are unable to see how much emotional turmoil, drama, and Substitute Sense of Self–oriented fear would disappear from your life once you have restored your Sense of Self.

This and other benefits and challenges of a Restored Sense of Self will be discussed in the next section of the book – Part III: Recovery.

PART III

Recovery

Chapter 11

The Restored Sense of Self

Putting a Sense of Self in place where one was never experienced before is quite a challenge. The SoS Method encourages you to spend time and effort observing your thoughts and behavior; introspection on what lies behind them should be followed by an honest analysis of your findings.

If you haven't already done so, start out by consulting the SoS Comparison Chart on page 159. Going over the characteristics in this self-assessment checklist can help you recognize whether you are actually your Self or if you are Substitute Sense of Self–oriented. When you then find that you are not as directly motivated as would be good for you, you can decide to recover from this addiction to approval-based "Feel-good-about-self" that serves as your Substitute Sense of Self.

The first step in that process is to get a sense of what makes you decide to do or avoid certain things by monitoring your motivations. An effective way of doing that is by observing and recording the degree of intensity in emotions you experience when making certain decisions or performing an action or behavior. When emotions rise sky high and the degree of frustration is not congruent with the actual event, be alert: this could be an indication that there is more at play than meets the eye.

Fearlessly scrutinizing your motivations might reveal that, deep down, you are pursuing a Hidden Goal by means of living up to specific Hidden Agendas on a daily basis. The idea is to get in touch with the inner causes of your emotional states, ailments, addictions, and compulsions.

Once you have seen the absurdity of the role this Hidden Goal plays in your life, you will want to take action to replace your Substitute Sense of Self with a healthier Self-awareness, a Restored Sense of Self. From then on, you will finally establish a true, direct connection with your Self and lead a much happier, more productive life.

What Is a Restored Sense of Self?

Restored Sense of Self

The end result of working with the SoS Method, which is being healed from the dependency on a Substitute Sense of Self and which consists of a steady awareness of being one's very own person who is free to live life based on one's own essence, preferences, abilities, and limitations. There is an inner knowing of being separate from any parent or caregiver and free from any dependency on achievements or approval. There is an abiding sense of being (unconditionally) alive and "real."

A Substitute Sense of Self cannot simply be replaced by a Natural Sense of Self if one was not developed at the appropriate time; that missed opportunity is gone forever. But the good news is that it *is* possible to move on to restoring your Sense of Self – even if you have no memory of having ever truly owned your own life. What you can achieve through awareness, training, and exercise is a Restored Sense of Self. This (re)learned Sense of Self then fills your core where once was only emptiness.

I speak about *restoring* the Sense of Self, which implies it has already been there and is gone. I believe that having a sense of one's Self is an intrinsic part of every human being and that the seed for being connected to one's Self is always there. My point of departure is the assumption that the process naturally initiated itself but was aborted at an early stage. Depending on how you were nurtured by your caregivers, your Natural Sense of Self never had a chance to develop properly and fully. Through awareness and training – reconditioning – you can create and implement, within your being, healthy and appropriate boundaries to the outside world, as well as cultivate a sense of being at peace with and for yourself.

A Restored Sense of Self is experienced as having found a home within your Self, where it is your duty to take care of yourself. It is only natural to *put yourself first* in your own life; this has nothing to do with being egocentric or selfish. I believe that each of us is given a body to manifest our soul's intentions, and it is up to us to manage that body and our lives to make that possible. We were not meant to be ruled by others, neither consciously nor subconsciously. (I am not referring here to organizations that serve society, such as governments and the like.)

If you are serious about wanting to make that switch from being ruled by your automatic pilot, which was conditioned long before you could think for your (Real) Self, you need to actively spend time on reconditioning yourself. Ultimately, your Restored Sense of Self will function like a Natural Sense of Self, including all the benefits that come with it (see page 33).

A Restored Sense of Self versus a Natural Sense of Self

In the long run, a Restored Sense of Self will work for you in the same ways a Natural Sense of Self would have if developed at the right time. But they are not totally the same, which may need clarification. Let's take a moment to compare the two.

A Natural Sense of Self develops in childhood in a natural way, and a Restored Sense of Self is purposefully developed later in life. So, it is manufactured, if you will. And because it is a relatively new habit, it may be more vulnerable than a Natural Sense of Self is. On the other hand, it might eventually be stronger since you will have created conscious awareness around your Sense of Self. Over time, the Restored Sense of Self does become "natural" in the sense that it becomes fully adopted, integrated, automatic, and normal. In other words, it becomes a Healthy Sense of Self.

With regard to how the SoS Method defines *the Self* in general, you will find detailed information in Chapter 16: The Layers of Self on page 325. This will further enhance your understanding of everything that is at play here.

The Benefits of a Restored Sense of Self

If you are having all sorts of problems at this very moment and your life feels like a struggle, you may be in a place similar to where I used to be. It might be that these problems are caused, without your knowing it, by letting your need to gain a Substitute Sense of Self rule your life. In that case, it is crucial for you to become aware of how you function – or rather, how you are coping – and learn what you can do to become the captain on the ship of your own life.

By becoming your own boss, your quality of life will be greatly enhanced. By replacing a Substitute Sense of Self with an intrinsic awareness of your own values and your right to exist as your Self, you will automatically have the tools necessary to succeed in dealing with many issues. With this new conviction that you are okay just as you are and that you have the right to exist, you will feel calmer and more balanced. It will be much easier for you to get a grip on what you really want and what needs to be done. With a Restored Sense of Self, you will have a Direct Relationship with yourself and with the things in your life. Your motivation will be direct and straightforward. The need to obtain the "Feel-good-about-self" state will disappear. You will be able to get a real sense of *who you are* and make decisions and choices geared toward your well-being and the expression of your authentic Self. With a Restored Sense of Self, you will finally experience the freedom that is the birthright of every human being.

One major benefit of restoring your Sense of Self is that Ego-References turn into simple Quality-of-Life matters, and this change alone removes a great deal of stress. Those who have a Healthy Sense of Self are guided by their true and honest motives and have no Hidden Agenda. They marry the person they really love and decide to start a family because they would love to have children and be a parent. They pursue a career they truly enjoy in an area in which they are skilled. This as opposed to those with a Lack of Sense of Self who might end up marrying the person their parents want them to, choosing a job that makes good money to satisfy their father, and having kids only because their mother wants grandchildren. In short, it is safe to say that a Restored Sense of Self leads to a tremendous change for the better.

With the Substitute Sense of Self, you not only experience numerous dependencies based on the desired outcome of your actions and behavior, but you are also haunted by a hankering for a sense of satisfaction that will never be fulfilled, simply because your intent is not directed toward fulfilling your (Real) Self. When you have achieved a Restored Sense of Self, all this vanishes because you know that you are – and forever are meant to be – an independent being. You are the master of your life.

With a Restored Sense of Self, an endless road of improvement and personal growth has opened up to you.

How a Restored Sense of Self Feels

When you restore your Sense of Self, you feel much more balanced; you are able to look at things through the lens of your own perception and make sensible conclusions and decisions based on *your* values. Common sense kicks in! You feel at ease in your own body. What's more, you continue to improve every day!

So many things in life go much more smoothly: You sleep better, you don't quarrel as much, and your anxiety is gone. You have emotional balance and are not afraid of your own behavior! You have better focus and energy. Panic attacks and suicidal thoughts, if you had any, are gone. You have no desperate need for a high, whether from a substance or from the approval of others. Your calm inner knowing that you are okay makes you more approachable. It's easier to make real, lasting friendships that are not based on the desperate need to find acceptance. Your relationships stand a much better chance of being healthy, and there is less drama. You are the master of your own life!

It is important to know that sensing your Restored Sense of Self is a subtle experience, especially in the beginning. In the modern world, our senses are continuously exposed to loud and intense stimuli: television, movies, computers, cell phones, music, and urban noises of all kinds have made us less sensitive to the subtleties of the signals from our own bodies. In addition, the types of experiences we deal with every day – traffic and the attention required to navigate it, the continuous pressure to hurry in most aspects of life, both personal and professional – are totally different from our subtle internal experiences that can easily be overlooked when we finally decide to turn our attention inward to our Sense our Self.

Thus, if you want to know how a Restored Sense of Self *feels*, you will need to find or create quiet spaces in your life.

Quality-of-Life Experience

In addition to unhealthy Substitute Sense of Self–oriented stress, we certainly also have *normal stress* associated with everyday life. Every action that requires some sort of a special attention or skill brings forth a sort of mental tension geared toward the outcome: "Will I be able to do it?" There might be unexpected situations that interfere, which increases stress. This is what I call a Quality-of-Life Level of stress; it only affects us on the surface. This is the type of stress that everyone faces at one time or another.

Measuring Stress Levels as an Indicator for Approval-Oriented Activity

If you take a good hard look at how much stress you are experiencing and discover that the degree of stress is not really justified by the nature or the apparent goal of the activity, then something else is probably going on: your Substitute Sense of Self is likely at stake and is dependent on the outcome. This excess stress can help you identify whether you are working with a Healthy Sense of Self or a Substitute Sense of Self. In other words, measuring the amount of stress associated with the event or action, by means of introspection, and then comparing it with the normal amount of stress related to such an event or activity, can help you identify whether your motivations are direct or indirect.

What follows are more examples of the healthier ways you will experience life when your motivations are direct:

- Being independent from other people's opinions, tastes, and choices.
- Being independent from what other people mirror back to you about your Self.
- Being independent from your achievements.
- Feeling acknowledged and unconditionally accepted.
- Being able to bond with others (depending on your desire to do so).
- Feeling included.
- Being able to fully be yourself and live up to your potential.
- Sensing that you are your Real Self.
- Being realistic about your potential and your limitations.
- Finding and using opportunities to speak freely.
- Having a voice in a group (according to your nature).
- Sharing things about your life freely (when appropriate and according to your nature).
- Feeling balanced and not overly intense when experiencing emotions like joy, grief, sadness, and anger.
- Being able to judge situations fairly.
- Knowing fully on every level of awareness that you have the right to exist.
- Feeling good about yourself no matter what.[1]

A person with a Healthy Sense of Self still might experience moments of apprehension and/or fear on a regular basis. The difference is that, for this person, there is no Substitute Sense of Self at stake, so he or she reacts differently to it. Arriving late to work, having a disagreement with someone, or meeting a tight deadline can cause stress and uncomfortable feelings in all of us. However, other than the inconvenience of being late, missing the beginning of the event, or having to cram in extra hours at work, there is nothing at stake.

[1] Please note that there are two ways of feeling good about yourself: 1) the SoS term "Feel-good-about-self," which has a negative meaning as it indicates that it is a substitute for experiencing your Self, and 2) the normal, healthy feeling good about (your) Self, as a perfectly healthy way of feeling satisfied about something.

Thus, a fear related to quality of life has an entirely different basis from a fear related to a Substitute Sense of Self. The former refers to a healthy, temporary, everyday type of apprehension; the latter is a deeply rooted psychological, existential type of fear. Identifying these two aspects within yourself is important to be able to effectively reduce your stress levels.

All Ego-References have both a Quality-of-Life aspect and a Substitute Sense of Self–oriented aspect (see Figure 11.1 on next page). The light grey half of the leaf represents the normal, healthy part of a behavior (e.g., to be on time); it is very common to have a bit of fear of being late. The dark part of the leaf, though, represents the irrational, intense Substitute Sense of Self–oriented fear.

This complex dual-aspect makes the pathological behavior involved in Ego-References almost impossible to identify. For the person experiencing the fear, there always seems to be a plausible explanation. Excessive stress is justified by saying something like: "Some people are just more fearful than others."

So, every Ego-Reference consists partly of a Quality-of-Life aspect. It is the actual action or behavior that functions as the Vehicle. That is the part people use to explain or justify their anxiety. The mixture of Direct and Indirect Motivation has made it impossible (until now) to distinguish the real cause of the fear: the Indirect Motivation.

Rest assured that with a Restored Sense of Self, the dark part of the leaf vanishes, leaving the leaf entirely light. Imagine the relief that would bring.

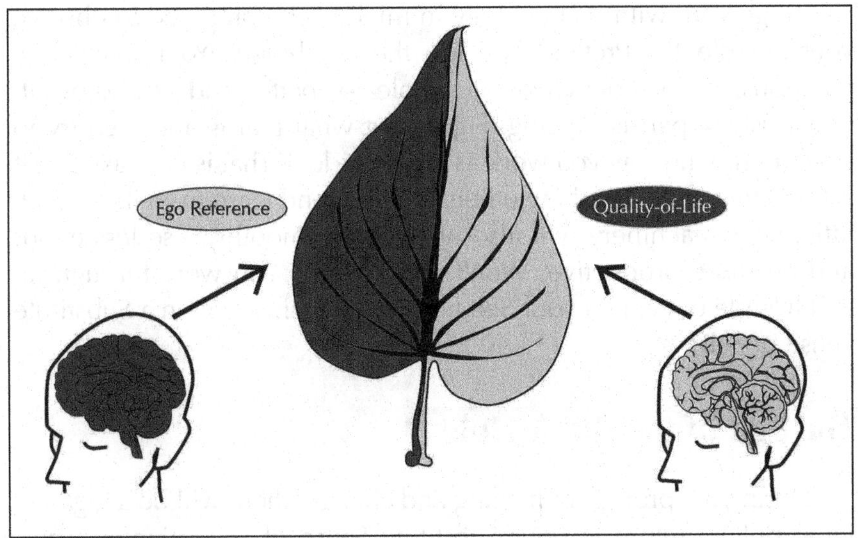

Figure 11.1: The dual aspects of stress in Ego-References.

The Challenges to Restoring Your Sense of Self

If you want a better life, your only choice is to restore your Sense of Self. Creating a Restored Sense of Self is intensive; there is *no quick fix*, and doing the work needed requires great persistence and endurance as you fight against a continuous tendency to fall back into old behavior patterns. But the only other alternative is to continue suffering with a Lack of Sense of Self. At times, in the course of the recovery process, using whatever you are doing to Score (see page 76) will seem more important to you than anything else, especially your own well-being. At those moments, you'll convince yourself, subconsciously, that it's a much better use of your time to work hard to take care of your Ego-References. Many moments of discomfort and even anxiety are to be expected as you move through the healing process, but it is all worth it.

Imagine that you have a piece of machinery that works in a stumbling but predictable way. For it to function more effectively and productively, a specific part that has been missing so far needs to be inserted. But that part is not for sale! So, first, you must find out what is missing and then, if you want to implement it, you will have to build that part yourself.

I urge you, with that analogy in mind, to be prepared to observe yourself intently. Pretend *you* are the machinery. Your machinery functions, but it could work a whole lot better and you know it. Obviously, a part is missing. Figure out what that is and then try to insert it into the way *you* work as an individual. That is not easy, but it is the only way! Study how others function and learn from it. Little by little, your machinery will also work more smoothly, use less effort, and be more productive. Won't you be glad you went through all that trouble of healing your Self from the dependency on a Substitute Sense of Self?

The Pull of the Black Hole

During the process of healing and change, there will be a gigantic inner pull to return to your Substitute Sense of Self–oriented ways, with its motivation to do things to Score and gain approval. With the power and intensity of a force of nature, this unhealthy survival system will push its way through your desire to change and do its job: suck up all the good outcomes you are finally able to get so it can fill the Black Hole. After all, we are talking about a survival system that needs to keep functioning at all costs.

So, it is the duty of your Early Childhood Survival Strategy (ECSS) to make you (subconsciously) believe that letting go of your old habits is not an option. Changing your ways is seen by the ECSS as an attack on its task of defending you and keeping you safe, and it will fight your newly made decisions with astonishing force and persistence.

Only by *immediately replacing* whatever you have been using so far to fill that Black Hole with real-life experience of your (Real) Self can you be successful in patching that void and stopping its pull. What you need is a deep understanding that the only way you can reach your goal of restoring your Sense of Self is with gentle perseverance, frequent exercises, mental rehearsal, continual awareness, and complete honesty toward your Self.

The Magic Cane

A man is walking mile after mile on a long and dusty road heading to the next village. Almost collapsing under the weight of an old backpack, he schleps along a shapeless bag while heavily leaning on an old red cane.

Suddenly he sees, leaning against a tree, a bright green cane with a golden knob reflecting the last sunrays of the day. He scurries toward the desired object and grabs it with his left hand. He would love to exchange this intriguing green cane for his old red one, but he is puzzled about how to switch canes while walking, and he must walk on; he has no time to lose. Walking without a cane, even for a single step, is not an option because he would collapse and crumble to the ground. Then suddenly he gets it, and without missing a step, he moves the new green cane next to his old red one. Now holding both canes in the same hand, he continues on his path with a grin. He sees what needs to happen.

He rids himself of his old cane by letting it slide down to the ground while still leaning on the beautiful new one. Now there is a secret to this green cane, and he knows it intuitively: it is going to dissolve over time, and on the day it disappears completely, he will be able to walk all by himself again.

The Substitute Sense of Self can be considered a crutch you have leaned on your whole life. Make sure you have parts of your Restored Sense of Self in place when you try to drop your old cane!

Habits and Backsliding

Let's get a clear understanding of the hurdles you have to be prepared to jump. Humans are creatures of habit, and therefore it is safe to say that you can and will slip back into your Substitute Sense of Self–oriented behavior. You should not judge yourself harshly for this; it's just a fact of life. Beating up on yourself for any slips will only cause suffering and slow your progress, so be kind to yourself!

Recovering from a Substitute Sense of Self requires continuous effort to install the new Restored Sense of Self and prevent falling back into unhealthy habits. There is no way around it: you have to go out of your way to make your sense of being your Self as strong as you possibly can by continuously checking in with your Self. Ask your Self some questions like: "Am I living from my own heart and thinking with my own mind in this situation? Am I in touch with my own feelings or have I fallen back into my old habit of allowing my life to be a performance?" With time and persistence, you will win.

Figure 11.2 is an illustration of the stress your brain is under during relapse. Similar to the representation of the two types of stressors at work in Ego-References, we have represented what the challenges are when recovering from the addiction to a Substitute Sense of Self. As mentioned earlier, there is the continuous threat of relapse. With a Restored Sense of Self, you walk the straight path of your (own) life; when relapse occurs, something triggers you to switch from the path of Direct Motivation to the path of Indirect Motivation, and you are pulled back into the whirling vicious cycle of Substitute Sense of Self–oriented behavior.

Beware of Denial

When you are living as your Self, your brain is light grey (green in our color version of this image) and generates the Quality-of-Life side of an action or behavior. But beware of denial when monitoring your behavior, as both shades, dark as well as light grey, are present in your brain when you are Substitute Sense of Self oriented. This enables you to be selective and just identify the (obvious) Quality-of-Life Level of your activity in order to fool yourself. Once under the spell of scoring a Substitute Sense of Self, there is a tremendous need to deny your own problematic psychological and emotional makeup, as the goal of being able to Score is the only thing that counts! It goes without saying that you want to have a totally "light" brain.

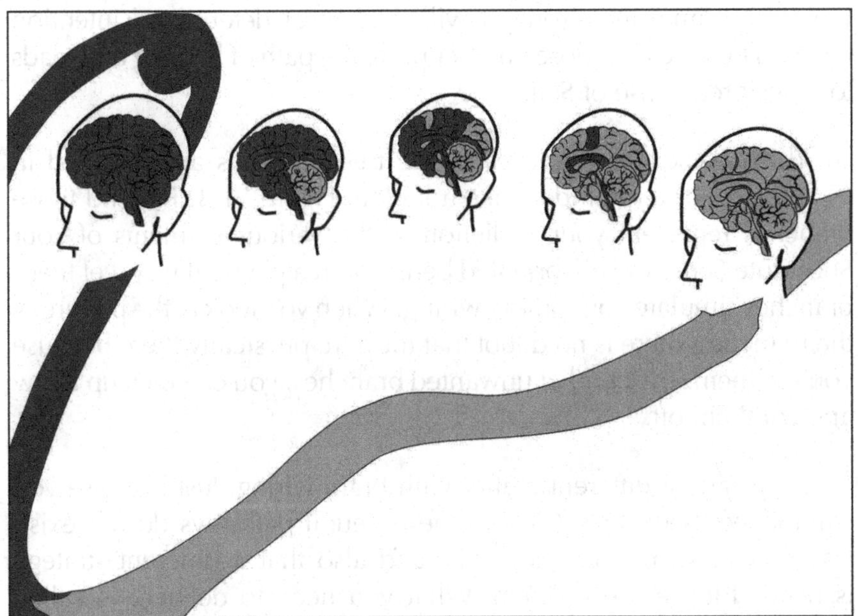

Figure 11.2: Stress in our brain.

It takes a lot of convincing/reconditioning to have new feelings, thoughts, and actions override the habits of your old behavior. You have been holding on to them for so many years that they have become hardwired in your brain. Yet it can be done. I did it – so can you!

To guarantee a successful implementation of a Restored Sense of Self, it is of great importance that the awareness exercises presented in Chapter 15 have a permanent place in your life to keep you from slipping back. Encourage yourself by keeping track of how your problems and pains are diminishing.

An Addiction

Gaining a Substitute Sense of Self is to be considered an addictive behavior because it has to be performed at all costs. That means we can deal with it in a similar way as with any other addiction. So to make things easier, compare yourself to a drug addict, nothing more and nothing less. Just like a junkie, you are continuously falling prey to the numerous triggers that lie within yourself and your environment.

Only with time, the strongest will, and most determined intention will you be able to choose another path, the path of healing that leads to a Restored Sense of Self.

Think back to the images of the tree branches as presented in Chapter 2. For a reminder, take a look at Figure 11.3. Pretend those branches represent your addiction to the various elements of your Substitute Sense of Self–oriented behavior in a physical way. Let these branches simulate your brain's wiring. When you look at the picture of the branches, there is no doubt that they are physically there because you *see* them. To get rid of unwanted branches, you can pick up a saw and cut them off.

It's clearly a different matter with brain wiring. Just because you cannot see them doesn't mean these neural pathways do not exist. It's good to know that they exist and also that a different strategy is needed to get rid of them. What you need to do here is called *reconditioning*, and it comes down to learning new ways of looking at your Self and sensing your Self; these new ways need to overrule the old ones.

Please be patient with yourself, though. It takes time to mentally and emotionally step away from those familiar pathways. You need to leave them behind and consciously and actively choose to create other pathways from scratch. These newly formed routes are then like a freshly cut path in a jungle: The moment you stop cutting the bushes and plants on your new track, they grow back – and they grow back fast! Before you know it, the new path toward a Restored Sense of Self that you created just a few hours ago is completely overgrown!

Figure 11.3: The branches of the tree representing your brain wiring.

There is hope, though! There *is* hope for complete recovery. Just as there is hope for alcoholics and drug addicts, there is hope for those of you who are addicted to approval for your Substitute Sense of Self. Is it accidental that people who are dependent on a Substitute Sense of Self are more likely to use drugs or alcohol? Technically, you could be addressing both addictions simultaneously. However, it is so much better if there is no additional physical addiction to a substance that must be dealt with first, especially the mind-numbing ones. Being able to think clearly and be committed is a must for this process to be successful.

During the beginning of the recovery process, just like many alcoholics and drug users, you will have moments in which you are like a "dry drunk": explicitly avoiding working on your Ego-References but mentally focused on them all the time. The problem is that you have to pay attention to them in order to single them out. How else are you going to become aware and remember what it is you do not want to do?

My Own Recovery Process

In my own recovery process, I started out by learning my list of Ego-References by heart. Some might suggest that it is better to focus on the positive. My truth was that I needed to be aware of the negative so I could turn it into a positive. For example, one of my Ego-References was being on time. Indeed, I was always late, and I had to become aware that I was really trying to avoid that. Just by stating, "I want to be on time" did not do the trick. So I explained to myself as often as needed (and that was very often): "I don't have to worry about being on time because I know it's not for the sake of the event or activity. It's only for fear that I won't get my Internalized Parental Voice's approval. How silly of me to still worry about that. But I don't blame myself for it. It's not because I'm silly. I just conditioned myself that way earlier in life because I thought it was the only way to get my mother's approval. All I wanted was to be seen and heard as a real person. I now know that 'not being late' is not going to do that trick for me. So I might as well not worry about it."

Fear and Blame

In the process of recovery from the addiction to a Substitute Sense of Self, you might experience feelings of anger and resentment or even self-blame. Remember that you developed this Substitute Sense of Self–oriented behavior because you were deprived of acknowledgment by your parent/caregiver during your childhood. This is heavy stuff. We are talking about serious existential terror. So cut yourself some slack without letting up on your will to heal. Expect those fears to come closer to your conscious awareness, and just have compassion for yourself.

You bear no blame in this; you did the best you were capable of as a child in an unhealthy situation. Do not impede your healing by blaming yourself for anything, including the idea of having "wasted" years of your life. You might also need, as part of your recovery process, to learn some forgiveness techniques that work for you. Regarding your caregivers, it is up to you how to get to a point of accepting what happened and how to move on. Just be advised that I found that any way that can stop the blame-game works wonders on the ability to live in the present, and forgiveness is definitely one of them.[2]

Special Challenges in Recovering from the Compulsion to Perform Ego-References

Recovering from being a slave to your Ego-References presents some special challenges because so much has been perceived to be at stake for such a long time. Separating yourself from your Ego-References may feel like it equates to losing the opportunity to anticipate your sporadic and tenuous grip on *any* experience of self, albeit a Substitute Sense of Self.

What you need to learn is to focus on yourself, on what you like or on what needs to be done based on Direct Motivation. Separating yourself from your Ego-References – recovering from the dependency on a Substitute Sense of Self – is hardly an option until you become utterly aware of your slavery to them and are determined to carve your path to freedom. Realizing this task is what the SoS Method hopes to help you with.

In trying to fulfill your Ego-References, you are like Don Quixote battling against windmills. You are striving for a fictitious, unattainable goal, but you cannot allow yourself to see that.

How deeply can you be trapped in this pattern? Consider this: At some point in my own healing process, I experienced anxiety attacks and moments of terror. This terror came up despite the fact that I was the one who had consciously made the decision to counter my compulsions!

While I was carving my own path to freedom, I would resist trying to fulfill my Ego-References, such as compulsively practicing piano or violin, working on my website, or cleaning the house. I would deliberately choose to not do those things and do other things (or nothing) instead. It was almost impossible to resist the pull of the

[2] For help with this process, I recommend *Radical Forgiveness* by Colin Tipping (Louisville, CO: Sounds True, Inc., 2009).

Black Hole and not try to fill that emptiness inside, and this led to anxiety and undefined feelings of frenzy. When your only way (the substitute way) of experiencing your Self is not allowed to take place (even when based on an initiative instigated by your Self for healing purposes), you can feel a frantic fear that may result in rage and possibly violence as well as in symptoms like insomnia and depression.

So very much seems to be at stake. You feel threatened by the collapsing of the inner structure that has been the backbone of your psyche so far. Your Early Childhood Survival Strategy (ECSS) simply will not tolerate that. Your subconscious reflects what you have been programmed to do since early childhood and is (misguidedly but sincerely) trying to warn you that you are doing something dangerous to your very sense of existing! That is why it is not an option to throw away the crutch you are leaning on, your Substitute Sense of Self, without first putting in place a more positive, healthy beginning of a Restored Sense of Self. (Remember the story of the man with the red and green canes.)

The Substitute Sense of Self–oriented patterns of behavior are very tricky. They can co-opt your healing process. Your habitual behavior will try to kick back in and do anything to seduce you to Score and reach your Hidden Goal after all. Please be on the alert! Do not let your new experiences become your Substitute Sense of Self in disguise. Inspect your intentions conscientiously, and honestly assess whether or not you are allowing yourself to feel alive through your problems.

You have to take that step and get in touch with *who you are as your own person,* based on your own criteria, as opposed to blindly and habitually being led by memories of what made you feel (close to) accepted by your caregiver. The moment you enter this world of recovery, your new life may feel gray and undefined simply because you no longer experience emotional extremes. Chances are you became used to those, and it is not unlikely that you will, at first, miss the great highs and lows you are trying to give up. Until now, these have made up your sense of being; the drama in your life gave you a sense of being alive. Your new life will color up beautifully, though – trust me on that!

Discover Your Stressors

Recognizing what triggers stress for you is necessary to free yourself from it. You have to discover the connections between your life as you are living it now and the missed opportunity of having been allowed to cultivate a sense of your Self in the past. You have to become consciously aware of what your observations were as a child, the adjustments you made, and what you hoped to achieve with those adaptations. That will not be easy since most of these processes took place on an entirely subconscious level. But you have to work with what you can remember and then connect the dots. It is like creating a map of your stressors as they manifest in your current life and figuring out what the initial reasons for these were. You then can play with all the elements in this chain of emotions and become familiar with them. Once you can recognize them as they come up, you can learn to draw different conclusions based on how you now view the causes of these stressors and repeat the new conclusions so often that they overrule the old ones.

Here are a few tips for how you can play with these concepts, while realizing that your goal was always to avoid Annihilation. Keep in mind that the reason you felt you had to do that has been dismantled. Consequently, you can now free yourself from, and eliminate, the addictive need for an unhealthy substitute and replace it with a true, healthy acknowledgment that *you exist* and that you do not need to do anything to prove that.

To help you reinforce this conclusion, you need to do the following:

- Connect to your body as the ultimate proof that you are *real*.
- Realize that "Yes, I already *am*. I already exist. I do not need any external or internal (i.e., IPV) approval; I do not need to achieve a 'Feel-good-about-self' state because that is my default state."
- Realize that "I do not have to pursue my Hidden Goal anymore because it has become obsolete. I don't have to continuously improve my Ego-References anymore. I now know where all of that came from, and there is no need for me to comply with these Early Childhood Survival Strategies any longer now that I am restoring my Sense of Self."

- Realize that "I don't have to use my daily activities and behavior as Vehicles anymore. I can do the action or activity for its own sake."
- Realize that "I no longer wish to convince my parents that I am better than they think as it was not my fault they were not able to acknowledge me in the first place. I'm already good enough just as I am."

Whenever you notice that you are stressed, you need to *stop*, draw strength from the depths of your being (your Real Self), and wonder, "What do I authentically – as my Self – think of this situation?" By asking yourself what you are actually after and actively making it a point to think with your own mind, you might discover that you are chasing after approval from your parent (or yourself) or proving yourself in some way or other. Asking those questions and then seeking and finding the answers will have a healing effect on your life.

Tools and Time Are Needed

To be able to get that Restored Sense of Self, you need many tools to support you: imagery and visualization; body work; creative expression through crafts, arts, music; and the like. Additional tools and resources you might find useful are offered in the chapters that follow and on www.healthysenseofself.com. Please be fully aware that this recovery work is hardly something you can do on the side. If you want to succeed, you must give it a lot of attention and devotion. For the time being, you have to make *becoming your Self* the master plan for your life.

I should let you know that a halfhearted recovery attempt might cause more suffering than relief. The fears and blame mentioned previously will emerge big time, and you might feel like a failure as your old habits and addictions keep reemerging because you are not fully committed to addressing them with your increasingly stronger Self. However, if you are determined to succeed and proceed on the path of restoring your Sense of Self, you are entering a new world, a world where your life is about *you*.

Achieving a Restored Sense of Self *Is* Possible

Come and step into the future, where you are less attached to what happens in and around you because nothing is at stake on an existential level. There will come a time when your Restored Sense of Self is strong enough to change your motivations in life from indirect to direct. Then the Hidden Agendas will cease to pull, and the Ego-References and the Substitute Sense of Self will have lost their appeal to – and their hold on – your subconscious mind. At this point, you will sense your Self in a direct way, which will have become more natural and automatic to you. See *yourself* as the master of your life.

Looking Inward

Discovering what was missing in me and repairing the damage done had me digging deep into my psyche to figure out how I developed that big Hidden Agenda. The answer was found in what happened in my early childhood – or, rather, in what did *not* happen in my childhood. That may be the path you'll have to go, too.

To take advantage of the SoS Method, you will be required to do some serious exploration of what is going on inside your head – and body. Knowing yourself more fully will enable you to make smarter decisions from which others will also benefit. Self-knowledge is power!

The fastest route to understanding yourself is to get familiar with your real motivations: Why are you doing what you are doing? Why do you avoid doing certain things? What are you after? What do you seek or wish to avoid? What are your goals, your agendas, for doing things? Questioning your motivation and coming up with sincere answers is the key to getting the insights you need. What exactly is driving you to get to a certain outcome at all costs? What are the *real* reasons for the particular choices you have made in the way you live? Once the insights are there, the potential for healing will be created.

Without knowing what you are/were all about, that change will be impossible. Until you have full understanding, you are like a monkey learning a new trick. You do not want to be a monkey!

In the SoS Method, we do not focus on the obvious universal motives of securing food, shelter, warmth, and so on. Instead, we are looking at other kinds of motives rooted deeply within, beyond the surface of appearances: Are your choices in life *really* motivated by what you *believe* your motives are? What is the relationship between your goals and your *real* motives? Are you in touch with what drives you? Are the choices you make in daily life indeed directly linked to what seems, on the surface, to be your goal?

You must examine all of your behaviors, even the most commonplace. For example, ask yourself the following: "Why do I want to dress a certain way and how important is that to me? Is it to express myself, to manifest my own identity? Am I flexible about it, and can I make minor/major compromises depending on availability and/or budget? Or is there more at stake? Is it more of a statement, maybe? Has it to do with wanting to belong or giving certain impressions?" Many more questions could be relevant to a thorough inspection of the trivial decision of what to wear.

You might assume you have freedom of choice in everything you want or do not want, but you might discover that changing your choices isn't easy at all. Your actions and behavior may turn out not to be as optional as you might have believed they were. Do you sometimes feel as if you are being driven by an invisible power? That is one clue that your choices are somewhat addiction-based. All motives around gaining a Substitute Sense of Self are addictive. Whether geared toward approval to gain an artificial spine or toward rebellion to establish your own identity, they need to happen at all costs (see page 140 to review the discussion about reactionary Ego-References).

> *Knowing your true motives is important because your health and well-being depend on which motives are operating.*

When you know your *true* motives, you can use the SoS Method to help develop strategies for improving your quality of life.

Willingness to Be Honest with Yourself

Discovering your motivations is key to recovering from an unhealthy Substitute Sense of Self. However, it requires total honesty with yourself. That might sound easy enough. It isn't. Finding out the truth about your deepest motivations is not obvious, nor is it simple, easy, or pleasant.

The SoS Method offers a variety of ways to help you dig down and understand your own motives – including motives for wanting to deceive yourself about your motives! Getting that clear is a huge part of the healing process and the way to become healthier, happier, and more successful – in other words, a life free from the addiction to approval and free to be your own true Self.

Admitting to yourself that you depend on the outcome of your Ego-References to "Feel-good-about-yourself" is a big step in overcoming what is, in fact, an inauthentic way of living, based on a fictional self-experience. Being totally honest with yourself is an absolute requirement for investigating – via introspection – which of your current thoughts and feelings are actually Substitute Sense of Self oriented. For the sake of recovery, you have to be willing to get to the bottom of every thought and feeling, to find the truth hidden underneath – often *actively* hidden by yourself from yourself!

The Aggressive Nature of Indirect Motivations

During my twenty-five years of introspection, self-discovery, and uncovering my motivations, I realized that my mind was full of agendas and motives that had been hidden, for decades, from myself as well as from others. There always seemed to be a good reason that served as the conscious justification for my actions and hid the true motives from myself. The way that worked was to guarantee the continuation of the pursuit of my Hidden Agenda. You can definitely say that there was an addiction operating here!

Here is an example from my own life: Even though I had a good job as a bassoonist in various symphonic orchestras for years, I was dissatisfied with what I had accomplished. I was unable to live up to the level of mastery I had aimed at and worked for throughout a good part of my life. I strongly felt I would have been a better violinist than a bassoonist. So when my kids were still little and went to Suzuki Music Education,[3] I benefitted from the opportunity to start my own violin lessons as well.

For about three years, I practiced like mad – and here comes in the Substitute Sense of Self–oriented drive: even when there were days in which it was impossible to find time to practice, and that happened quite a lot in the life of a mother with small children, I felt compulsively driven to do it anyway. I would explode in rage and resent my role as a mother, or blame my family members and provoke a drama with behavior that I regret deeply in hindsight.

What was the real reason for it? Was it truly because of my wish to be able to play the music I liked so much? Partially yes, but 60 percent was because I was unwilling/unable to let go of my intention to finally become that "great" musician I so desperately wanted to be and convince my mother I was worth the adoration that she had chosen to give to someone else.

An interesting detail, perhaps: the music I liked most was Hungarian Gypsy music. Was that for the music itself? Perhaps, but it was mainly because this type of passionate music represented for me the ultimate freedom, something I didn't feel I had.

When my family and I moved to a different city and a different setting, playing violin was no longer on my mind. From then on I started working on this method, which took up all my time and later helped me accept that I didn't need to gain a "Feel-good-about-self" state anymore because *I ALREADY WAS*. However, for a long time, the Black Hole within would still push at me.

I was lucky enough to realize that I would be a whole lot smarter to counter that pull and learn to be present to my Self and to my (real) life. I first had to try to really enjoy music performed by others without experiencing symptoms of high stress. Because maybe then I could consider playing some myself.

[3] Shinichi Suzuki is the creator of the Suzuki Method, which is based on the same principle that children learn to speak their mother tongue. For more information, please visit www.suzukiassociation.org.

The Challenge of Being Honest

How can the existence of this unhealthy phenomenon of Indirect Motivation not be common knowledge? Because it is not visible and people with a Healthy Sense of Self do not have any idea there can be such a problem. If you are in need of a Substitute Sense of Self, though, you are a master at fooling yourself and live a continuous lie. Remember, when you live with a Substitute Sense of Self, nothing is really as it seems; you are living in the past and continually trying to overcome barriers from your childhood. The only way to discover your Indirect Motivations is by being completely honest with yourself.

Restoring your Sense of Self comes down to recognizing and dismantling the Substitute Sense of Self you have become reliant on. For your inner child who is in survival mode, blowing the whistle on that game feels as if it will result in your Annihilation as a being. The inner child will tell you this is nothing to mess with, not even for the sake of healing. Too much is at stake to start trying something new! You need to acknowledge and even appreciate that part of you (the inner child in survival mode) that is (understandably) resisting. Denial is in the *self*-interest of the inner child but not in the *Self*-interest of you as a person!

Until you are ready to assess your motives honestly, true introspection is impossible. It requires a great deal of courage to face your Fear of Annihilation, the causes of your stress and discontent in life, and your Hidden Goal in its full and devastating reality.

Summary and Looking Ahead

With a Restored Sense of Self, you are able to sense your Self without using performance-based criteria. It comprises a reconditioning of yourself to a new inner reality: being fully in touch with and connected to the physical, emotional, and psychological aspects of your own being instead of being enslaved to controlling circumstances and to other people's rejection or approval.

All along in this book, I have been referring to the possibility and the process of replacing the Substitute Sense of Self with the healthier means of Self-experience: The Restored Sense of Self. Now that you have an idea of what a Restored Sense of Self might feel like, it is time to look more deeply at the SoS Method and process of *how* to gain one – the topic of the next chapter.

Chapter 12

Recovery from the Addiction to a Substitute Sense of Self

This chapter introduces you to a tool to assist you in recovering from being compulsively focused on gaining a Substitute Sense of Self. The **Motivation Check** helps you identify whether your actions and behavior are based on Direct or Indirect Motivation. Using this tool will help you gain knowledge about yourself and you will be able to map your journey from the addiction to a Substitute Sense of Self to becoming your own independent person. It also discusses the Stages of Change based on the work of author and social worker Virginia Satir and applies it to the situation at hand.

Motivation Check
A Tool to Detect Indirect Motivation

Earlier you saw that there are two types of motivation – Direct and Indirect – and that the type of motivation is indicative of the type of Sense of Self you have: respectively a Healthy Sense of Self or a Substitute Sense of Self. With the help of the SoS Comparison Chart on page 159, you initially self-assessed which category currently describes your Sense of Self. Learning to become aware of your motivation is the next step and an important part in the process of restoring your Sense of Self.

Being fully committed to actively working on gaining a Restored Sense of Self is required of you as this is not an easy adventure. By manifesting a clear intention to work your way through the many obstacles and relapses you will encounter, you'll be able to break free from the unhealthy motivational patterns described in this book.

Once a Restored Sense of Self is moving gradually into place, your motivation will automatically clear up. *There is no longer any need for a Substitute Sense of Self if you learn to sense your Self and truly connect to your own person!* When there is no need for a Substitute Sense of Self, there is no need for you to bring your Ego-References to a good ending, because the Hidden Goal no longer exists. Automatically, your Vehicles lose their importance and no longer function as carriers for your Ego-References. Finally, your motivations become straightforward (Direct Motivation). From then on, you do things for their own sake or because it pleases *you* to do them.

Indirect Motivation is Highly Personalized

Detection is not simple, because the way your Indirect Motivation shows up is very personalized, and it is hard to identify a common denominator in the variety of its manifestations. That is why you may not have been able to discover your Indirect Motivation yet.

The Hidden Agenda of getting approval shows up in everybody's life differently; it wears many different faces. On top of that, a great variety of Vehicles disguise it. So far, you may not have been able to recognize the double function of these Vehicles, but the bottom line for the Hidden Agenda is always about the *same* thing: finding ways to be seen, heard, acknowledged, and validated.

The need for approval manifests itself in different ways for each individual. It all depends on what worked for you when you were a child. What made you feel the closest to being acknowledged? Was it through being complimented, getting attention, being taken seriously, being smiled at, being hugged, being asked for advice, solving a family issue, being the peacekeeper? Was it a certain look in someone's eyes or hearing a certain tone of voice? Was it *not being frowned at* by someone who always seemed to disapprove of you? Or was it being allowed to participate in certain family activities that you were often excluded from? Maybe it was any of a thousand other faces.

The *feelings/thoughts/self-judgments* (lumped together as "Feel-ing-good-about-self") that result from successful achievement of the Hidden Agenda also has many faces, including:

- Feeling acknowledged
- Feeling taken into account
- Feeling admired
- Feeling accepted
- Having a sense of belonging
- Feeling safe
- Feeling alive
- Having a voice
- *Not* experiencing ridicule or humiliation
- Feeling valued
- Feeling a sense of relief
- Experiencing intimacy

The **Motivation Check** serves to do the following:

1. Detect Indirect Motivations and Hidden Agendas.
2. Record and become familiar with your Ego-References, Hidden Agendas, and Hidden Goal.

Overall, doing this exercise makes you become consciously aware of the following:

1. Which specific activities, actions, or behaviors function as Ego-References for you.
2. What actions, activities, or behaviors you've subconsciously chosen as Vehicles to serve these Ego-References and your Hidden Agendas.
3. What types of activities or behaviors are vulnerable to becoming contaminated by this Indirect Motivation and may potentially turn into Vehicles.

Motivation Check

A crucial (verbal) tool, which serves to a) detect your (Indirect) Motivation and b) record your Ego-References and Hidden Agendas, and to get insight what your Hidden Goal is.

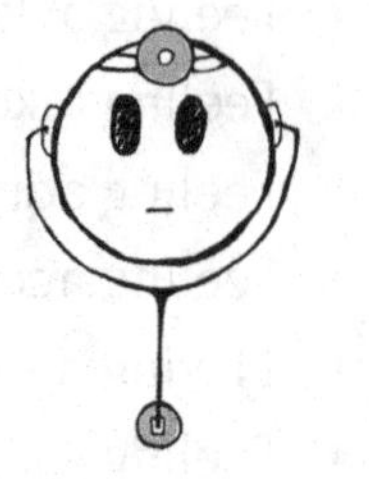

Below you will find four overviews of the Motivation Check process for you to work with.

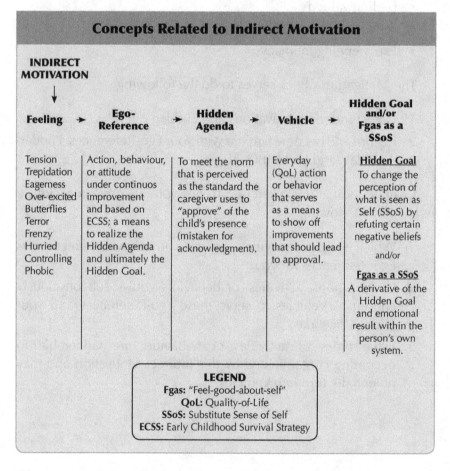

Concepts Related to Indirect Motivation

INDIRECT MOTIVATION ↓

Feeling →	**Ego-Reference** →	**Hidden Agenda** →	**Vehicle** →	**Hidden Goal and/or Fgas as a SSoS**
Tension Trepidation Eagerness Over-excited Butterflies Terror Frenzy Hurried Controlling Phobic	Action, behaviour, or attitude under continuos improvement and based on ECSS; a means to realize the Hidden Agenda and ultimately the Hidden Goal.	To meet the norm that is perceived as the standard the caregiver uses to "approve" of the child's presence (mistaken for acknowledgment).	Everyday (QoL) action or behavior that serves as a means to show off improvements that should lead to approval.	**Hidden Goal** To change the perception of what is seen as Self (SSoS) by refuting certain negative beliefs and/or **Fgas as a SSoS** A derivative of the Hidden Goal and emotional result within the person's own system.

LEGEND
Fgas: "Feel-good-about-self"
QoL: Quality-of-Life
SSoS: Substitute Sense of Self
ECSS: Early Childhood Survival Strategy

Figure 12.1: Concepts related to Indirect Motivation.

Figure 12.1 outlines each of the concepts in Indirect Motivation. It gives you a better understanding of each one as it describes in detail what type of content they cover. This overview shows the relationship between 1) the emotion you predominantly experience, 2) the Ego-Reference you perform, 3) your Hidden Agenda as the initial motivator, 4) the Vehicle you choose as a carrier for the activity, and 5) your ultimate Hidden Goal, or its substitute, the "Feel-good-about-self" state.

So, to perform a Motivation Check, you need to come up with the information about yourself that involves the following concepts:

- **Emotion**: Become aware of the feelings that are predominant in the moment of performing or anticipating the performance of an Ego-Reference.
- **Ego-Reference**: Describe the specifics of what you intend to get from performing the Ego-Reference, other than the obvious result (the directly motivated part) – e.g., "I want to show/prove that I am not selfish."
- **Hidden Agenda**: Describe in colorful words how and with what result you would love to perform the underlying activity (or behavior) – e.g., "I want to show that I can think of others and not only of myself (as I have been accused of in the past). I would be so happy if my parent (or other person/group in authority) would see my actions and conclude that I am better than they thought."
- **Vehicle**: Identify an action or behavior that you found has been contaminated with Indirect Motivation – e.g., "I always bring flowers whenever visiting someone."
- **Hidden Goal (Fgas/Substitute Sense of Self)**: Describe what high-quality result you are ultimately aiming for and how achieving that result would make you feel. Based on the SoS Theory, what function would that feeling have in your life? – e.g., "It would make me so happy to finally feel accepted by the person/group all this is aimed at and know that they are really proud of me. Knowing that they are proud of me is the only way I can feel proud of myself."

Attentive readers could ask themselves what the reality of this situation describes: "I have been accused of being all about myself, but I want to show that I can think of others so that my parent/educator/ group that I am associated with values me as a better person than I feel I really am. The fact of the matter is that all I wanted was to prove that *I was able do it.* I was not in the least bit concerned with the receiver of my behavior (Indirect Motivation). I wanted to demonstrate that I was able to think of others' interests, but it really wasn't about their interests, nor about mending my ways. What I wanted to achieve was solely to refute my caregiver's negative opinion about me and accept me as a valuable person." (Compare also: Chapter 6, the aspects of Indirect Motivation on page 111.)

Below you will find explicit meanings of the words used in the Motivation Check for clarity or better understanding.

Emotion (as defined under Indirect Motivation): a feeling that arises from displaying or anticipating an activity or behavior that has a disproportionate high degree of intensity in relation to its reality.

Ego-References: actions or behaviors that are based on conclusions, reflected in an Early Childhood Survival Strategy (ECSS), and aimed at realizing the Hidden Agenda.

Hidden Agenda: the strategy to show off one's best behavior/ performance with the purpose of changing your caregiver's perception of you by meeting his or her perceived standards.

Vehicle: an activity or behavior used with an ulterior motive, which is to display specific skills or characteristics (Ego-References) rather than being executed for the obvious, ordinary goal.

Hidden Goal: the ultimate objective of getting your caregiver's approval, which then functions as an unhealthy substitute for feeling acknowledged as a "real" person ("artificial spine").

"Feel-good-about-self" as a Substitute Sense of Self: a temporary emotional state of relative well-being and increased sense of safety due to the absence of Fear of Annihilation and urgency to pursue your Substitute Sense of Self.

What the Motivation Check tool comes down to is asking and answering the question: "Is my emotion proportionate to the reality of my situation?" Here are the concrete questions that need to find their answer when you are investigating your motivation:

Am I feeling these particular feelings because ...

I am about to perform an Ego-Reference?
What could my particular Hidden Agenda be?

Am I using my activity, my behavior ...

as a Vehicle,
to satisfy my Ego-Reference ...
and realize my Hidden Agenda
to achieve my ultimate, overarching Hidden Goal ...
so that I can get my caregiver's (or substitute for this person's) approval and feel accepted ...
or at least "Feel-good-about-myself" ...
which functions as a Substitute Sense of Self?

Figure 12.2 contains real-life examples of each of the concepts listed in Figure 12.1. In the case of Direct Motivation, the action or behavior serves the overt goal. If that were the only motivating factor, it would be a healthy motivation.

The overview, though, shows what happens in the case of Indirect Motivation, including everyday activities or behaviors that are only used as an excuse to perform Ego-References. Take a moment to fill in your own activities and/or behaviors that you suspect to be connected to Indirect Motivation and Ego-References.

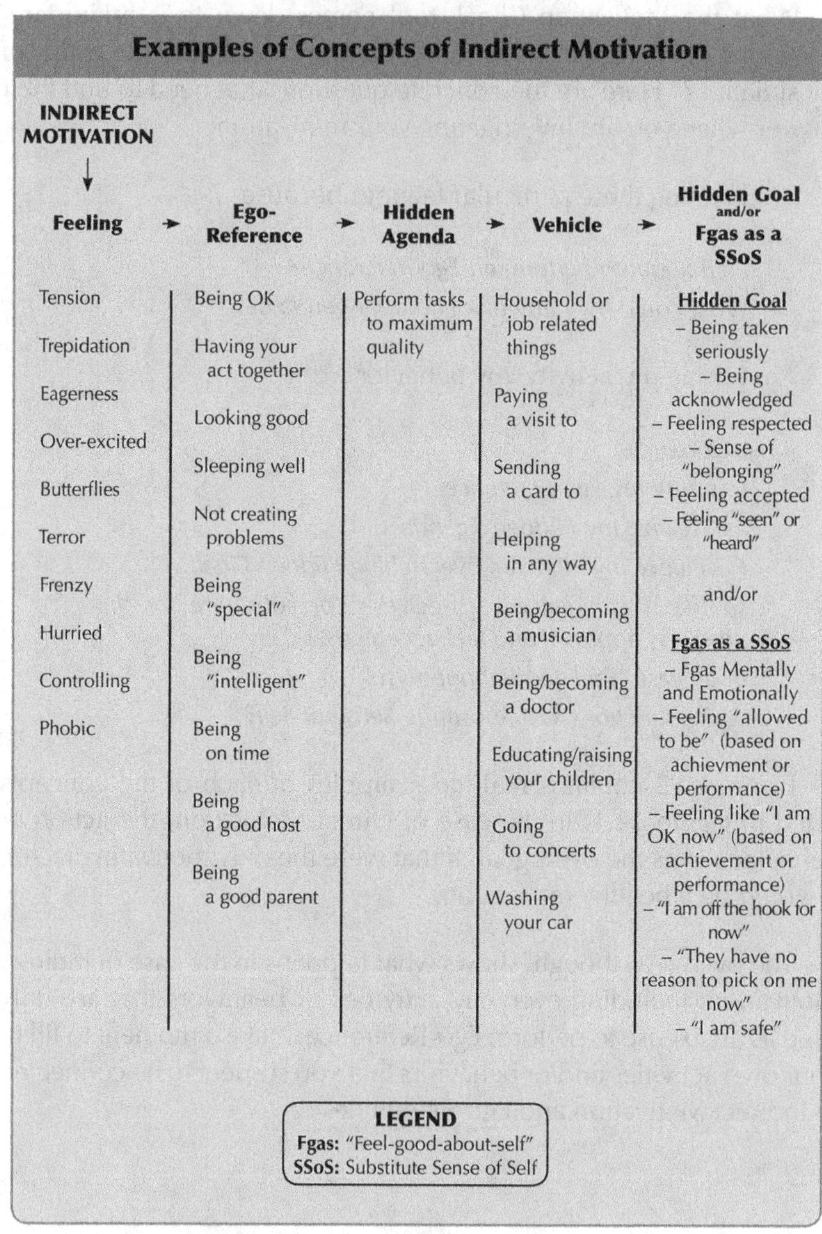

Figure 12.2: Examples of concepts of Indirect Motivation.

These lists will help you get more clarity on how, through Indirect Motivation, you might be using a Vehicle to work on improving yourself with respect to those conditions that form your Ego-References.

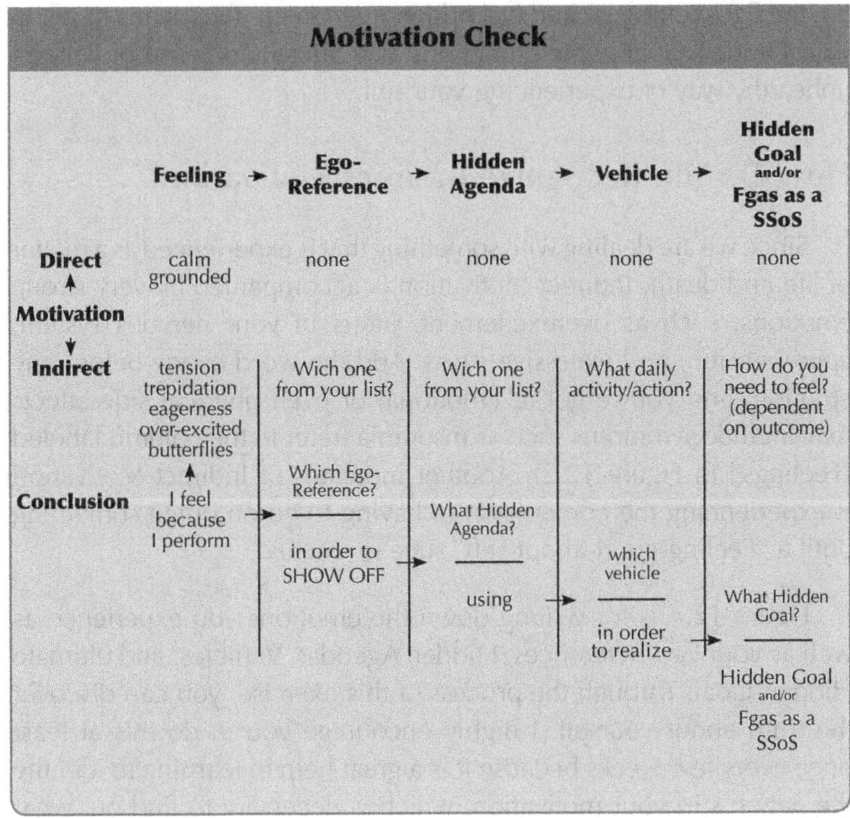

Figure 12.3: Motivation Check Questions.

Figure 12.3 shows the difference between both types of motivation. When motivation is direct, a behavior and/or action is performed for the sake of an obvious goal. What you see is what you get. There is a healthy congruency between the means and the goal. The feelings involved in this process are regular and healthy Quality-of-Life Level feelings.

When motivation is indirect, the focus of the activity shifts from what would normally be the goal to its functionality as a Vehicle that is meant to show off a specific quality or a characteristic. This activity or behavior, called an Ego-Reference, has the Hidden Agenda of proving that you can do better on this specific action or behavior than (you perceive) your parent thinks. The ultimate Hidden Goal of this subconsciously motivated activity is to be valued and acknowledged by your parent or other significant authority figure.

So, the Ego-Reference and its Hidden Agenda are the means to get to your Hidden Goal, which functions as a Substitute Sense of Self, an unhealthy way of experiencing your self.

How Do You Recognize Indirect Motivation?

Since we are dealing with something that is experienced as a matter of life and death, Indirect Motivation is accompanied by very strong emotions, such as overexcitement, jitters in your nervous system, apprehension, and excessive stress. Add the word *overly* before any emotion, and you've got it. Emotional or even physical side effects may include symptoms such as insomnia (refer to the column labeled "Feelings" in Figure 12.2). Another indicator of Indirect Motivation is experiencing the compulsion of having to go on doing something until a "Feeling-good-about-self" state is reached.

Figure 12.4 is for writing down the emotions you experience as well as your Ego-References, Hidden Agendas, Vehicles, and ultimate Hidden Goal. Through the process of this exercise, you can discover the truth about yourself. I highly encourage you to do this at least once every few weeks because it is a great help in learning to identify the patterns in your motivation, which is necessary to find out what your ultimate drive is and what that means in your life.

The Motivation Check is a crucial tool in getting a clear idea about the crooked nature of your Indirect Motivation. If you are serious about recovery, it is essential for you to work with these forms. You can do the work either mentally or in writing, whichever works best for you; however, I recommend initially going through the forms in writing until you are familiar with the Motivation Check process.

Here is what you can do to make your own lists: photocopy Figure 12.4 or download it from https://healthysenseofself.com/resources/motivation-check-process and fill in your information. Use this form every time you need to clarify your motivation. As you study the SoS Method and learn more about your Self through introspection, you will become increasingly better at it! So, filling out a new copy of the chart every few weeks will help you track your progress and gain a much deeper understanding of the root of your motivation.

Identified Patterns of My Indirect Motivation

Feeling	Ego-Reference	Hidden Agenda	Vehicle	Hidden Goal and/or Fgas as a SSoS

Figure 12.4: Identified patterns of my Indirect Motivation.

Helpful Tip

After I had diagnosed myself and discovered that I was fully addicted to "earning" a Substitute Sense of Self, I had to find, invent, and test out tools for recovery. I had to work hard before I was able to effectively feel less dependent on, less of a slave to, and less harmed by my everyday battle to live up to my Ego-References. The Motivation Check process has helped me, and I hope it will help you, too.

Like most people, I was reluctant to take time out of my busy schedule for myself. Interesting note: that schedule was full of tasks and plans that were there to help me gain a Substitute Sense of Self, but at the time, I was not sufficiently aware of that to focus comfortably on my healing and real well-being! So be prepared if you feel resistance to making the change. Shifting your habits that you – mistakenly – think your (well-)being depends on requires a gentle but determined approach.

The Stages to Restoring Your Sense of Self

As has been discussed in previous chapters, having a Substitute Sense of Self is an addiction. The reason it may not look like or feel like an addiction is because the harmful effects are not obvious and occur over a whole lifetime. I have found it very helpful in my recovery from a Substitute Sense of Self to look at and compare it with the recovery from substance abuse. To replace any unhealthy behavior with a healthy one, you need to go through various stages of change.

The Stages of Change

While pursuing my studies to become a chemical dependency professional (CDP), I was introduced to a model of *the stages of change*.[1] It is a tool used by addiction counselors to show their clients what it means to go through a process of change. It can help soothe the worries of a person who is recovering from alcohol and/or drug abuse and make them understand that there is a beginning and an

[1] James Prochaska and Carlo di Clemente, *Changing for Good* (University of Rhode Island; Trans-theoretical Model (TTM) 1977–1983).

end in the process, as well as what to expect in the various stages. You can use this model as a compass to tell you where you are in the process of change. It shows you that there *is* a shore on the other side of the ocean that you are trying to cross in your little ship of life, even though you are unable to spot it while you are in the turmoil of trying to survive a storm!

The model distinguishes five stages of change:

- Stage 1: Pre-contemplation
- Stage 2: Contemplation
- Stage 3: Preparation
- Stage 4: Action
- Stage 5: Maintenance

This sequence is also valid for recovering from dependency on a Substitute Sense of Self. Here is a short overview of the stages:

Stage 1: Pre-contemplation

This is the first stage of change. Seriously consider whether you are actually addicted to a Substitute Sense of Self. Do you have the symptoms of the addiction? Take this opportunity to review the SoS Comparison Chart on page 159.

If you have symptoms of being ruled by a Substitute Sense of Self, there hopefully comes a "tipping point" in your awareness. In this brief moment, the notion flares up that, yes, you would be wise to look into what is causing your unhappiness, stress, and addiction to approval. It is a crucial moment, even if it seems minor at the time. After that first awareness, you need some time to let the motivation for recovery grow before you embark on your journey of healing.

Stage 2: Contemplation

If indeed you find you are addicted to a Substitute Sense of Self, you will likely ask yourself, "What does this actually mean for me? What benefits would recovery get me, and what does it take to get there?"

By now, you know that you have to dig deep. You may want to start by posing the obvious questions: "What am I all about? What is motivating me to do what I do? What is my ultimate goal with any given action, activity, or behavior?" Now that you know motivation can be direct or indirect, you can ask yourself which type of motivation is at work in you, especially when you are dealing with important decisions.

There is a very efficient way of asking questions that I learned from one of my mentors, Wendy Lipton-Dibner.[2] Here is an example of how that goes:

> *"I want to become a medical doctor."*
> *"Why? What would that get me?"*
> *"I would be able to help people."*
> *"Why? What would that get me?"*
> *"I would be able to establish myself in a small town and be part of a nice community."*
> *"Why? What would that get me?"*
> *"I would be surrounded by family and lifelong friends."*
> *"Why? What would that get me?"*
> *"I would feel safe."*

This sequence of questions and answers does not have a negative conclusion, fortunately. Feeling safe seems like a legitimate motivation to do or avoid things. However, this sequence could also lead to quite unexpected, less healthy goals:

> *"I want to become a medical doctor."*
> *"Why? What would that get me?"*
> *"I have been interested in helping people since I was a kid."*
> *"Why? What would that get me?"*
> *"I would have found a way to do what I seem to be good at and make money as well."*
> *"Why? What would that get me?"*

[2] Adapted, with permission, from the best-selling book *Shatter Your Speed Limits: Fast-Track Your Success and Get What You Truly Want in Business and in Life,* by Wendy Lipton-Dibner (Wilton, CT: Professional Impact, Inc., 2010), www.ShatterYourSpeedLimits.com.

12 Recovery from the Addiction to a Substitute Sense of Self

"I would be respected by my dad and do something he really admires."

"Why? What would that get me?"

"I finally would know that I can please him!"

Go ahead and ask yourself the questions that apply to your own situation. Knowing the ultimate answers to your questions is key to assessing what your ulterior motivation is – in other words, finding out what you are all about.

Stage 3: Preparation

Once you know what your deepest issues are, you can get a clearer view on how they affect your life and your choices.

Next, start addressing the items from your list of things you need to work on to recover from the dependency of a Substitute Sense of Self, which comprises:

1. Understand the terminology and know what the SoS Theory is about.
2. Determine whether or not you have a Healthy Sense of Self.
3. If not, create a list of your Ego-References, Hidden Agendas, and your ultimate Hidden Goal.
4. Do the Motivation Check as described above.
5. Practice the Twelve SoS Reconditioning Statements (which will be addressed in the next chapter).
6. Always stay aware that you can and will relapse and learn the ways to step back out of that hole.

In this stage, you also need to make decisions about practical and emotional steps you can take to help you implement the desired change in your life. I am referring here to decisions such as distancing yourself from people who have a toxic influence on you.

Stage 4: Action

In this stage, you need to be absolutely honest with yourself and ready to admit when you are indirectly motivated.

During this phase, you are actively involved with the various exercises and affirmations presented in the next two chapters. You do frequent Motivation Checks and continuously question the motivations underlying your behavior.

You start to see that there is no need to be afraid of Annihilation because you actually *ARE already*.

You actively cultivate the necessary deep, abiding sense of being your very own "be-ing," separate from your "do-ing."

You learn to connect to your body, which forms a big part of your being.

You act, in this stage, with the ultimate goal of redirecting your energy, attention, and focus away from fulfilling Ego-References.

Instead, you actively and consciously notice, record, and remember that all the parts of your body belong to you and they are part of your Self. You own them, they are you, and consequently you do not have to exert any effort to "earn" them. There will be that AHA! moment in which you start to truly feel that you already *exist!*

That moment is your savior. Know that it will slip away from time to time, especially in the beginning, and that sometimes you have to work hard to feel it again. Over time, though, it will become easier.

Exercise and meditation are your daily companions. The self-reflections included in the following chapter are for exploring and mapping the territory of the Self by finding landmarks and road signs on your path to a Healthy Sense of Self. It is important to keep an open mind and not expect the world of meditation to be similar to the world outside of meditation … it is another reality. You need to be ready to explore.

Stage 5: Maintenance

This is a very important phase in becoming and staying successful in your recovery toward a Restored Sense of Self. You need to actively and consistently maintain awareness of your Sense of Self so it deepens and stays with you throughout the day, throughout the night, whatever happens. Know and respect that the old system can easily flare up and take back the reins of power over your behavior. The Black Hole of your (former) Lack of Sense of Self is like a ferocious beast opening its disgusting maw with a relentless hunger; it is always ready to suck in any remotely successfully performed Hidden Agenda (Ego-References performed with a positive outcome). When your conscious awareness falters (and it will!), it'll make you want to Score, and there you are on your way to relapse!

And here is again some irony at play: now that you are improving your quality of life, everything starts to work out better than before, and that especially tends to lead to many a relapse (remember the desired outcomes of the Ego-References). When relapse happens, you have to hang in there; there is no option. Never give up! Remind yourself that there is everything to gain! Brush up on the tools that are offered in this book and use those you may have developed for yourself over time. Persist in your awareness of Self with exercises and practice, and you will find your way back to your Restored Sense of Self. There is a minefield of potential fallbacks when you go through the process of change. Relapse is inevitable; it is not a failure but simply a part of that process. It is true, you will need a significant amount of determination and motivation (keep it "direct" at all times) and gentle understanding of your own situation to work your way through.

Figure 12.5 represents the process of change and speaks pretty much for itself.[3] Imagine the line as a path you are walking on, beginning at the bottom of the illustration. It highlights the second stage of change in which you have made a conscious decision to start a change. You are going to take that leap into a better future. The jagged line marks the place where you start to actively implement different behavior. With your list of what needs to be done in front of you, you start to undertake more and more based on what you have decided is good for your Self (the new behavior).

As you go forward, you leave your old habits behind, and at some point, there will be confusion and chaos. You have to remember the rules for your new behavior and keep yourself from falling back into

[3] Illustration based on an original piece by Virginia Satir (1916–1988) American (family) psychotherapist.

old habits. Your body and mind start to object and display symptoms of stress from being deprived of the old input that you previously perceived as the only way to survive. People around you act differently because you are changing: some of them might support you and reinforce your change; others might resent it, and even try to sabotage you, because what is a positive change for you threatens their status quo.

This image can be helpful. You can look at it over and over again and take comfort in the knowledge that the chaos and confusion is natural, and that it lessens over time. Once you get through the jungle, the path becomes easier to follow and your efforts will be rewarded. You will be better able to keep up the new behavior. You will have made the foundation for a healthy Restored Sense of Self. Stay alert, though! Even after having passed through that jungle, you have to prevent the Black Hole from using your achievements to Score. Over time, relapse becomes easier to overcome, and your Restored Sense of Self stays with you and becomes more natural – until you can't even remember how it used to be to live in the prison of being Substitute Sense of Self oriented.

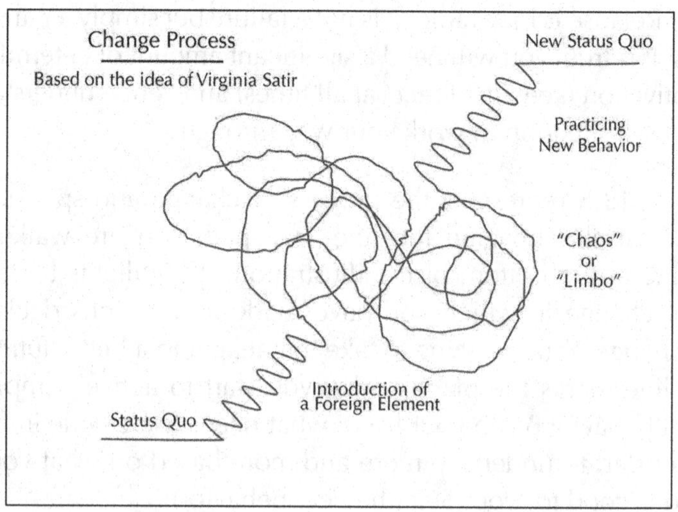

Figure 12.5: The change process.

Recovery from the Addiction to a Substitute Sense of Self

By *recovery,* I mean restoring and/or strengthening your Sense of Self. I mention strengthening as well because it is possible that you are *not totally* missing the healthy way of sensing your Self; it is just not a strong sense, and you are inclined to give in to other people's demands, both spoken and unspoken, too easily.

What you are recovering from is the *addiction* to experiencing your Self in an unreal, incorrect, and substitute way, through "Feeling-good-about-yourself." So far, the sensation of being temporarily freed from the urge to tiptoe may very well have been the closest point to experiencing some sort of self. You are recovering from the urge to realize this state of "Feel-good-about-self" at all costs to avoid the risk of feeling Annihilated.

You need to come to the conclusion, through sensing your individual characteristics, that your existence – your Self – isn't determined by anything you do or avoid. I am referring to characteristics such as your body, your mind, and the ability to direct your intention and energy, your inclinations, and your strengths and weaknesses – everything that makes you who you are. Remember, you are recovering from a set of behaviors that operate subconsciously and used to function as your way of connecting to what you thought was your Self. Now you are shifting toward truly sensing your Self, and you are getting in touch with who you really are. Please note that these processes do not necessarily occur in a linear way but may mutually influence one another.

Once you have the beginnings of a Restored Sense of Self, you'll find that some self-destructive habits that used to take place automatically change for the positive, because now you have something to lose: your Self! These changes then are here to stay, because *you* have changed yourself. So, if you begin with only one behavior, after beginning to implement a Restored Sense of Self by learning how to sense yourself correctly, you can begin to hope that you will be successful in recovering from *other* self-destructive behaviors.

A Word of Caution

A short warning is needed once again as I do not want people to think that there is a quick fix for any of the problems that result from the dependency on a Substitute Sense of Self. Rather, consider tackling this issue as a thorough lifestyle change: The way you have been living your life has proven to be harmful for you. It has not been serving your needs, and it must be replaced by a healthy way of living. On the surface, you cannot expect everything to go on as if life were continuing as normal.

Restoring your Sense of Self is a reconditioning process that doesn't happen overnight, although at given moments in time you will experience a breakthrough or feel inspired and think you have forever changed in the direction of a Restored Sense of Self. To truly end up in better shape may take anywhere from a few months to several years. It also takes dedication, but now your dedication is geared toward yourself, toward improving your own life. This process is necessary to be successful in freeing yourself from unwanted and self-destructive behaviors as well as in ridding yourself of the excess stress of living with a Substitute Sense of Self and its related result: disease and dysfunction.

Do not be discouraged! You can work on changing the way you sense your Self at any moment and in most any situation. If you do not tell anybody, people will only notice a shift has taken place in you for the better. After all, this change comes down to a shift within yourself. Your family and friends will only wonder how you have gotten to be so balanced and patient. They will register a change in you that might make them curious. Then it will be up to you to step up and take the chance to make the world a better place by introducing them to the SoS Method.

In the recovery process, the order in which you tackle things is important. To eliminate the unhealthy behavior of being dependent on a Substitute Sense of Self for your self-experience, you first need to have a healthy replacement operating. In other words, to be able to outgrow/replace the compulsion to "Feel-good-about-self" you need to have in place – at least partially – a healthier way of experiencing your Self.

I'm sure you are eager to begin replacing your bad habits with good habits, so I need to give another short warning that is related to the same issue, which is best worded as follows:

"It is impossible to live in a vacuum." In other words, even though you want nothing more than to live from your own core of being, so far you have been filling that void – where the true and real Sense of Self should reside – with conditions and achievements you thought you had control over. These conditions and achievements need a lot of attention and input from you, which has become a very predominant habit: we call it a compulsion. Just stopping the compulsion is not going to work, as a sort of vacuum would arise. And since your self-experience depends on these conditions and achievements, you can't just remove them all of the sudden. Remember, the Substitute Sense of Self used to function as the backbone for your psyche. Suddenly removing it would be highly anxiety provoking and you would (virtually) fall apart, because the real backbone (your Restored Sense of Self) is not in place yet. Of course, this is just a metaphor I use to help you understand the importance of holding on to the old crutch while in the process of change (compare the story of the old man and the cane on page 229).

If you systematically work your way through the steps and exercises described in the next chapter, you will build up your healthy Self-experience from scratch. Your first step is body awareness. Once that awareness is well in place, you can increasingly start to let go of living up to your Ego-References and throw away the old cane.

Summary and Looking Ahead

Now that you are aware of the wonderful benefits that are awaiting you when you take the time and invest your best effort into restoring your Sense of Self, you will want to know how to proceed. The Twelve SoS Reconditioning Statements are an important change agent on your way to restore your Sense of Self, and they will be explained in depth in Chapter 14. The next chapter serves as preparation.

Chapter 13
Learning to Sense Your Self

This above all: to thine own self be true,
And it must follow, as the night the day,
Thou canst not then be false to any man.
– Shakespeare, *Hamlet* (Act I, scene 3)

In this chapter, you will learn to see what it takes to move from being stuck (trapped in your involuntary and often self-destructive habits) to becoming a free person – one who can effectively make use of your birthright (your Self) and start making decisions based on personal choices or what genuinely matters most in your life, and then live accordingly.

Imagine you are one of those people who would be happier with a bit more of that Healthy Sense of Self. Most likely, there was a time in which you were living and doing things based on what you thought were your own initiatives. But, in hindsight, it turned out to be based on a coping strategy that was part of your Early Childhood Survival System. Then there came a time when these things stopped working so well for you, and, at some point, you had to start questioning what was going on. It was a time of struggle and self-deception.

At this point in the book, you have likely come to understand that there always was a Hidden Goal in your life that you were not even aware of. This Hidden Goal weighed so heavily on your subconscious mind that your daily life was sprinkled with Hidden Agendas you felt you had to achieve, which took a lot of time, effort, and energy. Perhaps the concept of changing the Hidden Goal into becoming your own purpose in life is starting to grow on you. In fact, it may seem like the best dream ever, but in the process, you already notice that it is not easy to change your old habits and patterns of thinking and make way for the desired new ones.

This chapter deals with the particular Substitute Sense of Self–oriented habits and ways of behaving that you identified in your Motivation Check (see page 245). You will learn how to turn them around into behavior that is truly self-serving and that will enable you to fully bloom into the person you were always meant to be.

If you want to make changes on such a foundational level, simply deciding that you want to is not enough. It requires a lot of persistence and repetition to change your ways; most of all, you need presence in the process. In fact, the changes you aim to make here are all about becoming more present to your Self. So you need to continuously monitor whether or not you are truly being present to your Self and to what you want to achieve: fully being your Self always and in everything. Learning on such a deep level of your being is called *reconditioning*.

Here are two explanations of the term *reconditioning*:

- According to *Merriam-Webster Dictionary, reconditioning* means "to restore to good condition by repairing, cleaning, or replacing parts."
- In *The Penguin Dictionary of Psychology,* Arthur S. Reber says: "The use of the prefix 're-' can make understanding 'reconditioning' a bit more complicated so there are two meanings:
  1. the new conditioning of an old but weakened response and
  2. conditioning of a new response in order to replace the old one."

Whereas the first explanation gives a general idea of the word, we refer to the second definition given by *The Penguin Dictionary of Psychology* when we say "recondition."

What you learned early on – especially about yourself – is the foundation for who you become as a person later in life. Your caregivers were not necessarily always in the right position to teach you what you needed to know. This is the reason you were unable to become an integrated, happy, and healthy person. For a long time, you used to think that that was just the way it was; it was a given. Those were the cards you were dealt, and they determined your position in the game (of life).

What if you could restore your Sense of Self, though, and unlearn the negative beliefs that, so far, have caused you to be in your own way? What would your life look like if you could replace these beliefs that block your health and creativity with positive ones? What if the beliefs you hold about yourself truly worked in your favor? You even might become the happy, healthy, and productive person you feel deep down inside that you are!

The SoS Method

Once you see that the conclusions you drew as a child are not serving you as well as you might have thought, it is likely you'll start to consider how those early conclusions can be overwritten by new ones. Once you start to notice how your well-being, creativity, and productivity are blocked by your earlier learned behavior, it is time to zoom in on it, asking yourself what actually lies at the bottom of it. You are right to question these so-called truths and to start truly thinking for yourself. When you conclude that the self-deprecating and self-stifling ideas your mind has been programmed to believe might not be true at all, then it is time to start the daunting task of reconditioning yourself.

The SoS Method aims at training your mind so you can learn to give priority to more self-affirming conclusions about your Self and about your potential in life. You might have already decided that you want to take action based on what you learned about yourself in the previous chapters. If you are ready to replace those instigators of behavior that serve neither yourself nor others, the SoS Method will give you the tools to do so. This is your opportunity to rethink certain formerly accepted "truths" about yourself and take charge of your own life. Step up and reprogram yourself to live your life *as* you and *for* you! You have the power to do so.

Don't give up!

We know the proverb: *The road to hell is paved with good intentions*. Well, that proverb is especially true here. And if it is for you as it was for me, it could take a lot more than good intentions to stick to the mission of reconditioning yourself. Real discipline is needed before you can effectively divert your focus and energy from the reality you used to live in to a new one.

> *You need to learn to shift from aiming at "Feeling-good-about-yourself" at all costs to truly sensing your Self.*

The only way to do that is through reinforcing the new knowledge that you do not need a Substitute Sense of Self because *you already are*. You'll have to practice to become proficient in experiencing the proof of that fact: body awareness.

Next, you'll have to convince your *subconscious* mind to let go of old patterns of behavior and trust the signals from your real Self. Learn to actively listen to your Self and obey its (your) needs and wants, and live up to its (your) potential. Often these signs and signals are not generated by your mind but arise from other areas of your body (Self). We call them gut feelings, or intuition. Sometimes these signals come from your heart and manifest as a sense of love, being aroused by something or someone for no apparent reason. You owe it to your Self, though, as well as to your loved ones, to make the right choice. You don't want to skip your life altogether. You deserve to live on your own authentic terms; the reward for all your hard work will be priceless.

> *Reconditioning yourself means leaving your Substitute Sense of Self–oriented ways behind, and looking at yourself and your life in a new way.*
>
> *In this new way, you are at the heart of your existence, where your purpose is your own well-being, based on your own criteria.*

As with any change in behavior or routine, a learning curve is involved and relapse is always lurking. Imagine two opposing energies, the old and the new. The old energy is strong because it was reinforced over and over again for a long time. It has established a clear path in your brain, which has almost become hardwired. You could think of it as having become a physical characteristic in your brain, which is why it can be so difficult to get rid of.

The new energy is full of good intentions and may even be based on desperation because you cannot go on in the old way any longer. The continuous need to obtain a Substitute Sense of Self may make you feel, at times, as if you are Sisyphus from Greek mythology: eternally pushing a huge boulder up a steep hill and, just before reaching the top, an unknown force rolls the boulder back to the bottom.

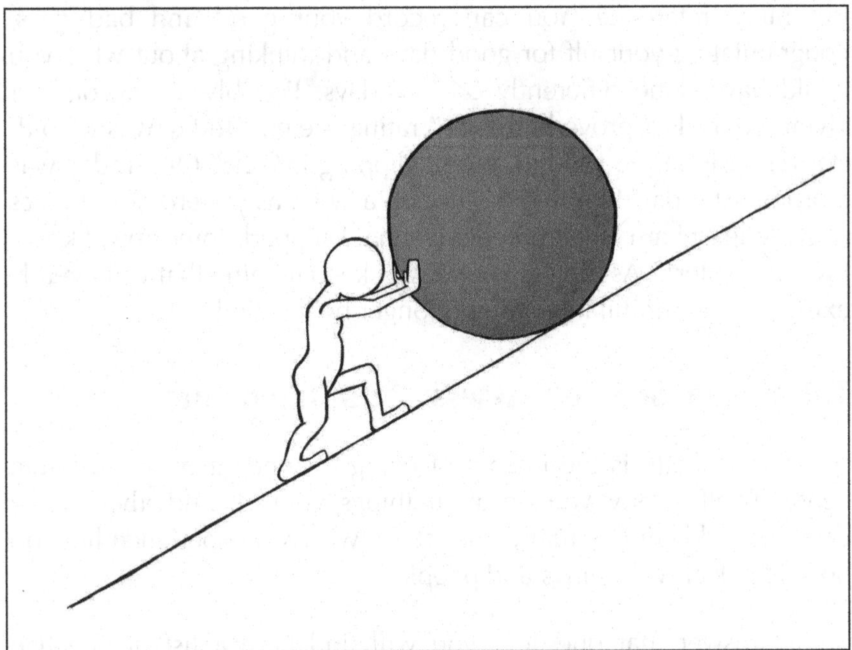

Figure 13.1: At times, you may feel like Sisyphus ...

Preparing for the Twelve SoS Reconditioning Statements

In a little while, you will be introduced to the Twelve SoS Reconditioning Statements – *twelve very important key phrases* that form the stepping stones to reprogramming your mind. They function as thinking prompts on specific topics that will wake you up to the fact that *you really are* your own person and therefore your own boss.

The prompts form an essential starting point for learning how to sense your Self. I urge you to sit for a while with the content related to each statement to gain the maximum benefit and create awareness of your own Self. It is important that you follow the course of thought as it is outlined to get the full idea of how these statements can help you recover from the addiction to a Substitute Sense of Self.

You might want to keep a special journal to describe your experiences and insights with this reconditioning process: track your progress and document your experiences, thoughts, and feelings for future reference. You can record your good and bad days, congratulating yourself for good days and thinking about what you could have done differently on bad days. Possibly, even consider giving yourself a proverbial "star" rating – e.g., "Today was a gold-star day. Each time I found myself slipping into …" Or, "Today was a bronze-star day. I know I did not do as well as yesterday, but that's okay. At least I am able to recognize that I slipped. Tomorrow, I know I will do better[4]." As long as you always keep in mind that you already exist, Fear of Annihilation can no longer by justified.

The Twelve SoS Self-Assessment Statements

What exactly is the impact of being dependent on a Substitute Sense of Self for how you feel about things, yourself, and others? How does that addiction actually impact the way you experience life and how you deal with things and people?

To answer that question, you will find here a list of negative statements: The Twelve SoS Self-Assessment Statements. These statements are based on their positive counterparts, which form the active, positive Reconditioning Statements (listed below and covered in detail in Chapter 14). First, though, it is necessary to recognize more details around your own negative mindset so that you become aware of what you will have to address when you begin changing your ways. Note that I say *changing your ways,* but what I actually mean is *changing back to your Self.*

[4] For more help with learning independent thinking, check out my book *A Guided Journal to a Healthy Sense of Self: Thoughts to Inspire Peace Within and Around the Word.*

1. You are not aware that you are first and foremost a physical body.
2. You are more connected to *what you do* than to *who and what you are.*
3. You function on automatic pilot.
4. You are busy repairing the damage done in the past and skip the present.
5. Your senses are not used for taking in life or for keeping you safe but are abused for scoring.
6. You are living in the dark grey circle of addiction to your Substitute Sense of Self so your natural feelings are hidden by the (much stronger) Substitute Sense of Self–oriented ones.
7. You are unable to really "see" your Self and others for who you/they are.
8. You do not really hear what others have to say as communication is geared mostly toward gaining a "Feel-good-about-self" state.
9. You are not fully in touch with the content of your work as your main goal is to get an outcome that makes you "Feel-good-about-self."
10. You want to believe that "everything is fine" and are willing to cover up the truth.
11. You spend most of your time daydreaming, convincing yourself that one day you will really be able to live your life the way you want to.
12. You feel alone, and you likely missed out on big chunks of your life.

The Twelve SoS Reconditioning Statements

The Twelve SoS Reconditioning Statements presented below may seem like simple and straightforward truths, but chances are they are being violated continuously throughout your everyday life. These twelve statements are positive and Self-enhancing exercises in thought, feeling, and the use of your body as well as your senses. They were born from turning the negative reality of being Substitute Sense of Self oriented into their positive opposite. Now please take some time to consider these positive counterparts to each of the earlier negative statements:

I My life and my body are mine.
II I experience myself directly.
III I am present to the Here and Now.
IV I think for myself.
V I am consciously aware of my senses.
VI I have access to my own feelings, preferences, and opinions.
VII I see other people for who they are.
VIII I have conversations to transfer information or to connect with others.
IX My work is aimed at the obvious, direct outcome.
X Relapse is always lurking and I am prepared to deal with it.
XI I am ready to share my life with others.
XII I am ready to be part of a healthy community.

Here We Go!

The next chapter elaborates on each of the Twelve SoS Reconditioning Statements followed by some exercises and activities to enable you to address the root of your problem.

Changing your strategy or your reaction to something on a subconscious level requires an extreme degree of conscious awareness. The Twelve Reconditioning Statements help you reinforce your new beliefs and actively promote their seeping through into your subconscious, overriding your old conditioning. The goal is for you to gain a thorough awareness – consciously and subconsciously – of your new truth, which is that you do not need a Substitute Sense of Self *because you already are*. The prompts are presented in a logical, progressive order, beginning with body awareness.

By repeating the words of the prompts, eventually a light bulb will switch on as the content starts to get through to your subconscious mind. You will learn to break through the wall of denial built around your issues. If you can memorize the Twelve SoS Reconditioning

Statements, that's even better since they will eventually start to resonate with the truth inside yourself. "Fake it until you make it" is a valid part of this process.

Recovering from dependency on a Substitute Sense of Self means learning to sense your Self and change your Hidden Goal!

Summary and Looking Ahead

In this chapter, it became clear that reconditioning is not a quick fix. You owe it to your Self, though, to do the work necessary to free yourself from an erroneous mindset that no longer serves you in the present. Of course, focusing on the positive is very useful, but you also need to know *what* you want to change and *why*. Now you know how, and to that purpose you were asked to create an overview of the negative aspects in your attitude and behaviors you want to change.

In the next chapter, you will learn to integrate these positive statements into your Self.

Chapter 14
The Twelve SoS Reconditioning Statements

Remember how your orientation toward gaining a Substitute Sense of Self has led you to develop an unhealthy relationship with a number of elements in your life. Maybe you always knew that other people had less difficulty with feeling true compassion for others or that they were less inclined to become jealous. You may have wondered why some people seem to know exactly what they want.

These and other aspects of your mental and emotional makeup that haven't been of service to your happiness, productivity, and well-being are now going to be turned around into positive statements. Through the reconditioning process, you are going to learn to own these healthy attitudes and outlooks. What you need is time, awareness, exercise, conviction, intention, and confidence. Let that confidence be based on the progress you have already gained toward restoring your Sense of Self as you worked your way through this book: you have the right to trust yourself and fight to feel that you are a whole person who enjoys living your life just like anybody else.

By repeating the words of the steps over and over, you will find that you end up becoming aware of the content. You will wake up to see that wall of denial you had built around the issue. By repeating the words – and faking it until you make it – the words will start to resonate with the truth inside your Self.

For a visual overview of the Twelve SoS Reconditioning Statements please check pages 37 and 38.

I. My Life and My Body Are Mine

The following activity and its variants will help you restore your Sense of Self through gaining awareness of your physical presence. To be able to access your *real* Self, you need to be aware that your physicality is your vehicle in life. So first you have to become aware of living in and through your body by learning/practicing to sense it before you can truly believe that your body, and thus your life, is yours.

It's a funny thing, realizing that you really both *have* and *are* your body. So this exercise is to gain understanding – by means of sensing – what it means to be *in* and *with* your mind and body while being both of these things at the same time. Doing this exercise will initially result in a "knowing" that you *are* and *have* a body, and, in the long run, this intellectual knowledge will transform itself into "knowing" on a deeper, more integrated, almost physical level.

As you repeat this exercise and become aware of all the different areas of your body, you might want to pause and consider what more there is to *you* as a person and what life is all about. You might want to reflect on these questions, but here we enter the realm of spirituality or religion and addressing these questions it is not within the scope, nor the intention, of this book.

The exercise serves as a tool that can help you feel and function better in your everyday world as you gain a Healthy Sense of Self. To be able to do that, one thing needs to be crystal clear:

> *You* are *(the owner of) your body.* Your body is you. You *deserve your attention, and you need to become fully aware of it. You are worth it!*

The Three M's: Master, Manager, Maintenance

It's so natural to take your body for granted; you have always had it and therefore you may not think about it much, but it is what allows you to be physically present in the world. Countless people focus on taking care of others while bypassing the needs of their own bodies. It is tempting to overlook the responsibility you have toward your body, especially if you have never experienced physical problems, but if *you* don't take responsibility, then who will?

After all, *you* are the master of your body and the life granted to you. Not only are you the master, you are also the manager of the energy that is yours to spend throughout your life. Lastly, you are the maintenance person as well, who ensures that all aspects – physical, mental, and emotional – of the entity that is *YOU* keep functioning. You have an obligation to your Self to keep your body in good health.

If, thus far, you have perceived your right to exist as depending on the approval (real or virtual) of your parents/caregivers, you need to become aware that your right to live is not dependent on all the conditions you thought you had to fulfill to get other people's approval.

That perception is a fiction! Please think through the following statement: "In order to (know that I) have the right to exist, I have to make someone (a special person) feel good about *me* so I get his or her approval." Or even this: "In order to (know that I) have the right to be, I have to make someone 'Feel-good-about-themselves' so I get a good mirror back and 'Feel-good-about-myself.'" Strictly speaking, this comparison doesn't make sense. It is like comparing apples to elephants, but it made sense to you when you were a child.

The following exercise aims to help you acknowledge, oppose, and dismantle the Fear of Annihilation.

Sense Your Body Activity

Find a quiet place where you will not be interrupted and work through the following steps: Look at your body as if you are seeing it for the first time in your life. Like an inquisitive toddler, explore all the areas of your body in a nonsexual manner. Stand up straight and sense how your feet are touching the ground and how your legs are supporting your whole body – supporting you.

Now reach down to touch your toes with your hands and tell yourself *aloud* what you are doing. It is important that you direct your *awareness* to those areas as you mention them. Keep your mind present to the parts of your body that your hands are touching, and allow the sense of your body to fill your mind. In summary, experience your Self as a closely knit unit.

You can follow this script literally or modify it in ways that feel more natural to you and your body. Keep in mind that the point is to feel how all of the parts of your body that form YOU are interconnected physically as well as mentally, from the inside as well as from the outside.

- With my hands, I am touching my toes. I feel my nails, the soles of my feet on the floor – I am touching the tops of my feet, my ankles, my shins, my calves, the back of my knees, the front of my knees. My hands rest on my knees for a while. They feel nice and warm. Now I feel my thighs, my hips, my belly, my chest, and my shoulders. I feel my arms, my wrists, my hands, and my fingers. I feel my legs attached to my feet, my limbs attached to my torso. I feel my neck and my head and my hair.
- I touch my eyelids. I touch my ears, my nose, my mouth, and my skin.
- This is all me; this is all mine. It is the physical part of my Self; this is my tangible "I."
- I feel my heart beating, sending my blood traveling through my veins. I feel my lungs expanding and contracting as I breathe in and out. I imagine my liver; I imagine my kidneys, spleen, and gall bladder. I imagine all my inner organs. *I am all of that.*
- I am my nervous system; it starts in my brain and extends into the remotest areas of my body.
- I am my hormonal system, the biochemical messengers in my body.
- I am my reproductive system.
- I am my lymphatic system, part of my immune system, the soldiers of my body.
- I am my digestive system, processing the nutrients that keep my inner fire burning.

- It is all mine. It is all *me*. I've got the use of this wonderful machine called my body, my Self.

The following variations offer a different way to practice awareness, again, to help you become familiar with having and being a body, your body, through effectively sensing it. Sensing your body is the first step in sensing your Self.

Variation 1

Instead of using your hands, you might want to try directing only your *attention* to the various body parts as mentioned above. Following the same order, move your attention from your toes, up to your feet, to your ankles, to your shins, and so on, gradually climbing your entire body until you reach the top of your head. (No hands this time!)

Variation 2

Now instead of traveling from bottom to top or vice versa, you take a different approach: Focus your awareness on a random area of your body, for example, your knees. Use your hands to touch the skin of your knees, concentrating on that action, and say aloud: "I am sensing my knees." This way, you bring your awareness to your knees from the outside, through your hands, and from the inside, through your attention. Let your awareness linger in your knees before hopping to the next area of your body, chosen at random, that you mention aloud while putting your hands and attention in place. You are free to continue doing this as long as you like.

Variation 3

This variation is a little more advanced and is about memorizing the awareness you created earlier. You can move your awareness and your hands randomly from one place to another while maintaining awareness in each place you've previously given your attention. As you progress, bit by bit, your awareness will occupy your entire body.

As you explore who you are in this way, you may notice how your attention hops from one place to another. Think about *what* (or who) it is that is doing the hopping. For example, you begin in your toes and you decide to hop to your right elbow. You stay there and give this part of your body your full attention, then you move on to your left ear until it is present to you along with your toes and right elbow, then you skip to your stomach, and so on. That something/somebody who registers what happens and commands what needs to happen is *you!*

Variation 4

Another way to do this is not to hop from one place to the other but to travel there. Let us say your attention is in your knees and the warmth of your hands penetrates the area of your knees while your heart (attention) is also in your knees. Now you decide to go to your right elbow, but instead of hopping there, you follow a road, as if your heart had legs and feet, to slowly walk to that place on the inside of your body. Imagine your body as a road map and your awareness as a little white light that travels along the highways, intermittently brightening the areas you pass through to show you where you are. Your hands travel with the light as well.

Becoming aware of and, even for a short while, just *being present* in your body is a great way to help you begin restoring your Sense of Self. Mastering this activity will allow you to sense that you are physically real; you are existing both within and through your body – there is no need for a Substitute Sense of Self!

II. I Experience Myself Directly

When you have an Indirect Relationship with yourself, you are *not* fully aware of yourself; the only thing you live for is that moment when you know you have done something *"right,"* which then gives you the green light to "Feel-good-about-self." By now you know, though, that this "Feeling-good-about-self" state is only a substitute for the real Self-experience.

Having an Indirect relationship with yourself does not mean that you are not existing as yourself, but it does mean that you are not aware of it. From your earliest days, you have been trained (by your parent) to focus on securing a "Feel-good-about-self" for your self (and for your family members), instead of on building a relationship with your Self and developing a sense of your Self. You are simply not used to experiencing people and things *for and through* your Real

Self, because you never learned how to do that. Instead, your primary focus has always been on gaining or maintaining this state of "Feel-good-about-self," which includes perfecting your Ego-References, by means of their Vehicles, so you can reach your Hidden Goal. You were never in the position to focus on your Self. Your Self-experience is broken.

Vehicles can include the project you are working on, the errand you need to run, the chore that needs to be taken care of, or a condition you need to fulfill (e.g., to sleep, to be thin, to become a doctor). You are possessed by the need to bring these tasks to a good ending because you perceive them to be a way of earning that Substitute SoS. Since you have no active connection with your Self and therefore lack the skill of questioning your own strategy, you are in no position to identify that this compulsion-to-score is fictional.

You are not aware of your body, of your potential for independent thinking, or of your own personhood in general. It means you are fixated on whatever it is you think you have to do to compensate for what didn't happen in your past: feeling acknowledged as the valuable person you are, YOURSELF.

When you have grown up with a Lack of SoS, you are still focused on avoiding that sense of Annihilation you experienced back then, even as an adult. It is the reason why getting positive results is still a matter of life and death to you. However, it is a compulsion rooted in the past rather than a desire based in reality. Your efforts serve only one goal and that is, in one way or another, to "Feel-good-about-yourself," which then serves as your Substitute SoS.

In those moments, you are what I call a *floating brain* – it is as if you are nothing but a mental process that makes sure everything you perceive to be necessary to earn a Substitute SoS is being executed. It is as if you were a head without a body; some might say it is like living from the head up.

You are not being real with yourself or as your Self. Well, here is the bottom line: When you are not in your body, you cannot live in the present. When you live in the past like that, you miss out on your real life. But your life clock keeps ticking and time moves on regardless of whether you live your life or skip it all together.

Restoring your Sense of Self is about freeing yourself from this unhealthy way of living, and learning to sense and experience all the aspects that form your Self in an immediate and direct way.

There should not be a bridge between how you experience your Self and what you do or sense; in other words, you should not be dependent on something else for your Self-experience. There should not be a *need* for achievements, approval, or a state of "Feeling-good-about-self." You have to learn how to cultivate a Direct Relationship with your Self and to be unconditionally present to your Self. Being present to yourself means you are whole!

When you are in a Direct Relationship with your Self, your focal point shifts from being one with your activities and self-imposed conditions and the Feel-good state that is perceived to be at stake to being one with your own person, with your own life, and your own well-being. YOU become the determining factor in your decision-making processes.

Direct Relationship with Self Activity

Here is what you can do to reinforce this Direct Relationship with your Self:

- Complete frequent Motivation Checks (see page 245).
- Engage in physical activities while maintaining awareness of your body.
- Consciously touch and feel things – a chair, a wall, a book – so you become aware of having a body. This exercise is specially geared toward drawing your attention to the fact that it is this body that gives you the ability to interact with the world outside yourself. You ARE this body. This body is YOU!
- Practice saying "I" aloud and feel that word thoroughly while merging the physical, mental, and emotional aspects of your Self into a whole.
- Explore all of your emotions – positive, negative, and neutral. Notice how they feel. Wonder what triggers them and where in your body you feel them.

- Bring conscious awareness to the fact that all of this is what makes you uniquely *you!*
- Tell yourself repeatedly: "I already am and my right to exist is not dependent on any condition."

III. I Am Present to the Here and Now

For people with a Substitute Sense of Self, all behavior is rooted in the past. It is as if you have no connection to the present because you are single-mindedly focused on repairing the damage that occurred during your upbringing. These behaviors are reinforced as you age. The place where you live seems to be of little to no importance because you are stuck living in your head, in the past. Even your age doesn't make a difference; your belief of having to live up to your (Substitute Sense of Self–oriented) program does not have an expiration date. If you don't stop yourself, you are doomed to pull this cart full of Ego-References and Hidden Agendas throughout your entire life. It makes your existence heavy, slow, and oftentimes unbearable. You need to put that burden down, relieve yourself of its dead weight, and become lighter.

Figure 14.1: The burden of the Substitute Sense of Self–oriented goal.

Reality Awareness Activity

The purpose of this activity is to become aware of the things in your mind that *do not exist* in the here and now so you can get in touch with the present. Anything you come across that does not belong in your current time and place needs to be examined in detail and recognized as alien to the present. Over time, this exercise will create awareness of the discrepancy between your two worlds, and promote you giving yourself, as well as all things/people, the time and place they deserve.

As always, you can add your own elements to customize this script.

Walk around and sense your legs – this helps bring awareness to your body's existence and your physical presence in the world around you. Actively observe and note the following, saying each statement aloud:

- I am in [*name of your current location*].
- It is [*morning, afternoon, evening, night*].
- My name is ...
- I am a [*woman/man*].
- I am [*single, married, dating, etc.*].
- I have a [*partner, sister, brother, husband/wife, etc.*] named ...
- I have [*children, nieces, nephews, friends, etc.*] named ...
- So I am a [*mother/father, son/daughter, aunt/uncle, friend, relative, etc.*] to ...
- I frequently obey the instructions or commands of ... [*name one or more people that immediately come to mind*].
- Life is mine and about *my* experience of it, so I am now erasing from my mind the instructions and commands of these people *who are not ME.*
- Now I am alone in my mind, and I only owe responsibility for myself and to myself.
- Now I am alone in my mind on [*day and/or date*].
- I live life following my present needs and wants.

- I touch the walls of [*location*]; they are real. I can touch and feel the objects around me. They include [*name objects as you touch them*]. They are real, just like I am.

IV. I Think for Myself

Some people are capable of truly thinking independently, while others still use the criteria of their caregivers and mistake those ideas for their own. If you are one of the latter, as I was, it is most likely because you weren't given a fair chance to develop a Healthy Sense of Self. When you don't have a Self to consult or use as a point of reference, it is almost impossible to make up your mind about anything.

So far, living up to your Ego-References has taken the place of developing your own criteria and standing up for them. Not only did you not know that the criteria you were using were not your own but were values of your parent/caregiver that you had picked up on. You were too busy fulfilling conditions for your Substitute Sense of Self to survive, so you had no time to even question what you were doing.

But once you let go of all your heavy (Substitute Sense of Self–oriented) tasks and unrealistically high goals in favor of just living and being, you can do so much *more* because you are present to it and have the right (Direct) motivation. Now dependency on fulfilling Ego-References makes space for exploring and executing your own opinion, based on your own reasoning and needs.

Think for Yourself Activity

Practicing this activity will reinforce what you have already learned by now: you no longer need to live up to the conditions based on your caregiver's values. What you need is to *practice awareness*: start rethinking your long-held beliefs, forming your own judgments, developing your own values. You do this by continuously questioning the values you currently use to judge yourself and others. Ask yourself, "Is this really what *I* think? Is this true? Where did this thought/judgment/value originate – whose criteria is it based on? **What do I actually think of it myself?**"

With a healthy purpose in life (remember, you are your own purpose), you will notice that when you no longer perceive there to be so much at stake, forming your own opinions and standing up for them feels a lot less risky than before.

First, you need to wake up and be present to your Self before you can create that possibility. To that purpose, you can do the following exercise:

1. Imagine your body and mind: your system.
2. Then imagine the two opposing forces – one is your true Self (color it green), and the other force is the Substitute Sense of Self–oriented system (color it red). Think of these two forces as clouds filling your entire system; they are continuously in motion, exchanging places, colliding softly or violently, and separating again. Picture them like a bad weather pattern in the sky; in this image, *you* are the sky.
3. Now imagine holding a magic wand; lightly touch these entangled red and green clouds with your wand, and *poof*, a shift takes place immediately on your command.
4. The red clouds separate from the green. Now two groups form: the green group, your naturally healthy and joyfully productive Self filled with your authentic thoughts, feelings, opinions, judgments, and values; and the red group, all of the elements tied to your Substitute Sense of Self.
5. Quietly and gently (remember, the red clouds were part of you at one time) start to grow and strengthen the green clouds, your healthy Self, until eventually there is no room left for the red clouds, which shrink and shrink until they are gone.

Once you have successfully banished the red clouds (your old automatic way of thinking), you will be the true ruler of your system. You have become the master of your thoughts!

V. I Am Consciously Aware of My Senses

Maybe you have noticed that your eyesight has worsened, and you wonder if it's due to aging. Perhaps you don't hear so well anymore, either. Did the sensitivity of your taste buds change? Do your favorite dishes seem to have lost their appeal? When you flatten your hand to straighten the sheets on your bed, do they ever feel odd, as if your hand isn't able to register all the sensations? When in the shower, did you notice that there are areas on your body that seem insensitive to water temperature?

If your senses have become dull, the problem could be that you have lived from the head up, focused on achieving or perfecting your Ego-References instead of using your senses to experience life outside of your mind. After many years of this detrimental habit, your senses might be slowly declining. That is a very alarming condition. When your senses dull, it could be a warning sign that, instead of really living, you have identified with whatever it is you are doing, buried as you are within your Substitute Sense of Self–oriented system; you have become your doing. It is more than likely that your stress levels and degree of exhaustion are very high.

It is time to become actively aware of your senses, after ignoring them and taking them for granted for so many years. You'd better start to appreciate them and use them as they were meant to be used. They should no longer be simply a means to getting to your Substitute Sense of Self, but little miracles that allow you to interact with, and appreciate, the world around you. How wonderful it is to distinctly see the faces of your children, a beautiful landscape, the sheet music on your piano, or an arrangement of freshly cut flowers? Once you become aware of your senses, you realize that you need to be utterly grateful for them; you need to actively enjoy them by using them with intent and not neglect them.

Primary Senses Activity

You can work on the following exercises to become present to your primary senses. Some of these you can do at home, at work, or even virtually, in your mind; others require you to go outside.

1. Repeat these statements related to each of your primary senses and make yourself conscious of them:

    - I watch and see. I am present to the process and sensation of watching the things around me and to what I am seeing.
    - I hear and listen. I am present to the process and sensation of listening and to what I am hearing.
    - I use my nose to smell, and I register scents as my nose detects them. I am present to the sensation of smelling and to what I smell.
    - I taste and register all the various flavors. I am present to the process of tasting and to what I taste.
    - I touch and feel. I am present to the process of touching and to what I am feeling.
    - I sense my Self. I am present to sensing my Self.

2. Take an afternoon walk in a park, work in a garden, or enjoy a five-minute break in the open air; stand in the light of the sun or a brilliant full moon.
3. You can visualize scenes you would like to experience in your life, things you think are beautiful or that move you. While creating your mental image, exercise your senses one by one. As an example, here is what I like to imagine:

    > "I stand in front of a huge castle, and I touch the marble stones with my hands. I look up at the crisp blue sky while I feel the fresh green grass under my feet. I listen to the song of the birds. The garden of the castle is full of colorful flowers that spread a heavenly fragrance. I taste the nectar that a hummingbird drops on my tongue."

VI. I Have Access to My Own Feelings, Preferences, and Opinions

First, you have to be able to acknowledge that you are not really listening to the signs and symptoms of your body, and that you are not present to your own needs and wants. You may even suspect that you are being deprived of various feelings, except for anger and resentment. You are obsessed with making things work within the scope of the way you perceive life to be. What you take for your tastes, opinions, and even feelings are, in reality, opportunistic choices rooted in your compulsive need to Score:

> *"What's the best thing I can do/say to get a good reaction mirrored back to me?"*
>
> *"What would be the best thing for me to do so I can 'Feel-good-about-self'?"*
>
> *"Let me stay vague in my opinion so I can avoid confrontation and being left without a sense of approval or, God forbid, being rejected entirely."*

But what about you? What do *you* really like that is *not* aimed at scoring? What truly gives you pleasure? What do you like to do that is purely for your own enjoyment? What are you really interested in just for the sake of the experience? What does your heart long for? (Please be alert; do not count your long-standing craving for acknowledgment, which is Substitute Sense of Self oriented.)

If everything you do, want, need, think, or invent is intended to be of service to your Hidden Goal, you are skipping your *own* life altogether. There is no connection between what you are doing, how you are living, and your personal inclinations, talents, and aversions. In this state, you are intrinsically unable to experience any true feelings of joy or even sadness. Because every norm that you apply is based on the efficiency of the Substitute Sense of Self–oriented system, you experience emotional roller coasters and remain trapped in a reactive state. These intense emotions, however, have nothing to do with a healthy experience of living on a Quality-of-Life Level: true feelings and inclinations; passion and compassion.

Discover the True You Activity

What do you have to do to develop a healthy level of emotions? How do you gain access to your true likes and dislikes, your opinions and feelings?

- Remove the Substitute Sense of Self–oriented goal from its throne and take that seat for your Self.

- Explore what makes you feel light and what makes you happy after removing your Hidden Goal.
- Undertake new activities that are not geared toward scoring.
- Spend time doing seemingly useless things that make you feel relaxed.
- Make a list of topics that interest you or are relevant to your life, situation, or surroundings, things you know you should have an opinion on. Read about them, formulate your opinion, and express it aloud.
- Figure out what styles and fashions appeal to you, what types of food you enjoy, or what genres of music make you feel good. Explore your likes and dislikes further; in short, start to live your life *for you.*

VII. I See Other People for Who They Are

Due to my own recovery from being addicted to a Substitute Sense of Self, the role of other people in my life has shifted completely. While living in Enmeshment with my mother, most everything I did or thought was ultimately meant to make sure *she* would get her fix of the Fgas state. I didn't do this because I was such a good person; it was purely based on my selfish fear that she wouldn't approve of me and not let me into the Castle of Enmeshment. Since she needed to achieve that Fgas state as her Substitute Sense of Self, and my own Substitute Sense of Self depended on her getting hers, I too, needed to have things my (or her?) way.

We are talking narcissism here, and this is what it is all about: You have no doubt that you are the center of the Universe and that the rest of the world revolves around you. You think everything and everybody exists to cooperate with and facilitate your needs and wants. Let us be clear, though, that we are not talking about the actual needs and wants of the authentic Self that are accessible when we have a Healthy Sense of Self. Narcissism is a classic example of dependency on a Substitute Sense of Self and not being present to your Self. To fully understand a narcissist's mindset, you need to look at it through the perspective of the SoS Theory, and then you may come to agree that a narcissist is not the ultimate egoist. The narcissist squirms and squeezes the juices out of their life, not because they personally benefit from it but for the sake of a perceived need to survive.

People Living in Their Own Bubble

To put what is commonly condemned as *egoism* in perspective, we can state that each person has the right to be his or her Self. You are the king or queen of your own life, and you can decide what to do or not do. You must also become aware that this then is valid for everybody else. Everybody has the right to direct their own life.

If this is a new concept for you, it may help you to visualize each person on Earth as living in big individual bubbles. Each person is the center of his or her own bubble. Sometimes your bubble touches others and bounces away – sometimes you are allowed to occupy a little space in someone else's bubble (your spouse, best friend, or parent). But the main concept is that it is not natural or normal to invade another person's bubble all the time, nor is it healthy to live in the same bubble with somebody else (Enmeshment).

Figure 14.2: Each one of us is living in his or her own bubble.

Being Egocentric Is Okay

It is natural for people to be preoccupied with themselves; others are not your personal pawns, nor do they exist to mirror back to you that deadly desired Fgas state. Becoming fully aware of this reality may shift your perspective of what living is all about. If you accept that others focus on themselves, you may feel better that you, in your bubble, focus on yourself. The mistaken belief that you are a better person when you are not egocentric inevitably causes you to believe that you always need to make room for others: that you would need to prioritize their wants and needs, give them unlimited amounts of your time and energy, and so on.

Direct Motivation Creates a Better World

Here we need to make an important distinction between giving so you can receive (Indirect Motivation) and giving for the sake of giving (Direct Motivation). If giving comes from the place of Direct Motivation, it is genuine and healthy. However, if you are still very needy and fear rejection, you tend to go out of your way to do things for others only for what you think you can get in return: approval and acceptance. That is not what I call "giving," even though it may look like it from the outside. You first need to focus on working out your own issues and become less dependent on the opinion of others before you are able to help or give to others. Only when you can do things for others without expecting a certain outcome, and you can allow others to do the same, are you directly motivated. If we could all do that, wouldn't the world be a better place?

It is important to be aware that your life is ultimately about your very own personal experience. Spending time and energy on searching for what is missing in your life, healing what is wounded, and patching what is leaking (Black Hole) is the best thing you can do both for yourself and for the world. It is part of managing your system. You can only live the life of a (directly motivated) giving person when you are not needy yourself.

So, the next time you look at your spouse, be aware of the fact that this person is not only there for you. He or she is in your world but, ultimately, lives to fulfill his or her own dreams and goals. You and your spouse are different people, or perhaps I should say your spouse is a separate person from you. Stop expecting both of you to have the exact same ideas and intentions. We are all born with the equal right to be ourselves, and that means that nobody has to be like anybody else. If you are eager to do what you want to do, so is your spouse, your son, your daughter, etc. Look into the eyes of your friend and give it a try. Gauge the depth of their being. It's funny how that deeper dimension doesn't show on the outside. You just see a tangible body, but behind those eyes and in that body is a whole world: a past, a present, and a future, and *you* are just a small part of it.

Personal Bubble Activity

Actively undertaking the effort to develop this new way of thinking about yourself and others while being with somebody will give you the right perspective on your own position in their life as well as their position in yours; it will teach you to see others as being just as real as you experience yourself to be or vice versa. At least that is how it worked for me.

1. Just look at people and observe how they are.
2. Imagine them living in their own bubble and you in yours.
3. Imagine that you open up your own bubble, knock on the door of theirs, and ask them to let you in for a while.
4. After a while, back out of their bubble and return to your own – then close the door.
5. Now turn the activity around: Imagine someone is knocking on the door of your bubble. You get to decide whether you will let that person in or turn them away.
6. Once you have someone in mind who you want to allow into your bubble, think of being fully there for them and with them while they are with you.
7. At some point, when a natural impulse arises, imagine each of you going your separate ways.

VIII. I Have Conversations to Transfer Information or to Connect with Others

The purpose of conversation is to transfer information or to connect with others. Contrary to what Substitute Sense of Self–oriented people think, conversations are not meant to provide you with the Fgas state that functions as a Substitute Sense of Self. If you happen to be someone who thinks that everything and everyone in this world exists to facilitate your needs and wants, you may be making the mistake of expecting others to be all about giving you that Fgas state because it is the only thing you crave. If you are like I used to be, you are working so hard to realize your Substitute Sense of Self that others having their own goals might actually come as a surprise. If you are as I was, you might squirm when trying to get a conversation to end on a note that makes you "Feel-good-about-self."

Can you tell when you are actually not interested in what others want to discuss? Can you see how other people talk about the subject itself, purely for its own sake, and that it is not the goal of the conversation to end it with a Substitute Sense of Self? Keep these questions in mind when you talk with others as it may help you change your perspective and therefore your attitude toward others in conversations.

Let me give you an example: I am at a party where I hardly know anyone, so I need to make an effort to meet new people. I feel like nobody is interested in talking to me even though I am being nice and doing everything I can to make them feel good. Digging deeper into myself, I find that all I want from them is a pleasant chat so I can then part from them with a Fgas state.

The truth is, though, if all I want is to achieve a Fgas state, I have a (subconsciously) premeditated goal, and I am not really participating in the conversation. I am not open to others! I am just trying to be pleasant and say the right thing at the right time, so, in the end, I can go home with a Fgas state.

Usually, you can get that done by making others feel good about *themselves*. What is the result of all this? You might be surprised: People with a Healthy Sense of Self sense that something odd is going on. They sense that you are not being authentic, and they turn away from you, not interested. People with a Healthy Sense of Self are interested in "the real thing" – real conversation or interaction. They do not want to waste their time on playing a game of lies and flattery. People with a Lack of Sense of Self might be drawn to you because you are like them, understanding the need to play the game for your Substitute Sense of Self.

Awareness of Your Problem

When you accept that conversations are either about transferring information, sharing ideas, connecting with others, or simply for fun, it rules out what you used to use them for: as Vehicles for your compulsion to end up in a Fgas state.

Do you remember conversations that left you utterly frustrated when, upon ending the conversation, you felt you'd just been left there, dangling, with no emotional closure, without satisfying your craving to "Feel-good-about-self"? By internalizing this principle, you will gradually become aware of what you are doing when you talk with others. Our goal in the process of recovery from the addiction to a Substitute Sense of Self is to learn how to have conversations with people for the sake of the conversation, to exchange useful information/ideas, to get to know people, or to have a pleasant time in their company. To be effective in getting there, you need to analyze what has happened in many of your past conversations.

I Am Already

To be able to make this shift in perception successful, you need to become convinced that *you already are*. You already have what it takes to be yourself. You do not need this Substitute Sense of Self, this Fgas state, provided by, and therefore *dependent on*, others.

You need to become fully aware that you are a closed living circuit for as long as you exist and that you have the ability to interact with other closed living circuits. This doesn't mean you cannot influence each other, just not at the level you have been used to: depending on others for your artificial spine. Can you sense how stressful it is to get that outcome at all costs, and how forced it feels for those you try to involve as well?

You can practice this new mindset and attitude by being utterly aware of what you want from the person you are conversing with. You need to learn to remember that your existence is not at stake or dependent upon the way a conversation ends. It does not matter whether it ends on a pleasant note or has a neutral ending. Even disagreement is okay. You do not need to end it on a Fgas note. All that matters is whether the message was delivered or received, or the connection was attempted, or whether or not you had a good time (on a Quality-of-Life Level).

Compulsion to Endlessly Prolong Phone Calls

If you want to endlessly prolong the conversation until the moment you feel safe to leave, chances are you are compulsively trying to reach that Fgas state and are unable to accept that the conversation is ending until you have what you came for. It all depends on the degree of the emotions that go with the conversation. If they are normal, the situation seems healthy; if your feelings approach the intensity of anxiety, fear, or desperation, it could be an indication that the situation is far from healthy.

The moment you are able to *get over* that compulsion to end a conversation with a Fgas state at all costs, you will be able to truly see and interact with other people.

Conversation Awareness Activity

The following is an outline of the awareness you have to cultivate during conversations with other people while you are in the process of restoring your Sense of Self:

- Ask yourself, "What are my expectations for this conversation and what could my Hidden Agenda be?"
- Keep in mind at all times: "I *am* already. I already have what it takes to be myself."
- Another key phrase to keep present in your mind is: "I am safe, and I do not need to 'Feel-good-about-self' at all costs. I do not need a Substitute Sense of Self. I have my Restored Sense of Self."

- Practice holding this awareness while conversing with a friend or spouse and just let the conversation take its natural course. (Consider it a skill you have to learn!)
- Purposefully set up a conversation with a person who does not need to know you are doing this activity. It may be a Hidden Agenda of sorts, but if your intention is to help get yourself to a better, healthier place, you'll be fine.

IX. My Work is Aimed at the Obvious, Direct Outcome

Work needs to take place to get you from A to B or Z because that is how the world operates. But work needs to be done for the sake of itself or for its own purpose, and never to provide you with a Substitute Sense of Self.

You have to separate your work from you as a person. When you get so involved with your work that you *become* your work, you identify with what you are *doing* and not with what and who you are *being*. Chances are you are obsessed with working to get the desired outcome to "Feel-good-about-self" at all costs. Not only do you lose a healthy sense of boundaries, but you are also not paying attention to your body and general well-being. I believe that the root cause of what turns people into workaholics is, in fact, the dependency on a Substitute Sense of Self. Getting an outcome at all costs can mean that you are not in touch with yourself as a whole person.

This is what this unhealthy relationship with work looks like: While at work, you are unable to take a break. Even when you take a moment for the absolute necessity of having to eat, you are hardly aware that you are eating, as your mind is busy with the next phase of your work. Having to go to the bathroom is a nuisance that leads to irritation.

The fear of not bringing an Ego-Reference to a good end is the reason why you live under this continuous burden of stress, frenzy, and anxiety. You are monitoring yourself and everybody else in your environment in order to control your circumstances, thus creating the highest probability of getting a good outcome.

Your dependency on a Substitute Sense of Self for experiencing your self translates into your inability to leave the jobsite and go home until you have reached the relatively relaxed state of "Feeling-good-about-yourself." After all, that is what you are working so hard to achieve. Without that Fgas state, you face Annihilation.

Work for Work's Sake Activity

Here are some suggestions to implement this new way of looking at work:

- Learn the following by heart and repeat it many times: The reason for work is to get from A to B or Z; never to provide me with a Fgas state as a Substitute Sense of Self.
- Do a sincere Motivation Check: Take what you are doing at work and find out if it might be functioning as a Vehicle for a Hidden Agenda. Remind yourself of what those are.
- Choose two days of the week to set aside some time to assess one thing that you truly enjoyed completing at work and why you enjoyed it. Were you able to Score a Fgas state with it?
- Then, turning it around, assess one thing you truly despised at work and why you despised it. Did it not serve your Substitute Sense of Self–oriented efficiency?
- Pick up an activity that has no scoring potential but that you've always wanted to try. Find out what *you* really like and do it.
- Secretly help somebody else out with something that has no scoring potential, and make sure he or she does not notice you were the one who did it; stay anonymous.

X. Relapse Is Always Lurking

The moment your Restored Sense of Self is somewhat settled in, you need to remind yourself, more than ever, that the Black Hole is always waiting. After exercising your reconditioning program for some time, you may be well equipped enough to initiate actions and activities that used to be indirectly motivated but that now come from a healthier place. You know that you do not need to worry about living up to certain conditions because you do not need a Substitute Sense of Self. But there is a hidden danger.

Because now your action that used to be an Ego-Reference was initiated as a Quality-of-Life-level action, you have a better chance of succeeding. However, there is a danger that what you started with the right (Direct) motivation will be co-opted and pulled into the Black Hole anyway since your mind has a long history of being wrongly (indirectly) motivated. This is what relapse looks like in the context of recovering from a Substitute Sense of Self: the Black Hole that was conditioned to suck up any successfully performed Ego-Reference in the past is activated by things that were historically used to Score, and you fall back into that old pattern.

When you are using these Twelve SoS Reconditioning Statements in your recovery process, make sure that the Black Hole has been patched by creating good body awareness, as described in Statement I; otherwise, when things begin to go well for you, the successes may trigger the Substitute Sense of Self–oriented system to kick back in. After all, it was your life's purpose to perform certain actions and behavior to perfection and be rewarded for it by a Fgas state or parental approval. Now that your actions make you feel authentically good, the temptation is too great (for the Early Childhood Survival System) to not use your directly motivated successes to Score, and have them turn back into indirectly motivated ones.

You need to develop continuous awareness to avoid falling back into that old system. That can be quite difficult since the desire to forget about it and put it behind you is intense.

Remember, though, that pull is coming from the Substitute Sense of Self–oriented system.

Keeping up an ongoing awareness of what triggers your desire to Score, and that those triggers can arise at any time, will be greatly beneficial to your Restored Sense of Self.

So you need to make an extra effort to maintain Direct Motivation and keep your eye on your real goal. The moment you sense jitters, frenzy, anxious sweating, or a rapid heartbeat, you need to be alert and interpret these symptoms as warning signs: you might have shifted from the direct path back onto the indirect one (see Figure 12.3 on page 253). Also watch out for frustration beyond reason, sleeplessness, or other signs of depression. Those are symptoms of an active Substitute Sense of Self–oriented system.

If you have reason to believe that you have relapsed and the Substitute Sense of Self–oriented goal has reactivated itself, you need to STOP what you are doing and consciously repeat the SoS Reconditioning Statements to bring you back to your Real Self.

Sidestepping the Black Hole Activity

The following are a few examples of how I managed to overcome the danger of the always-lurking Black Hole. You are also invited to use your imagination and creativity in coming up with ways to avoid the Black Hole.

- I envisioned the Black Hole as an actual hole in the floor that went all the way to the other side of the Earth. I taught myself to be careful not to step in it.
    - **a)** At some point, to help myself see the situation as less dangerous, I created a bottom for that hole by imagining a piece of wood shoved underneath it.
    - **b)** Later, I came up with the idea of putting dirt on over the wood at the bottom of the hole and sowing grass seeds in it. As the grass grew, I put a little fence around it so I would not inadvertently step on it.
- Other times, I envisioned (and almost felt) that the Black Hole was located above my left hip. For a few days in a row, I imagined a scab growing over it, sealing it off, and healing it.
- I made a drawing of the Black Hole to create more conscious awareness of its existence.
- I would go over the **Magic Formula** (see page 320 in Chapter 15) and thoroughly sense its meaning.

XI. I Am Ready to Share My Life with Others

Once you have restored your Sense of Self enough to consider yourself the master of your life, once you know you are no longer living on automatic pilot, it is time to celebrate your life and share yourself and your life with others! But this time around as a *non-needy person*; you are not dependent on the outcome of your achievements or on what other people think of you. You are also becoming more and more skillful at shutting up that Internalized Parental Voice.

It is necessary to first have your act together before you can socialize with the hope of a healthy outcome. If you present yourself to other people in your former needy state, no doubt you would encounter those who are attracted to that situation and who radiate negativity, rejection, and dependency. But if you wait until you truly sense and experience your Self as your home and anchor, you will bring value to your interactions with others. If you bring a sense of independence, you attract others who have that same ability. Together you can work, have fun, or simply be while not being a heavy burden on each other – people with a Healthy Sense of Self can sense *your* independence very distinctly.

Warning

It is so much easier to stay grounded when you are by yourself. You will find that the moment you are with other people, even with people close to you, you face a bigger risk of relapse. It can be a challenge to stick with your new ways. You will likely have to experience that a few times before you learn to be extra alert to relapse and avoid becoming Substitute Sense of Self oriented and make the Fgas state your main goal once again.

Interaction with others, especially intimate interaction, tends to pull you toward the old desire of getting the keys to the Castle of Enmeshment. It feels like you want to share your bubble with the other person at all costs – it becomes difficult to keep in mind that you are separate people at all times. This can be a bit of a problem after having been physically intimate with someone; it is the nature of lovemaking to be together with another person in one bubble. Just be alert to the danger of wanting to stay there, wanting to prolong that moment, or having problems sleeping afterwards comes from. With awareness, this too shall pass.

Your sense of who you are must be independent from someone else's opinion or emotional reaction to you. You can still be affected by what other people do or say to an extent, but it shouldn't hit you on an existential level. With a Healthy Sense of Self, you can help each other and be of service to each other in more and better ways. However, the process of getting there isn't easy, so it is smart to take as much time as you need to process your conclusions.

The reason relationships so often crash is because of one or both parties' dependency on a Substitute Sense of Self.

For example, avoiding Annihilation is a strong incentive for not wanting to give in during arguments or for rehashing old arguments that you did not previously bring to a satisfying end. If your Sense of Self is sufficient, you can function as healthy, interdependent teammates, community members, and fellow citizens, no matter your religious, cultural, or racial differences.

You can start out by making it an important factor in the education of your children, encouraging them to be their own person and lead their lives based on their interests and potential. Make sure your kids *get it* so they can pass it on to their kids. A Healthy Sense of Self is a prerequisite for being able to be who you are, and if we help one another achieve that, together we can create a huge shift for the better in the world.

Centering Activity

The idea is that upon arriving at Statement XI you have at least memorized and are reasonably able to stick to the previous statements. What you are getting to, from here on, is the crown of the reconditioning program. It is only, and naturally, achievable when you have thoroughly worked through all the other statements. If that is not the case, keep working on the preceding prompts until all ten of them have become familiar to you.

Here is what you could work on every day, or apply when in need, to center yourself:

- Think about what role you have in a particular group; it helps to become aware of when you slip back into the automatic and destructive habit of living for your Substitute Sense of Self.
- Envision yourself in a specific setting that appeals to you and that you would like to see in reality. For example, I see myself giving a party for my numerous friends and family members. I see big dining tables loaded with healthy food and overflowing with wine. I hear music and see my guests dancing. I see happy people of all ages surrounding me, and I am poised and balanced while thoroughly enjoying the feast and the company.
- Actively undertake steps to find groups you feel comfortable with or organize a night out or a coffee date with a friend, no matter how busy you think you are.
- Take the initiative to set up a party or celebration for somebody you value or spend some time alone with them and actively listen to what they are willing to share.
- Give a few hours of your time to volunteer in an environment you like.

XII. I Am Ready to Be a Part of and Contribute to a Healthy Community!

Now that you are on your way to developing your Restored Sense of Self, your criteria are changing. The values you use to judge things and yourself by are shifting tremendously. You come from a situation in which everything revolved around getting a Substitute Sense of Self: what you did, what you planned to do, what you achieved, what you thought was important, as well as what you avoided and rejected. You used to evaluate all of these aspects of life by whether or not they could facilitate your Ego-References, help you realize your Hidden Agendas, and finally get you to achieve your Hidden Goal.

Congratulations! Now *you* have become the most important person in your life. Your life is now about yourself, and you live in a healthy, natural way. No longer are you constrained and limited to chasing your "Feel-good-about-self" state. You have discovered the freedom to be yourself and the joy of living your own life. You get to choose your preferences based on who you really are. You are continuously discovering what you really like and developing your own opinions.

The abundance of life will flow your way for as long as you live! No more Hidden Agendas, so you can apply all that richness to your own authentic satisfaction. If you are healthy, you will automatically be grateful for that. If you are not yet healthy, you now have a tool that may prove very efficient in improving your health and providing healing in every aspect of your life. You are on your way to consolidating your Restored Sense of Self.

It is my expectation that, with a Healthy Sense of Self, many of your physical processes will become normal again. In the light of the intimate connection between mind, body, and emotions, I would not be surprised if restoring your Sense of Self would take care of many ailments. Not being a doctor, I am not in the position to give medical advice or make any predictions, but, in my mind, it makes sense: if your system functions naturally, then your body should also be healthy. (Of course, I do not want to suggest that it is always easy to spot where the problem lies or what cards you were dealt at birth.)

Once this final Reconditioning Statement has been internalized and activated within you, life has become about living it! You know your Self now; you have become *real.* That means you have a better sense of what your potential is and where your boundaries and limitations lie. You are aware of your body, and now nothing is needed to aid your experience of your Self; you think for yourself and are present to what takes place in your daily life. You really see other people and are able to hear what they have to say. You work for the sake of getting something done. You have developed personal preferences and you know you can act on them when you chose to do so. You are also ready to share what you think about things with others. You find satisfaction in playing the hand you were dealt and are aware of the triggers that lead to your past need for approval.

Reconditioning Activity

The following are a few suggestions for how to implement all of the reconditioning tools:

- Enjoy the fact that you have a body.
- You can develop skills that strengthen and help in the maintenance of your body and keep it in shape: go to the gym, take up yoga, or play a sport. You can explore any physical activity you think you might enjoy.
- You can make love while being present to your body and to your partner.
- Practice feeling less victimized by your personal circumstances; now that you have a Restored Sense of Self, you can spend 100 percent of your creativity and energy on improving your situation.
- You can decide to actively share your experience of the SoS Method to reinforce everything you've learned while helping others gain a better life.

Summary and Looking Ahead

The Twelve SoS Reconditioning Statements may give you food for thought for years to come. They can also function as an emergency brake to stop the behavior you want to shift. It is important to repeat the statements often until you know them so thoroughly that they are readily available when you need them.

In the next chapter, you'll find a number of exercises and affirmations meant to support your intention of leaving behind your old ways of serving a fictional goal so you can become your own goal.

Chapter 15

On the Threshold …

Affirmations, Awareness Exercises, and Advice

The following affirmations are abbreviated versions of affirmations and suggestions provided earlier. It is best to learn them by heart and practice them repeatedly, so you "own" them and they can work for you once you leave this book behind and continue your journey on your own. They may seem obvious in the beginning, but after numerous repetitions, you can expect to suddenly get it.

Affirmations

- I already AM.
- I accept that others create and have a life, just like I do.
- I feel good about myself no matter what!
- I practice constant body awareness.
- I am aware of the always-lurking suction of the Black Hole.
- I no longer need to comply with other people's wishes because I no longer fear rejection.

Now let us zoom in on these lifesaving statements.

Recovering from the dependency of a Substitute Sense of Self, or from the addiction to approval, is all about embracing the fact that you already exist and that there is no need to "earn" that existence in any way.

I Already AM

My life is first and foremost about being.
Not until I truly sense that "I already AM"
can I consider thinking about my doing.

As often as you can, put aside your work – or whatever type of "doing" provides you with a sense of identity. For a set time, experience "nothing." That might involve being physically still and allowing your mind to slow down. Try to make a shift into observing your thoughts rather than being trapped in them. In other words, practice *being more than your mind*. Incorporate all other aspects of yourself: your body as well as your nonverbal Self-awareness.

I Accept That Others Create and Have a Life, Just as I Do

I accept that others ARE, just as I AM. I admire and appreciate what they do and who they are. In other words, I do not have to have what they have. I do not have to have the same skills. I do not have to have the same circumstances. I do not have to be like them. I am myself, and they are themselves!

I Feel Good about Myself No Matter What!

As often as you can, simply choose to feel good about yourself *no matter what!* Please note that I am not referring to the SoS term "Feel-good-about-self" here, charged as it is with the addiction to approval and a Substitute Sense of Self. What I want you to do is to simply feel good about who you are and about what you do on a Quality-of-Life Level. Just consider for a moment how you are out there in the big world, look at yourself with your very own eyes and conclude: I am okay! I see the reality of life, which always ends in death – it is only a matter of time, so I am making my time count.

I Practice Constant Body Awareness

Body awareness will help you reduce anxiety and reclaim authority over yourself, your opinions, your goals, and your desires; in short, it strengthens your Sense of Self. As you are repeating the above affirmations, you need to keep constant awareness of your body, as described in Reconditioning Statement I (see page 278). It will remind you primarily of the fact that you already *are* and that you are not in need of a Fgas state to function as a Substitute Sense of Self. Being imbued with that knowledge (you can't repeat it to yourself enough!) will help you step out of the cycle of addiction to a Substitute Sense of Self and stop complying with the (overt or assumed) wishes of others (see the Maps for Restoring Your Sense of Self in Chapter 17).

I Am Aware of the Always-Lurking Suction of the Black Hole

Be aware that during your recovery from the dependency on a Substitute Sense of Self, when things go well, they still tend to be sucked into the Black Hole. It follows the old established pattern that was based on your need for approval. When this happens, *you relapse* and fall back into Substitute Sense of Self–oriented living, unless you catch yourself! And you *must* catch yourself!

Repeat aloud the following statement:

> *"Whatever I achieve has the potential to be sucked in by the Black Hole, which is a trigger that pulls me back into the Substitute Sense of Self–oriented system."*

Do you see the irony of what can be at play in such a case? You struggle to do things as well as you possibly can. You think you are really doing them for yourself now. But your efforts are being thwarted by the effects of your anxiety or even depression or insomnia. Wake up to see that it means you are still performing Substitute Sense of Self–oriented activities: the symptoms speak for themselves. The need to gain a Substitute Sense of Self is a habit your automatic pilot knows all too well; however, keep in mind that the only person the physical symptoms of your stress and anxiety have an impact on is *you,* and I mean the *real you.*

When living for a Substitute Sense of Self, you give all your efforts to a fictional purpose that takes away from your own life. *You* are the only one who is suffering the pain of migraines or the lousy feeling of not having slept well. *You* are the one who misses out on friendships and relationships. Make sure you change that and come from a place of Direct Motivation!

Sometimes you need to approach it more lightly and tell yourself that, after all, it is about time you uncover the buried adult in you. It is within your reach to truly grow up and start acknowledging your Self as an autonomous person. It is time to stop making your life harder by forcing yourself to live up to these self-imposed conditions that are being sucked into the Black Hole again. Now that you know it has everything to do with a need for approval, you have the ability to disrupt the process. You can leave behind the internalized voice of your parents/caretakers, who may even be deceased, and live your life based on your own criteria.

I No Longer Need to Comply with Other People's Wishes Because I No Longer Fear Rejection.

You know that you *already are* a body and a mind of which you are the master, the manager, and the maintenance person. There is nothing to lose! Therefore, you can STOP worrying about screwing up other people's Fgas states. It is important to see how that worry is based on the fear of getting negative feedback and losing your chance to earn your Substitute Sense of Self. Remember you do not need that anymore. Complying with other people's wishes (people pleasing) is no longer your set way of experiencing some sort of selfhood. You are your own person and you radiate your own Self, regardless of whether other people like it or not! Gaining full awareness of that truth will STOP your physical symptoms, such as migraines and insomnia. These symptoms were based on that Early Childhood Survival Strategy to get approval at all costs, which no longer serves you.

You now know you are safe in and with your Self, so you no longer care if these physical symptoms prevent you from gaining a Substitute Sense of Self *because you do not need it anyway!* This is the moment where you get closer to your Self. These physical symptoms DO MATTER. You want them gone, and guess what: they will be once you gain that awareness.

A good way to get started on this new path is by repeating positive affirmations on a daily, even hourly, basis.

The following list of affirmations is only a sample of what I worked with. It is by no means complete.

- I have presence! Others really do see and hear me.
- I have a voice; I have a face (look in the mirror!).
- I *am* already; others are ready to give me their attention!
- I am my own person.
- I have a home where I belong; my Self is my home.
- I am emotionally safe and free to express myself.
- I am free to be myself!

When creating your own affirmations, it is important not to use negatives or future-tense verbs! For great affirmations, you need to find a way to express things in positive present-tense language.

Awareness Exercises

Next to these and other affirmations, there are a few exercises to help you to turn off your automatic pilot. The only way to change something that has become so much a part of you over time is by making that change as consciously as possible, step by step. Every day you can discover a new layer of what this habit actually meant to you when it was invented. Then you can ask yourself, "What effect does it have on me in the present?" Only by knowing what the motivation is behind your behavior, can you dismantle it and implement a new one that really serves you.

Try to Reconstruct the Path to Your Substitute Sense of Self Aloud

Here is another way to help you make the transition: Keep reasoning and analyzing aloud how you proceeded through the process of gaining a Substitute Sense of Self. How did you become so good at it? What were the landmarks? This type of self-analysis will make you proficient in understanding that the Fgas state results from the need for approval that you used to mistake for acknowledgment. That withheld acknowledgment is what led you to the Fear of Annihilation. But, remember, acknowledgment was not withheld from you because you were not good enough; *it was because your caretaker had the problem of not being able to truly see you due to their own Lack of Sense of Self.*

By living up to Ego-References, you have been aiming to get acknowledgment from that one person who wasn't able to give it to you in the first place. It is unfortunate, but odds are that you will never get what you are after. Why? Because the reason you didn't get acknowledgment was never *your* fault! There comes a moment, though, in which you will break free of that perceived necessity to live and behave following that unhealthy pattern of self-imposed conditions. That will be the day you finally realize that your ultimate purpose in life is *being you!*

Practice Mindfulness and Being in the Moment

Take command of your life/body. Get away from the past and live in the reality of the present. Try to look away from your inner world. Shift your focus from being caught up in memories of your emotions to what is real, what is happening now.

The emotional shift you can make by doing just that is big. From the confusing state of inner turmoil and the desperation to find ways out of it, you can experience a sudden oasis of stillness and inner peace. Once you are fully in the now, you know that you are safe and that you are no longer just like Don Quixote fighting with the windmills.

Please know that persisting or returning symptoms are an indication that you are not clean: you are still, or have fallen back into being Substitute Sense of Self oriented without being aware of it.

This awareness exercise (as well as the others) needs to be repeated as often as possible. At some point, you will have moments in which you realize "being terrified of something that isn't even real is too silly to be true." And those moments do come.

Methods of Self-Optimization and Problem-Solving

From my own process of recovery, I have concluded that if my *perception* is "I am not being seen and heard; I have no voice or face," then I will continue to *create* that reality! This statement is based on the Law of Attraction, which is a powerful approach to healing yourself, and it is worth your attention.

There is a wide array of relatively new problem-solving techniques and approaches, which include Neuro-Linguistic Programming (NLP), visualization techniques, Emotional Freedom Tapping techniques (EFT), and various ways to apply the Law of Attraction. It may be good to learn about the many tools out there for solving emotion-based issues. They worked well for me. Finding out which tools work best for you and your individual needs takes time, patience, and effort.

Within the context of this work, I do not elaborate on these topics, but I wanted to mention them as a potential next step on your ladder of Self-healing. There are many books written on these subjects, and they are intriguing, to say the least. Look into these methods of Self-optimization; it is only smart to change your belief systems in positive ways and express them aloud to yourself to help you create a reality that fits your needs and desires better.

Advice on the Threshold ...

You are approaching the end of this book and are about to leave it behind and continue your journey of restoring your Sense of Self on your own. The way I have experienced my own healing process urges me to encourage you to keep actively busy with your reconditioning process. What has been ruling you for ten, twenty, or even sixty years has made a strong trail in your brain. What you now want to be ruled by are your new insights and conclusions, and they have to start carving their own path in the jungle of your brain wiring. Be to your Self like a good gardener to his beloved garden – and keep the weeds out! Here are a few ways to help you do that:

Hold On to Your Newly Restored Sense of Self Using Arts and Crafts

Make staying in touch with your Real Self the most important task of the day, the week, and the month. This seems logical in hindsight, but when you are right in the middle of trying to sober up from your addiction to earning a Substitute Sense of Self, nothing seems more important than achieving your Ego-References. Take into consideration that you are used to spending your time and effort to Score points toward your Hidden Goal. To flip this around and have all you do become Self-serving is challenging to say the least.

If it were possible to create a chart to measure your Substitute Sense of Self–oriented activity by marking your "score" each day, you would be able to get a better sense of its extent. That would also give you a better understanding of the progress you are making; on any given day, you would be able to see what your reality used to be and how it has changed as you are recovering from a Substitute Sense of Self. Unfortunately, it is not quite so easy to track. Just know that you need great mental discipline to restore and maintain your Sense of Self. You also have to be creative in this reconditioning process: create *visual aids* for yourself.

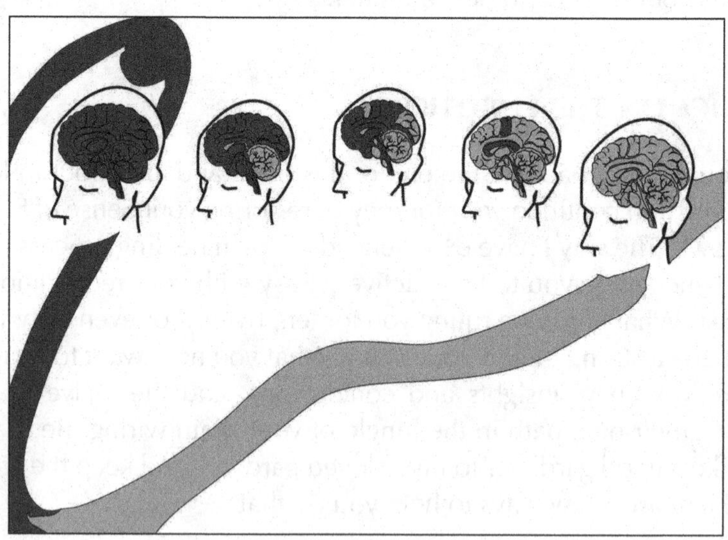

Figure 15.1: Switching from the addiction to a Substitute Sense of Self to a Restored Sense of Self.

Look at Figure 15.1, which you already saw in a previous chapter. Imagine that the healthy (light) path is the path you have to travel, instead of the unhealthy (dark) path. You can make a drawing/painting of it. That is what I did, and it helped me imagine the path more clearly. Use Figure 15.1 and visualize where you are at, at any given moment in time.

Of course, it is great if you can create drawings or paintings based on your own imagination and skills. Express your feelings or the goal you have in mind. It all helps to create clarity in the middle of chaos.

Learn Your List of Ego-References Using the Motivation Checklist

Learn the checklist thoroughly, by heart, so you know it inside and out, upside and down, to the point where you would be able to immediately recite all your Ego-References if someone woke you up in the middle of the night and asked you what they were. Look back at the list you made using Figure 12.4 (page 255).

Become Fluent with the Glossary Terms

The glossary on page 371 provides an overview of all the SoS terminology you have become familiar with throughout this book. Knowing the terms may help you deal with the issues they represent.

Know What *You* Are All About!

Do you still believe that working on your Hidden Agendas in the present is going to repair what went wrong in your past? Check in with yourself as often as you can, asking, "Is this how I think about things myself?" Are you truly on your way to living life according to your own criteria?

Create a Short Overview of Your Former Indirect Motivation

On a big piece of paper, write down (in big letters) the one thing that you were all about in your past: your Hidden Goal. In the past, there was a reason you were the slave to realizing your Hidden Goal.

- Does it still mean as much to you?
- Is that reason still active in your daily life right now?
- In what ways does the absence of acceptance by your parent(s) still show up for you?

For example:

If "the need to feel acknowledged as the person you are" is your long-standing quest, it may still show up in one or more of the following ways:

- Still looking to get approval and acceptance from your parent(s) (or from your Internalized Parental Voice).
- Still looking for ways to satisfy that sense of belonging.
- Still dealing with a need to feel as if you are part of something.
- Still not feeling truly safe if you have not complied with the wishes of the other person.
- Still having to prove yourself in order to feel that you are allowed to exist.
- Still having to do something special so you can feel alive.
- Still having an extreme need to being taken seriously.
- Still needing to know that others see you so you don't feel like a "ghost with a body."
- Still needing to see (extra) proof of being taken into account to avoid experiencing humiliation.
- Still making absolutely sure you are never in a position to be ridiculed.

Pay Attention to the Lurking Relapse

Relapse may jump up out of nowhere at times. Be especially alert after traveling (as jet lag can lower your resistance), while recovering from illness, after a good movie or, yes indeed, after sexual activity, or when there are other big changes in your daily living situation. Experiencing relapse a few times is necessary before you can learn to prevent it from happening. It is all a matter of staying aware of who you are.

New Freedom, New Now

Your former Substitute Sense of Self was, until now, defined by and dependent on all your Ego-References. These conditions had so much power over you that they kept you compulsive, addicted, and enslaved to your Fear of Annihilation. As this all fades away, out of your life, your recovery process dismantles your Indirect Motivation. You are finally free!

The conditions you were enslaved to were adopted in your past. Even though they were useful at the time, in the now, they are neither relevant nor helpful. Instead, they can be rather detrimental and limiting, as they may have been preventing you from reaching your potential. Stay at the steering wheel of your own ship (read: body, mind, activities, goals) by doing a Motivation Check every so often.

Imagine your mind as a room you want to keep clear of clutter. A Motivation Check makes you aware of why you do what you do, why you want what you want. Ask yourself questions such as "Do I have a Hidden Agenda attached to this or that? Am I still caught up in the cycle of Vehicles-Ego-References-Hidden Goals-Fgas-Substitute Sense of Self?"

Scrutinize the level of your emotions and your experiences. As often as you can, ask yourself, "What is the degree of my irritation and anger in this or that case? Are my emotions Quality-of-Life Level? Am I irritated or angry for a healthy reason, or is there a boiling volcano underneath (because of perceived Hindrances leading to rage) that I have difficulty managing?" The latter is indicative of Substitute Sense of Self–oriented activity. Keep your motives clean and manage your Self!

Listen to your body: "I am first and foremost my body" is an effective slogan to help you ground yourself and bring you back to being real. It can help you drop all Substitute Sense of Self–oriented activities or goals. Consider this slogan an emergency brake that stops the train from speeding toward the all too familiar (fictional) terminal: the Substitute Sense of Self. To give the slogan even more impact, you can add to it: "... and my well-being on a day-to-day basis is what counts most!"

I urge you to never give up. Have compassion for yourself.

Being Happy for No Reason!

The following is a simple exercise you can do anywhere. It is a great way to take a breather from your hard work and focus on your Self for a minute. The more relaxed your body and mind are while doing this exercise, the deeper and more lasting the effect it will have on you.

First, empty your mind. Then, imagine your chest has a large, spacious area around your heart and lungs. Take a deep, slow breath, expanding your abdomen first, then up through your ribcage. Slowly inhale air into your lungs until you feel as though you will burst. Then exhale. As you do this, your heart pumps fresh blood throughout your body. It feels good! Do this two more times, and notice how good it feels. This sensation is Self-contentment: happiness for no reason beyond existing and breathing in the moment.

Visualization

You can help yourself recover by creating positive images in your mind. It is most effective to do this for twenty to thirty minutes at a time. Each healing visualization should be done while sitting up straight to make sure you don't fall asleep. Once you have reached a relaxed state, see yourself in your mind's eye, as if on a stage, in circumstances that would erase your need to live up to self-imposed conditions (Ego-References). Images work better than words when you want to convince your emotional autopilot to learn to see things differently. So in your imagination, play out an alternative, positive scenario in which your own life situation could have gone from the time you were born until now; be a witness to your own story. You can do this as often as you want. It is fun, doesn't cost anything, and helps you grow toward becoming your own person. Doing this visualization frequently may lead to your early childhood memories being overruled by more positive images.

The Magic Formula

As a bonus, here is the Magic Formula! It will help you to remember the gist of the SoS Method. This single term carries in itself the complete complexity of the SoS Method. Remember how we started out with the concept of "Feeling-good-about-self," and how that is the most important drive in the life of a Substitute Sense of Self–oriented person?

Magic Formula

A way of remembering the gist of the SoS Method: Move away from the addiction to "Feeling-good-about-yourself." First cross out the judgmental word "about" – don't be about your self – be your Self! Next cross out the word "good" – no need to point that out: good is your default state. What remains is: Feel your Self = sense your Self = have a Healthy Sense of Self!

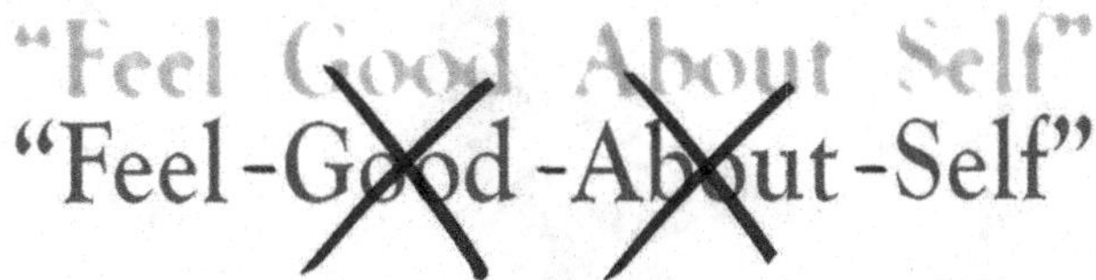

Move away from the addiction to
"Feeling-good-about-yourself."
First cross out the judgmental word
about – don't be about your self – be your Self!

Next cross out the word good – no need to point that one out:
good is your default state.

What remains is
"Feel Self = Sense Your Self!" Have a Healthy Sense of Self!
That is all you have to do!

Summary and Looking Ahead

In this chapter we have offered you a variety of tools and techniques to help you establish and strengthen your Sense of Self. For the time to come, it is best to keep these awareness exercises close at hand. The transition from a Substitute SoS to a Restored SoS is one that needs time and continuous maintenance.

Now that you have moved beyond immediate urgency and your quality of life has drastically improved, you may have time and space to give your patient attention to more technical details about the term Sense of Self and what comes with it.

The next chapters provide relevant details and delve into the scientific/therapeutic aspects of the material. Reviewing the concepts from this angle will certainly help you speed up your change process.

PART IV

Thoughts and Conclusions

Chapter 16

Self and Sense of Self

In the previous parts of this book, you learned that developing a Sense of Self is a process that can be thwarted or hindered, in which case you become dependent on a Substitute Sense of Self. However, if you are willing to do the work, you can regain your Sense of Self, and now you've learned how to do that. In this chapter, you'll find more details on what is meant by *Self* and by *sensing* in "Sense of Self."

Consider this chapter a refresher course and an opportunity to gain deeper insight and understanding.

What Is the Self?

The SoS Theory proclaims that restoring your Sense of Self – if you Lack a Sense of Self, or strengthening it if it is weak – is key to reducing and/or eliminating many aspects of human suffering. So what does this theory consider the Self to be?

The Self is a hard-to-grasp concept. The subtle difference between the Self and the Sense of Self is not so easy to pin down as the understanding seems to jump away the moment you think you've got it.

To make it easier, I see it as a sensory unit that is composed of six layers. Each layer needs to undergo healthy and adequate development in its own specific way so that it can adequately play its part in this healthy, fully functioning unit of interactive layers, the Self.

Note that even *the ability* to sense this Self therefore depends on the opportunity or circumstances to effectively develop these layers and have them unfold their potential and function interactively with one another.

Ideally, the process of developing a Healthy Sense of Self should go smoothly, but all too often people encounter obstacles that hinder this process from taking place.

Please note that the window of time in which this process takes place is of major importance. If that window is missed, the person might be forced to find other ways of giving his or her psyche the much-needed structure – in other words, a *Substitute Sense of Self.*

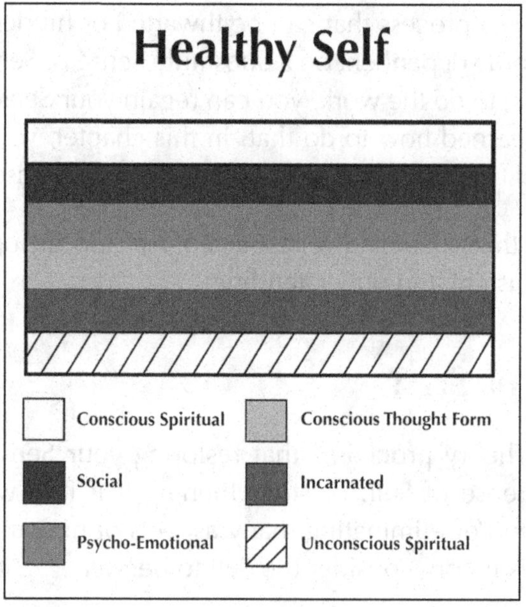

Figure 16.1: Layers of a healthy Self.

Imagine that we are putting the Self under a microscope. Pretend for a while that the Self is an object that we can magnify to better study its structure. What we then see are its six separate layers. Think of the layers as functions of the Self (see Figure 16.1).

Here is how I have named them:

- The first (bottommost) layer is the Unconscious Spiritual Self.
- The second layer is the Incarnated (Body) Self.

- The third layer is the Self Experienced as a Conscious Thought-Form.
- The fourth layer is the Psycho-Emotional Functions.
- The fifth layer is the Social Self.
- The sixth (topmost) layer is the Conscious Spiritual Self.

I have chosen this image because labeling the parts of the Self makes it easier to show what happens when things go wrong and where exactly that aberration is. Understanding how the layers of Self interact within both the caregiver and the child will enhance your understanding of the Sense of Self Method. Insight into how the caregiver's Self influences the Self of the child may also give you more insight into how (and which part of) your caregiver's Self influenced you in your childhood.

Lack of *Sensing,* Not a Lack of Self

I want to make it very clear that it is not a deficiency of Self that I consider to be the root cause of many ailments and dysfunctions, but an inability to *sense* the Self. The ultimate cause of a Lack of Sense of Self (LoSoS) is therefore the obstruction of the development of the ability to sense the Self during crucial moments in a child's upbringing.

The Layers of Self

Layer 1: The Unconscious Spiritual Self

All the layers of Self are carried by, and rooted in, the first foundational layer. You rarely consciously sense this layer because the Self exists within it as something indefinite – as the most primordial identity, the core essence, the pure awareness of Being. It is the foundation of "I" in "I exist." Most religions and spiritual philosophies point to this Self.

"I am."

Layer 2: The Layer of the Incarnated (Body) Self

More tangible and close to conscious awareness is that part of your Self that is aware of your physical existence as a living creature, of being incarnate within a body. This Self, and the sense of it, is also present in animals.

As an infant, you are immediately confronted with your body's demands and pleasures, which causes you to recognize your physical existence. These sensations create strong reactions, and if responded to in an adequate way during your earliest formative years, they helped you begin to develop a healthy sense of your Self.

As with all humans, you required a number of years to learn how to manage your bodily needs and wants, and receiving tender love and care was necessary during this time of life. The development of a sense of physical well-being reinforces your confidence in being in, and with, your body and helps you to (subconsciously) recognize and accept it as "Me."

"I am alive in this body."

Layer 3: The Self Experienced as a Conscious Thought-Form

In this layer of your Self, you experience that you are not just a living creature; you are a functional human organism with potential and limitations. This Self is more conscious than the second layer of Self – a "thought-form" of the psyche – although the sensations when sensing it are difficult to put into words: "I am a human being, a member of the human species."

From this layer arises your awareness of being a distinct and separate being from the entity that gave birth to you. The cut of the umbilical cord reverberates in this layer and awakens your sense of being unique. The development of this layer coincides with the time in your childhood when you discovered the ideas of "mine" and "not mine."

"I am alive as a (separate) human being."

Layer 4: The Psycho-Emotional Functions

With this layer, you experience life, others, and your Self on an emotional level. Your specific, individual Self-essence – your unique psychology, emotions, dispositions, inclinations, talents, weaknesses, strengths, and challenges – become part of your daily awareness of yourself as a unique human being. Through this layer, you use and observe these elements of Self and relate to them directly as "me."

The concept of "I" gains these qualities and characteristics, further developing the psyche and the emotional body as well. A growing sense of "me-ness" helps you consciously distinguish yourself from others: "I feel ..." and "I want ..." and "I believe ..."

"I am me."

Layer 5: The Social Self

The Social Self is formed by the social characteristics of your individual being. It enables you to function in society because it consists of, and influences, your relationships with friends and family, your associations at work, your roles in society, and so on.

The Social Self, if well established and well sensed, helps you contribute to the world. A Social Self that is able to function independently from others offers you the confidence that you, as a sensed Self, will not disappear when things go awry and the outcome is not what you expected. You can recognize yourself in a particular role, function, or status and are able to function interdependently.

"I am me in relation to you."

Layer 6: The Conscious Spiritual Self

The sixth layer of Self may not be considered a necessity for everybody. Many people consider life on earth to be the beginning as well as the end of existence. There is no need for them to include a spiritual reality because it is not realistic or important to them. So the sixth layer is for people who relate to this concept. It is the Conscious Spiritual function of Self, and when it is active, you have closed the circle and fulfilled the task of making the Unconscious Spiritual Self – the beginning of you as a person – conscious. In other words, it emerges into the conscious awareness of those who find that the Self is not simply what is encapsulated by the physical body. This larger

Self, as an identity, includes the preceding layers, which in turn are experienced as part of the "Ultimate," the "Divine."

"I am part of something (divine) that is bigger than myself."

Healthy Layers Form a Healthy Sense of Self

When the layers of the Self function correctly, the Self functions as the home and resting place for the spirit, or essence, of the incarnate "I." From this place, the person forms motivations and values that give shape to his or her life.

I like to compare the Self with the concept of the tonic chord in music: The melody starts from it, develops from it, and returns to it. Even if the complete chord is never sounded explicitly, it, as the root of the melody and harmony, is present throughout the piece, giving it functionality; in fact, it *determines* the functionality of the other pitches used. In just that way, a sensed Self provides functionality to your consciousness and to your psyche. Everything else flows from it, and it holds up the whole.

The Sense of Self

When you are appropriately aware of each layer, you have a *Sense of Self*. Being subconsciously aware of your independent existence as a definite, unique human being forms the backbone of the human psyche; it indicates to you on an ongoing basis that you exist and that you know who you are in that you experience your own being as uniquely yours.

Until recently, the skill of sensing your Self could be developed along one of two paths::

You develop a Natural Sense of Self (a healthy way of sensing your Self and your Being).

or

You develop a Substitute Sense of Self (an unhealthy, distorted way of experiencing your Self and your Being).

As you've come to see, a third possibility – a Restored Sense of Self – is attainable through working with the SoS Method. This method helps you analyze your Substitute Sense of Self and correct your detrimental views and behaviors. By understanding and righting what went wrong, you can achieve a way of experiencing your Self that is close to a Natural Sense of Self. This concept, and how to achieve it, has been discussed throughout this book.

The Natural Sense of Self

A Natural Sense of Self is the most rudimentary and natural awareness of your own Being and of your being alive. In this fortunate situation, every layer of the Self is healthy and, having developed correctly as you grew, performs satisfactorily according to its intended function.

As you've learned, a Natural Sense of Self is an abiding, unshakeable subconscious awareness – the sensation of being an autonomous human being, ultimately independent of others, especially from your primary caregiver(s). A Natural Sense of Self does not refer only to your physical independence, which typically does not happen until adulthood, it refers, most importantly, to your psycho-emotional independence. Having a Natural Sense of Self can be considered the anchor of your being. It is your ultimate inner home, or more exactly, it is who, what, and where you mean when saying or thinking "I" and "me." It is the place from which you act and are motivated.

If you have this type of Sense of Self, it feels natural, unquestionable, foundational, and intrinsic, because it has always been with you and it has grown with age. It is so natural to you that you do not even need to become *consciously* aware of it because of its steady, ongoing presence.

People with a Natural Sense of Self have one important, automatic characteristic in common: the ability to be at rest. A Natural Sense of Self provides you with the one and only safe haven you can expect to have in life; no matter what you do or do not like about yourself, you can always rely on the security of the "I am" bedrock it provides. Being rooted within, it cannot be affected by superficial matters. With a Natural Sense of Self, internal peace and confidence are the rulers of your being, even when the world around you is in turmoil and chaos.

A Natural Sense of Self makes you aware that you are a distinct "someone" different from other "someones." It allows you to fully *be* yourself and enjoy being alive as who you are. It opens you to the experiences of joy and personal satisfaction and allows you to be free to experience what you truly feel, to relate to others authentically without unhealthy filters, and to feel compassion. A Natural Sense of Self is a blessing that permits you to focus on the content of your life and get things done (without being distracted by an eternal search for the Self).

The Substitute Sense of Self

As you've learned, when a Natural Sense of Self does not develop in your early childhood, another structure develops in its place: a Substitute Sense of Self. It makes up for what is missing within you. When you lack a Natural Sense of Self, the foundation of what later turns out to become a compulsive drive for achievement-based approval automatically develops to enable you to experience a fleeting imitation of the lacking Natural Sense of Self.

If you don't develop an ongoing sense of autonomous existence, an inner vacuum is created that leads to an intolerable terror. Subconsciously, you then adopt various unhealthy strategies for getting positive feedback from your caregiver, be it physical, emotional, or verbal. This feedback becomes the closest you can come to obtaining a healthy regard for yourself. These unhealthy, subconsciously self-imposed strategies include various requirements (conditions) for feeling, acting, and/or behaving in certain ways to get recognition. Through successfully meeting these requirements, you "Feel-good-about-self," which is comparable to receiving a sort of validation that you exist. This substitute way of experiencing your self is called a Substitute Sense of Self.

The Substitute Sense of Self is the central part of a complex collection of psycho-emotional motives, goals, feelings, needs, desires, habits, and behaviors that, as a whole, is called the Substitute Sense of Self–oriented system. This system operates a great deal of your psyche and behavior, and has a profound influence on your health, relationships, work, environment, children, and spouse – in general, on your life itself. If you are ruled by this system, it causes a great deal of (unnecessary) suffering for you as well as for the people in your direct environment. Being dependent on a Substitute Sense of Self for your self-experience is a pathological condition, but being able to identify and label it, you can address your Substitute Sense of Self–oriented system and, with enough determination and effort, restore your Sense of Self.

The Layers of the Substitute Sense of Self

When a Substitute Sense of Self is in place, the layers of the Self are affected in particular ways. Let us zoom in on those layers one more time to explore what trauma does to them. We will take an up-close look at what the Self looks like when it is unhealthy or distorted.[1] (This section is not critical for understanding and applying the SoS Method.)

In Figure 16.2, you can see how the layer of the Conscious Thought-Form, the Psycho-Emotional, and the Social layers of Self are stunted, distorted, and/or warped when your Sense of Self does not have a chance to develop normally. They become abnormal when governed by the Substitute Sense of Self–oriented system. Note that the first layer, your spirit or inner essence, is unaffected. It's hard to tell what the development of a dependency on the Substitute Sense of Self might do to the layer of the embodied Self, but if you use your imagination, you could get a sense of the resulting invisible changes that take place in your mental and emotional makeup as well as in your physical body that might result in afflictions or physically detrimental coping mechanisms of some sort later in life.

The following are some brief comparisons between the healthy and distorted forms.

[1] For further and more detailed information, please visit https://healthysenseofself.com to view the videos and graphics showing the unhealthy relationship of the (layers of) Self in relationship to the caregiver, and the interactive influences among the many layers of Self.

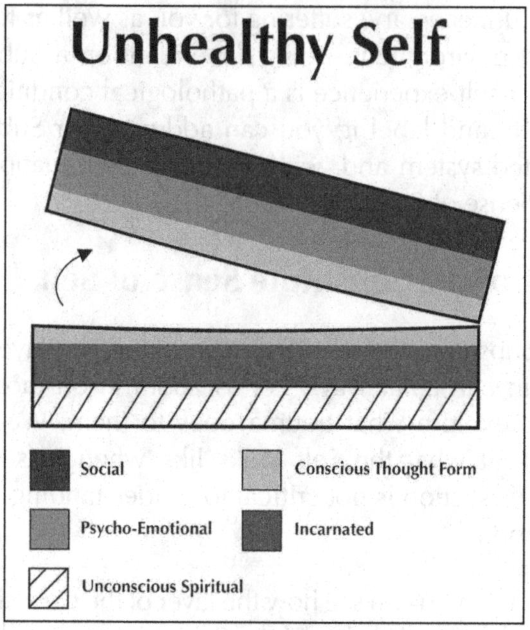

Figure 16.2: The damage done to the layers of Self of a person with a Substitute Sense of Self.

Layer 1: The Unconscious Spiritual Self

This layer forms at the beginning of a person's life. As such there is no change in the potential of the Unconscious Spiritual constellation between the Self of a person with- or without a Sense of Self. Read more on page 327.

Layer 2: The Incarnated (Body) Self

Most modern cultures emphasize that you are (mainly) your mind and your mental accomplishments, and neglect giving healthy attention to your physical presence. Often, you relate to your body in exactly the same way your caregivers paid attention to you when you were an infant: as a means to an end, not as a distinct being worthy of honor, attention, and care for your body's individual needs and wants. In that same way, you see your body as a means to an end, instead of something with its own unique needs and wants that you need to honor and pay attention to. Your body is the vehicle for your spirit (essence) in this world, and being out of touch with your body can become the root of illness. Therefore, later in life, to become a whole person again, you have to relearn that you are also – and first and foremost – your body.

Layer 3: The Self Experienced as Conscious Thought-Form

This layer is particularly vulnerable when you are a growing child without a Natural Sense of Self. A healthy development of this layer is crucial, which makes the timeframe in which it takes place an extremely important one. It is here that you need to get a glimpse of the idea that you are a separate person and you receive the appropriate feedback on your (potential and beginning) identity. It is during this time that the seed is planted for a healthy separation between you and your parent/caregiver. It is during this time that your parent/caregiver really needs to "see" you!

If this process does not take place, you become dependent on obtaining that visibility by complying with your caregiver's wishes for how they need you to be. If your caregiver is unable to give you, or mirror to you, the intrinsic notion that your existence is not dependent on the degree to which you fulfill their wishes, then what you learn is to keep on doing whatever it is that gets you their approval. You keep working on fulfilling their demands and feel a short sense of satisfaction ("Feel-good-about-self") when you are not rejected. On the other hand, you experience the terror of not existing in the eyes of others unless you are able to live up to their expectations; you develop a great fear of being invisible. Others may phisically see you, but your essence is ignored or discounted.

In Figure 16.2, note that the middle layer is divided. In case of a dependency on a Substitute Sense of Self, you have a tear at this level of your Self. As a child, you became enmeshed with your caregiver (see Chapter 7 for an explanation of Enmeshment) to the point that you identify your physical and psycho-emotional layers of Self more as parts of your caregiver rather than as parts of your Self.

One could say that children with a Substitute Sense of Self come to associate a large part of their Incarnated Self, Conscious Thought-Form, and Psycho-Emotional constructs as not belonging to them but rather as belonging to their caregivers.

Therefore, much of this book was devoted to further explanation of how this (third) layer of Self is affected by childhood deprivation of healthy acknowledgment as a unique human being and to studying the impact of that reality on your life.

Layer 4: The Psycho-Emotional Functions

In the case of a Lack of Sense of Self, this layer is especially hard-hit as it can be completely overwhelmed or co-opted by your caregiver as a result of the developmental disability that a Lack of Sense of Self really is. This layer of Self governs your mind, emotions, and motivations – all that is experienced as "me." Here, it is disrupted, distorted, and contaminated by the unhealthy functioning of other layers and specifically by the invasive activity of the caregiver's attempts to be, and stay the center of, the child's existence.[2] The consequence of this leads to further destruction by means of the implementation of detrimental forces, such as Indirect Motivation and Ego-References.

Layer 5: The Social Self

If you are dependent on the outcome of your achievements and on the high standards you have to live up to, you need your circumstances to cooperate with those tasks, so you desperately want to be in control. You cannot afford for things to go awry because that leads you to experience high anxiety or rage. You may even become violent or depressed.

However, there is a discrepancy to be aware of between what you feel and what others see when you are insecure and not forthcoming with others because you are not grounded in your own being. Your social behavior is saturated with influences that stem from your contaminated fourth layer (Psycho-Emotional) layer of Self and your split (third) layer of Self experienced as a Conscious-Thought Form. This causes misunderstandings and dissatisfaction in your interactions with others.

[2] When children are victims of natural disasters and war, we have a whole different story; I do not consider this part of the SoS Method and Theory.

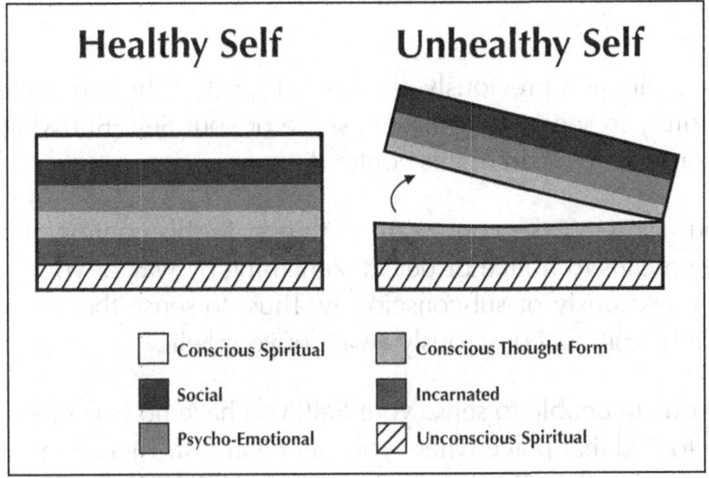

Figure 16.3: Layers of a Healthy Self versus an unhealthy self.

The Substitute Sense of Self – A Natural, Inevitable Development

Even though having a Substitute Sense of Self can lead to lifelong suffering, its development is completely natural and inevitable when a Healthy Sense of Self is not present. People who lack a Sense of Self are not to be blamed for their condition; their childhood experiences created a need for survival strategies, which were made quite below the level of conscious awareness.

If you are lacking a Sense of Self, you have (figuratively or metaphorically) no structure, base, or safe haven to return to. You are comparable to a ship without a set course, rudder, or anchor and thus are at the mercy of the waves of the ocean.

It is like this: For the development of a Natural Sense of Self, acknowledgment from the parent is needed, but if it has not been provided, a painful void exists. This void acts like a Black Hole; it sucks up everything that appears to be usable to gain the desperately needed acknowledgment. Note that acknowledgment and approval are often mixed up in a child's mind, and this can carry over into adulthood. Any outcome of an action or behavior that looks like it would qualify for approval is used to "Feel-good-about-self." That is the only viable goal in your life when you are ruled by a Substitute Sense of Self.

Defining *Sensing*

As mentioned previously, the central tenet of the SoS Method is your ability to sense, or to have a sense of your Self. But what does *sense* or *sensing* mean in this context?

Your senses make you aware of things. In this context, the term *sensing* means to notice or detect something by way of your senses, either consciously or subconsciously. Thus, to sense the Self means being more or less consciously aware of your Self.

If you are unable to sense your Self, you have no way of knowing where to find that place where you can be at rest. There is no way of even knowing there is such a place. All you know is that you have to work (hard) so you can "Feel-good-about-self" for a short-lived moment.

As discussed earlier, experiencing the Self can occur in two ways: directly or indirectly. Let's take another, closer look.

A Direct Relationship with Your Self

To experience existing independently from the outcome of your actions and behavior, you must have a Direct Relationship with your Self. That experience includes having a deep inner knowledge that you *are* a visible person in both body and essence, just like everybody else. There is no doubt in your mind that you can and will be seen and heard by others.

There is a deeply felt sense of "I" as an independently existing being that completely supports the surface experience of "myself" at all times. In your subconscious, you know fully and continuously that you are alive and have the right to exist as who you are. You never doubt that you have the right to occupy space and time in this world. Your sense of "I" is a given that is never doubted.

Having a Direct Relationship with your Self means that there is no need for other tools or tricks to get the sensation of being truly alive. Actions, activities, and behaviors are done because of their immediate and logical goal. For example, "I help my neighbor because he needs my help." My agenda is plain and simple and has no hidden aspects (compare this to "I help my neighbor because my father will be proud of me and like me for it").

When you have a Direct Relationship with your Self, you have good access to your authentic feelings, beliefs, needs, desires, preferences, and motives. No part of the Self is hidden from yourself or from others. There is no need to adopt anyone else's emotions, desires, or preferences or to fake your own for any reason. You know that whatever you do or don't do, your life (i.e., your sense of being allowed to be) is not at stake.

This Direct Relationship with your Self is found only in those who have a Healthy Sense of Self (that is, either a Natural Sense of Self or a Restored Sense of Self). Living with a Substitute Sense of Self creates an Indirect Relationship with the Self.

An Indirect Relationship with Your Self

If sensing the Self only takes place through experiencing a state of "Feeling-good-about-self" based on the positive outcomes of your achievements or the responses from others, you have an *Indirect Relationship with your Self.* An Indirect Relationship with your Self indicates that *self* is referred to (to yourself) by means of something outside your being. That element functions as a vehicle to this surrogate self-experience. It is put in motion when there is a positive outcome to your action or behavior: approval, which is then mistaken for acknowledgment.

Thus the state of "Feeling-good-about-self" is derived from approval, and obtaining it has become a need that is the best possible answer to the craving for acknowledgment. To fulfill this substitute for the need for acknowledgment, you identify with the tasks at hand and the process of getting the desired outcome instead of with yourself as your own person.

It is not that the Self is not there! It is just not sensed.

All your attention and energy goes somewhere else. It is that "somewhere else" that you identify with and mistake for yourself. You could say that a Substitute Sense of Self is a coping mechanism created and maintained over time that you identify with and that represents your "self." The result is that you aren't truly concerned about your life and your own desires and needs, but rather about attaining approval from others, which you have come to associate with the state of "Feeling-good-about-self."

A Sense of Self Is an Action, Not an Object

Contrary to what the language in the preceding discussion may suggest, you do not really *have* some*thing* called a Sense of Self. Rather, this Sense of Self is an awareness – not an object of perception. Though the term *Sense of Self* is a noun, it refers to your continuous acknowledgment of the *presence* of the core of your being. This presence to your own being develops to differing degrees from person to person.

These processes do not have to be consciously recognized as such when all goes well and a Natural Sense of Self is in place. But when healing is necessary, a full awareness of the six layers of Self can prove extremely helpful in restoring what should have developed further in you in the first place: your Natural Sense of Self.

So it seems reasonable to surmise that if the *sensing* is absent, then, in the *subjective* experience, the *Self* also seems to be absent. It might be there, but if you are unable to sense it, you will not know it is there. This is why the concept of "sensing" is important in the SoS Method.

Self-Esteem Requires a Sense of Self

The use of the term *self-esteem* is popular these days, as low self-esteem is often seen as the root cause of many problems. However, self-esteem and Sense of Self are not the same. According to *Merriam-Webster Dictionary*, *self-esteem* is "confidence and satisfaction in one's self; self-respect."

Within the SoS Theory, we cannot entirely stand behind this definition of *self-esteem* because individuals with a Lack of Sense of Self are unable to assess or validate themselves due to their lack of awareness of the Self. What these people do instead is base their confidence on the opinions of others and/or on judgments of others whose opinions they have internalized. The definition as described above is valid only for people with a Healthy Sense of Self. For individuals with a Lack of Sense of Self, self-esteem seems to be built on external validation, which then leads to pride in their achievements. This can be seen as an unhealthy validation that functions as their Substitute Sense of Self.

In general, self-esteem is not a part of the profound Self as it is referred to in "Sense of Self" within the SoS Method.

So, if you want to compare self-esteem, and its counterpart, self-loathing, to your Sense of Self concept, you need to agree with the following truth: Before you can esteem or loathe something, you must first be aware that it exists. You must *sense* it. In other words, you cannot have low or high self-esteem if you do not sense your Self in the first place. Therefore, self-esteem is something that people with a Natural Sense of Self can experience, but those with a Substitute Sense of Self cannot because they are unable to connect with the Self.

It is likely that, for me, this lack of awareness of a Self may have been the reason that my memories of my elementary and high school years are a blur. I may have performed well enough in school, but I was hardly there. I remember things and events not as individual instances but as an exhausting activity of keeping everybody satisfied. In fact, I am tremendously grateful to have been able to get enough insight to identify the hang-ups I was hooked on and free myself from them: fulfilling conditions and being apprehensive about the outcome.

It is my intention that you will gain crucial insight into your own life through the SoS Method. I hope that you will then be able to truly connect to yourself and consequently *own* your life, instead of running around like a juggler trying to keep your plates spinning in the air, like I once did.

Summary and Looking Ahead

You now have an understanding of what the Self is, viewed from the formal perspective of the SoS Theory and Method and its components. For your convenience and ease of understanding, the next chapter will make you familiar with the Maps for Restoring Your Sense of Self in Chapter 17, in which the crucial concepts of the theory are put in visual perspective.

Chapter 17

Maps for Restoring Your Sense of Self

If you have a Natural Sense of Self or a Restored Sense of Self, you do not depend on the outcome of your actions for your Self-experience. Regardless of outcomes, you always know who you are and that you have the right to be-as-you-ARE.

In the preceding chapters, we discussed the harmful psychological, emotional, and physical effects of the Substitute Sense of Self. This chapter offers Maps for Restoring your Sense of Self, which helps you gain a better understanding of how the SoS Method explains the many common problems and pains. The three different maps that you'll find in this chapter (pages 346 and 349), represent the main types of a Sense of Self: 1) Natural (Healthy) Sense of Self; 2) Lack of Sense of Self, which leads a Substitute Sense of Self; and 3) Restored Sense of Self.

Introduction of the Maps for Restoring Your Sense of Self

A Lack of Sense of Self leads to a dependency and/or addiction to a Substitute Sense of Self. This condition can be the root cause of disease and dysfunction because many forms of disease are tied into the degree to wich you are true to your Self. The wider the gap between how you truly are inside and how you show up in the world and in relationships, the more chance of disease. In fact, a Lack of Sense of Self is likely to lead to disease, sooner or later, if nothing is done to change this process.

The map that is most instructive is the Map of a Lack of Sense of Self. Often there are tensions between the different Substitute Sense of Self–oriented strategies, which have an aggravating effect on a person's health and ability to function. The relationship between these concepts is illustrated in the Map of a Lack of Sense of Self.

Comparing these maps will help you understand the importance of taking action to restore your Sense of Self.

Do These Maps Apply to You?

You start life with either an *Adequate* Mirror or a *Distorted* Mirror. If your caregivers held up an adequate mirror, you will most likely not need these maps, as you won't show any of the signs or symptoms displayed within them.

Adequate Mirroring leads to the development of a Healthy Sense of Self, which results in people who experience their problems and pains on a Quality-of-Life Level. While this doesn't guarantee an entirely problem-free life, no unnecessary stress is added to everyday difficulties, as there is no unhealthy preoccupation with Substitute Sense of Self–oriented strategies. Those who grow up with adequate Mirroring do not struggle with dependency complications that make even the most ordinary problems harder to solve. Life can be hard enough as it is!

When your caregivers turn out to be *inadequate mirrors,* you enter the realm of the concepts depicted in the Map of a Lack of Sense of Self. You develop a Substitute Sense of Self. That means that you come to depend on Ego-References, which are supposed to lead to parental approval or a "Feeling-good-about-self" state.

Growing up without an adequate mirror has consequences later in life. High anxiety is caused by the constant drive to achieve the Hidden Goal and fulfill Hidden Agendas. This will be experienced throughout your life unless you restore your Sense of Self.

This kind of anxiety is not present in the lives of people who had adequate Mirroring in their childhoods and were able to develop a Natural Sense of Self. It is normal and natural to experience a Quality-of-Life fear from time to time. However, these fears are tremendously amplified in people who also have Substitute Sense of Self–oriented fears. The ever-present anxiety can lead to exhaustion, depleting the body and mind of energy and health.

Looking at the causes of your problems and pains through the light of the SoS Method leads to two important conclusions:

1. When working with the principles for restoring your Sense of Self, you resolve the root of your problems and pains on a fundamental level.
2. You don't need a doctor to resolve your issues. You can help yourself by using the SoS Method.

The purpose of the maps is to show the differences in complexity of mindset between the paths you travel if:

1. You have a Natural Sense of Self.
2. You have a Lack of Sense of Self and have developed a dependency on a Substitute Sense of Self.
3. You have worked with the SoS Method and developed a Restored Sense of Self.

When you glance over the three maps, it becomes obvious: the second map is the most complex one. To live a healthy and productive life, you need to make life less complicated. This is exactly the goal of restoring your Sense of Self, which as you can see in the third map, leads to a less complicated existence.

The Maps as a Tool in Your Healing Toolkit

Now let's look at these maps. What are the various elements that you find in them? Each map contains the basic concepts of the SoS Method. Thorough understanding of these maps will help you get the gist of the SoS Method and will make it easier for you to gain a Restored Sense of Self.

Map of a Natural Sense of Self

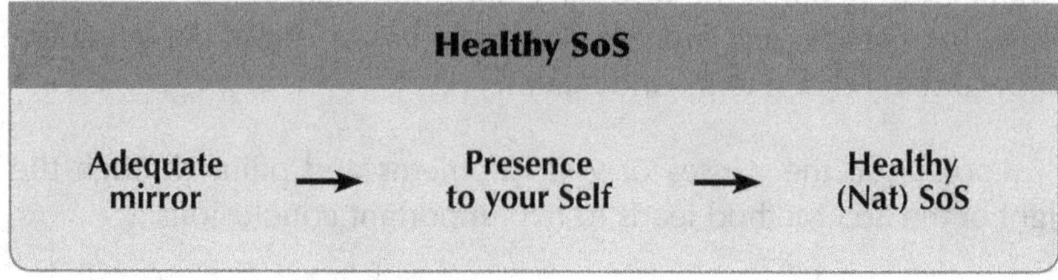

Figure 17.1: Map of a Healthy Sense of Self.

The first map represents the best-case scenario with the best possible result. When you have been acknowledged through adequate Mirroring by your caregiver, life is straightforward. Life is never simple, but things are more clear cut compared to the life of a person who is haunted by the perceived need to live up to conditions and to reach achievements. This means you can focus on the content of your life, on what you want to do, and how to get there.

What distinguishes a person with a Healthy Sense of Self is what it is all about: presence to your Self with a full awareness of your own personhood and knowing that your life is yours. Adequate decision-making that is of service to your Self is its positive result.

Map of a Lack of Sense of Self

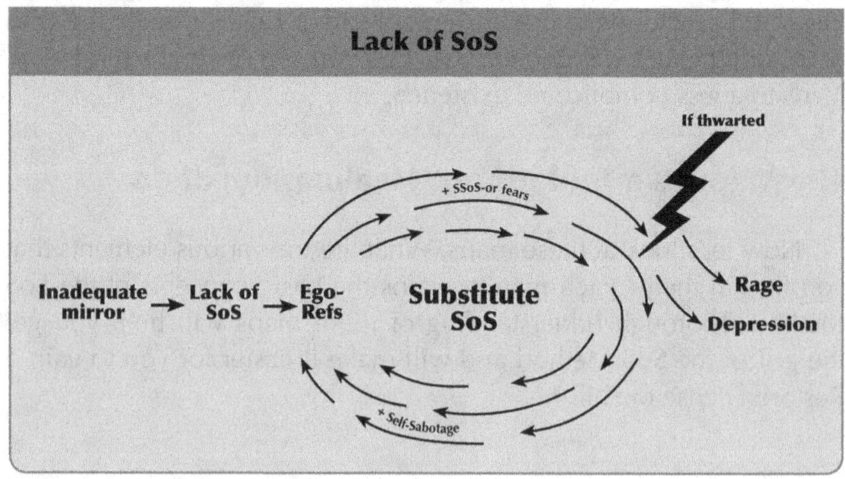

Figure 17.2: Map of a Lack of Sense of Self.

This map shows the root causes of a big part of human suffering: inadequate and distorted Mirroring as well as its immediate effect, a lack of acknowledgment of the child as a "real" person. The result of this inadequate Mirroring is that the child does not develop a Natural Sense of Self (and therefore a Healthy Sense of Self), which results in a Lack of Sense of Self.

Where there is a Lack of Sense of Self, there is an inner emptiness that forces you to develop a dependency to experiencing your "self" by means of a Substitute Sense of Self. This structure provides the closest thing to a self-experience that a person without a Healthy Sense of Self can get.

A Lack of Sense of Self leads to the formation of Ego-References, which form the conditions that you, as a child, decided you needed to fulfill. These conditions differ for each individual. Whenever successfully satisfied, these conditions enable the person to achieve fleeting moments of "Feel-good-about-self," which functions as a Substitute Sense of Self.

The arrows linking the concepts represent the force of nature: if inadequate or distorted Mirroring happens, then a flow automatically begins between the empty place inside the child's psyche and the Substitute Sense of Self. It is as if the child thinks: *"I am not being acknowledged as an independent person. I have no Sense of Self. I need some other sort of self-structure to be able to function. The next best thing for me is to make my caregiver happy so I will at least get attention and hopefully some positive feedback."*

The circle of arrows refers to the endless compulsive repetition of this pattern, which is inevitable because the experience of the Substitute Sense of Self must be renewed repeatedly. This circular pattern is the unhealthy "path of dependency," as opposed to the healthy path of living your own life.

Substitute Sense of Self–oriented fears drive a person's motivations. There are several types of anxiety at play that keep creating enormous amounts of stress and self-sabotage. The goal is always to maintain the Substitute Sense of Self. As long as no interference thwarts the flow, there is no rage or depression. There is a continuous severe level of anxiety though, about whether you can achieve your Substitute Sense of Self or, if you experience it, about what you have to do to keep it.

- A few examples of Substitute Sense of Self-related fears include common fear of failure, fear of abandonment, fear of not being able to function, and fear of change.
- Anxiety is a form of fear that can be very strong yet vague at the same time because its origin is often not identifiable. Anxiety is connected to being dependent on a Substitute Sense of Self for self-experience.

In the SoS Method, Self-sabotage is seen as nature's way of pointing you in the right direction, but you experience it as a big nuisance that thwarts your ability to achieve a Substitute Sense of Self. Please note that what commonly is referred to as Self-Sabotage really is the sabotage of the Substitute Sense of Self[3].

Imagine you are a singer and you are scheduled to perform. But the day before your concert you get laryngitis. This could indicate that this performance was based on Indirect Motivation. Most likely you were not focusing on performing music for music's sake but only to "Feel-good-about-yourself" by doing so.

These factors generate untold levels of stress on top of the fundamental, psycho-emotional stress of trying to function without a Natural Sense of Self. This combination of stresses is exactly the reason why a Lack of Sense of Self is the root cause of so many seemingly unrelated diseases and dysfunctions. Due to the extreme levels of continuous stress, a person suffering from a Lack of Sense of Self is more at risk of falling victim to disease and dysfunction than a person with a Healthy Sense of Self.

What happens if your attempt to reach the Substitute Sense of Self is thwarted? The immediate result is *rage*. Failure to achieve or maintain a Substitute Sense of Self is felt as Annihilation, and the obstacle in your path is addressed with tremendous rage. This rage is totally out of proportion with the obstacle.

[3] For more on Substitute Sense of Self-Sabotage please read: *How to Overcome Insomnia all by Yourself, A Healthy Sense of Self Guide to Getting a Good Night's Sleep.*

When you have a Lack of Sense of Self, you are dependent on the outcome of your actions for your Substitute Sense of Self. Sometimes, due to circumstances, you are forced to give up trying to realize your "Holy Grail." Imagine that you are forced to give up what is most important to you. What do you have left to live for? The result of being thwarted in your quest is depression: you are deactivated; you lose inspiration; you "deflate"; you feel unable to do what you perceive to matter most in your life, which is gaining approval and a Substitute Sense of Self.

Map for Restoring your Sense of Self

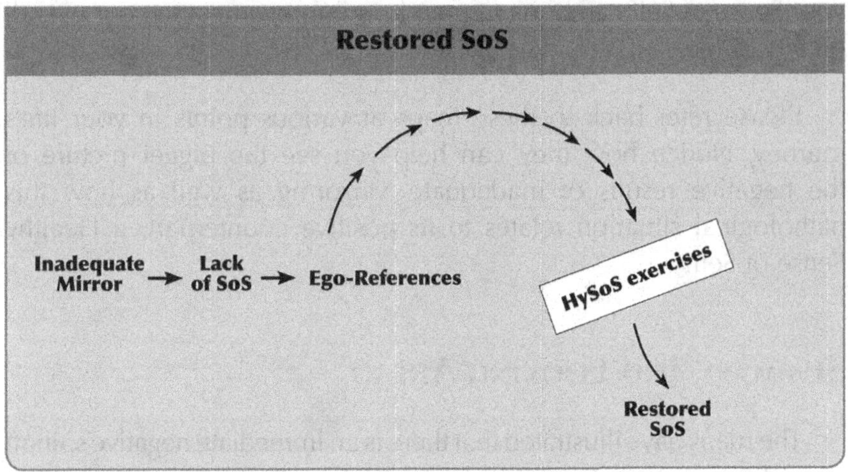

Figure 17.3: Map of a Restored Sense of Self.

A Restored Sense of Self is the result of going through the recovery process, which results in a Restored Sense of Self. The way to interrupt the vicious cycle of having to fulfill the requirements for your Substitute Sense of Self is shown in the third map, the flow that leads to a Restored Sense of Self. Despite having been subject to an inadequate mirror as a child, even after living with a Lack of Sense of Self, you can restore your Sense of Self – at any stage of life – by using the affirmations and doing the activities described in the previous part of this book.

Restoring your Sense of Self allows you to live your life through Direct Motivation. Ego-References have no influence on, or power over your goals anymore. Choices are made in the present and based on what is wanted in the moment. There are still issues and stresses to cope with, but they play out on a Quality-of-Life Level and solutions for overcoming these stressful situations don't cause rage and depression the way they once did. Anger and fear become manageable because you know what to do to restore balance in yourself and within your relationships.

The type of healing activities offered to you earlier are crucial to freeing yourself from the never-ending quest to achieve a Substitute Sense of Self. When done with dedication and commitment, restoring your Sense of Self can bring tremendous improvement to your overall quality of life.

Please refer back to these maps at various points in your life's journey. Notice how they can help you see the bigger picture of the negative results of inadequate Mirroring as well as how this pathological situation relates to its positive counterpart, a Healthy Sense of Self!

Summary and Looking Ahead

The maps have illustrated that there is an immediate negative spinoff toward many exhausting and intense emotional experiences when one is dependent on a Substitute Sense of Self. Those strong emotions, in turn, can lead to physical ailments, addiction, insomnia, or aspects of depression, such as the decision to end one's life. Please keep these maps in mind as you turn the page to the last chapter and see how the SoS Method has found a solution for various types of ailments.

Chapter 18
The SoS Solution

The SoS Method is all about restoring your Sense of Self. With a Healthy Sense of Self, you are more resilient to problems that are widespread in this day and age, and that can have a major impact on your own quality of life as well as on the lives of your dear ones.

Even though I am neither a medical doctor nor a psychiatrist, I dare to argue that there are many good reasons for professionals in the fields of psychology and neurology to investigate the relationship between depression, insomnia, substance abuse, and a Lack of Sense of Self. Once the correlation becomes more evident, we might even gain access to a solution for these problems.

The emphasis of the SoS solution to these problems lies in what you can do for yourself to help resolve these issues. It is, after all, a Self-help Method.

Because I wasn't officially diagnosed, I can't say with certainty whether or not I suffered from clinical depression during all those years I battled with insomnia and was easily provoked into a raging fury. Therefore, speaking formally about depression would be out of my wheelhouse. However, I do know that my insomnia had a profound effect on my life and I was overly concerned with the quality of my musical performance, mainly to preserve some sort of "Feel-good-about-self" state.

What I have offered you in this book is my way out of it all. I achieved this by learning to actively sense my Self as well as becoming aware of the difference between my *Real Self* and being ruled by something I mistook for a Sense of Self.

To truly sense my Self, I had to go down a very different path. Once I discovered that one, I was able to leave the whole map behind and carve that new path, the path of my own life, the way I wanted it.

I sincerely wish your takeaway from this book is that the process of sensing your Self in a direct way will lead you out of the darkness. Directly sense your Self through your breathing and through your notion that you are a human being. It is the most definite way to solve many issues, as it is not dependent on you meeting any self-imposed conditions at the cost of Annihilation. You are enough already, and no one and nothing can take that away from you.*

* Spoken within reasonability of course.

Insomnia

The inability to fall asleep or stay asleep is an occasional problem for some people and an ongoing nightly problem for others. In the latter case, we are talking about insomnia that has a detrimental impact on your life.

As with depression, the cause for insomnia is often unclear. Why do sleeping problems arise in the first place? Sleeping is a natural process, just like eating – you need it to function. If you are unable to fall asleep or stay asleep, there must be something interfering with this natural process. But doctors and researchers have not found a definitive answer to this question.

A lot of people suffer from lack of sleep, and it affects society more than you might think. (You can find convincing numbers on the Internet.) I will simply say here what has not yet been said: Insomnia stifles a person's development and Self-realization; it influences mood and social behavior, productivity, health, and even one's own and others' safety. Yet, for many people, the problem remains unresolved and the harmful consequences continue.

The medications most often used to treat insomnia are sedatives, antidepressants, and antianxiety pills. Alongside the fact that it takes quite a while to figure out the right type and dosage for each individual, these medications can be harmful and addictive. They alter the brain's chemistry and leave you passive in the process of regaining your good (sleeping) health.

It seems clear that sleeplessness is a symptom of an underlying problem, and by silencing this symptom, these medications merely mask the bigger issue. Not only do you become dependent on the medication, it also prevents you from getting in touch with what caused the problem in the first place and beginning the true healing process. If you don't address the underlying issue, you may enable other ailments and dysfunctions to develop.

The Way out of Insomnia

Although medical attention and taking medication might be necessary steps in some cases of insomnia, this is what the SoS Method can do for you:

> *Insomnia can be cured by changing the motives and needs of your unhealthy, Substitute Sense of Self–oriented behavior into healthy (directly motivated) ones, where you become your own purpose.*

Insomnia can be relieved if you learn to make the mental shift from the illusion of having to continuously feed a Substitute Sense of Self, which causes you to experience life as a series of performances – with the accompanying fear of failure – and blocks you from experiencing reality. You need to get your head and your heart grounded in reality: this IS *your* life – you'd better give it the full 100 percent! If you are no longer dependent on the outcome of actions or behaviors or the approval of others, if you can stand up straight, be yourself, and become truly independent, chances are you have found the ultimate solution to your insomnia.

Fear may be the root cause of the inability to sleep well.

- Fear of losing your hard-earned Substitute Sense of Self by falling asleep.
- Fear of not being able to function the next day so you won't be able to work your way up to your Substitute Sense of Self.

- Fear that others or circumstances will be in your way and cause Hindrances (the need to control others and circumstances).
- Fear that you may sabotage yourself by not sleeping!

Most of these fears relate to your efforts to obtain recognition/validation from others, to your indirect ways (Hidden Agendas) of obtaining attention and respect and your (perceived) dependency on the outcome of these efforts. The fact that most of them operate on a subconscious level makes matters even more complicated. To access what is subconsciously working for you – or against you – you need to be prepared to do a lot of *getting to know yourself*. You need to engage in introspection, recognize patterns in your thoughts and feelings, and understand how they lead you to experiencing yourself and your life the way you do.

The end result of your effort can be a whole lot more than just sleeping better; it can lead you to a better life! But it will only work for you if you do the work.

Encouragement to Look Within

Even though doctors and researchers have not found an answer to insomnia, there is a chance you know it yourself, on a subconscious level. You can get to the root of the problem by getting in touch with your Self. This is the path the SoS Method encourages you to take, because *you* have the power to put an end to the agonizing hours of restlessness while your friend or spouse is snoring their way to a productive and happy tomorrow. Make sure you use that power to investigate what is going on within yourself!

For step-by-step guidance, check out the Sense of Self Method online course at https://online.healthysenseofself.com.

Depression

Many people are labeled as being *depressed*. Potential causes may be well known but the fact that personal circumstances vary so much and are dominant factors means that the symptoms of depression are, too often still, suppressed by pharmaceuticals and that no actual cure is supported. Some people cope on their own; others receive medication and/or talk theraphy. These remedies seem to help some people, whereas, in others, the "remedies" actually worsen the depression, not to mention the many side effects. Medical professionals across different fields have not found a definite or universal cause of depression, thus making a cure difficult to attain.

Root Causes of Common Depression

The SoS Method sheds new light on depression, revealing what could be an important key in solving the mystery.

There are underlying, personal conditions that often result in unique behavior patterns. A person with a Healthy Sense of Self may therefore need a different approach to healing depression than a person with a Lack of Sense of Self. That said, I believe that people with a Healthy Sense of Self are much less susceptible to depression, if at all.

The thesis of the SoS Theory states that the quality of your life is strongly correlated with the quality of your Sense of Self. Think about the role a Hidden Goal plays in the life of a person who is addicted to a Substitute Sense of Self and how it affects them. It leads to the startling conclusion that one major cause of depression lies, ultimately, in the lack of a Healthy Sense of Self. Since this connection between depression and Sense of Self might not seem immediately obvious, let's go into more detail.

Looking at the Map of a Lack of Self (see page 346), we can see how the jagged line (it looks like a lightening bolt) indicates the onset of depression when a person realizes his or her Hidden Goal is forever thwarted, which makes reaching the "Feel-good-about-self" state impossible.

Depression Due to Changes in Circumstances Outside Yourself

> *Depression occurs in people with a Lack of Sense of Self when the attempts to improve on an action or behavior, perceived as crucial to achieving parental approval, become permanently obsolete; when the person to whom this action is (subconsciously) directed is no longer available (e.g., has died).*

Note that I do not say hindered or postponed – no, it is forever off limits! There is no hope to accomplish what is perceived as absolutely necessary to avoid Annihilation. Ego-References are a pattern of behavior that is firmly locked into the mind. They come forth from Early Childhood Survival Strategies, which after all are a *survival mechanism* to cope with what is missing (the acknowledgment, on a fundamental level, of you as your own person) by working on getting *approval*. Now if these agonizing intentions and efforts are pushed in the direction of what has become a dead-end street because approval is unavailable (e.g., the caregiver passes away), then the person's direction and meaning for life falls away. Since all of this happens on a subconscious level, it is not recognized and therefore the resulting depression is not addressed.

A Few Illustrative Scenarios

Example 1: You might have broken your arm while your Ego-Reference was becoming a swimming champion. Your father was a well-known sportsman, and he would be proud of you if you won a gold medal and this is your best chance. Now you have injured your arm, and the doctor told you that it is never going to work properly again so you better start looking for another career. If you were a person with a Healthy Sense of Self, losing that way of expressing yourself would certainly lead to feelings of grief, but you would be able to cope with it. Soon enough, you would adapt to your new situation and find something else you liked well enough to pursue as a career.

However, if being an athlete was (also) the only way to get some sort of access to your father, whose approval you desperately need to "Feel-good-about-self," being unable to compete in swimming competitions would have a deeply disabling impact on you. Now the way to your father's recognition is cut off forever, and that may lead you to depression or even suicide. Anticipation of feeling unable to reach the Fgas state would indeed be a *depressing* prospect, wouldn't it? There would be feelings of hopelessness about ever being able to feel like a person who really exists in your father's eyes.

Example 2: Meet three siblings: Janice, Jake, and Gus. Janice is a lovely little girl who has adored animals ever since she was exposed to them during a family vacation when they spent a few weeks on a farm. She wasn't fond of doing homework, and she did not have a knack for math. "When I grow up I am going to work on a farm," she used to say.

Jake was a clever boy, highly intelligent and with a broad interest in science. He ended up going to a good college where he developed a special interest in chemistry. He was also a good swimmer, and, at some point, an Ivy League university convinced him to join their team.

Gus, just like his father, loved pop music and knew everything about it. He also was a talented classical cellist and loved pursuing this branch of music professionally so he could become an orchestra musician.

Their father was a top-notch sportsman who adored pop music. He once confessed that he'd wanted to be a doctor but that never worked out. Imagine that these three children share a Hidden Agenda of truly being seen by their father, who didn't spend much time with them due to his busy professional life. Each of them tries to get closer to him in their own way: Janice, by becoming a veterinarian instead of a farmer; Jake, by spending more energy on becoming a good swimmer instead of a chemist; and Gus, by setting his sights on becoming a lead singer in a pop group instead of a classical cellist. Each one of these hardworking and well-meaning youngsters is oblivious of their Hidden Goal (to finally gain their father's acknowledgment). They are desperate to show off their achievements to their father and have no idea why they depend so heavily on the outcome of their activities to "Feel-good-about-self."

Most of us are well aware that children have a tendency to want to please their parents, and that parents have a crucial and powerful position in their children's lives. But it is often overlooked that this power can become a dominant factor, a dictator in the mind of the child (and later the adult). In those cases, a person can be unable to develop the ability to get in touch with or sense their innermost Self. What many fail to recognize is that these children/people mistake the feelings that accompany getting approval for Self-realization. What a misleading concept! We need to understand that dependency on outside approval/validation is what lies at the root of some forms of depression.

These examples may seem farfetched to you, but please make an effort to track (in your mind) a person's journey from infancy to childhood to adulthood. Begin, for example, with a small boy growing up without a Natural Sense of Self. Follow that boy over time and notice what he goes through, the amount of time and energy spent proving to his parents that he is worthy of their acknowledgment. Follow him all the way through to that moment of ultimate hopelessness of ever achieving that sense of acceptance. This scenario tends to be quite common these days, where parents have increasingly less time to dedicate to their children, so that we can consider it an epidemic. Just like depression.

Warning for People in Recovery

It is important to recognize the possibility of developing a "forced" depression. If you decide to restore and/or strengthen your Sense of Self, there will be moments when you feel deflated, depressed for not being able to follow through with your Early Childhood Survival Strategy. After all, it *is* a survival strategy that has been with you for a long time and it has indeed helped you survive until now. Your subconscious may not give it up easily. Rather than fighting it, try to respect it and gently guide yourself out of these old habits.

Hope

If depression is indeed a result of not having been able to build up your Healthy Sense of Self, there is hope. The answer to overcoming depression is within reach: restore your Sense of Self! People with a Lack of Sense of Self spend much of their time and energy on getting approval. Their happiness is completely dependent on outsiders over whom they have no control. The moment they become truly independent and able to live life for their Selves, they are free and will be less prone to depression.

The Way out of Depression

How do you restore your Sense of Self? Remember, as discussed previously, you will need to grow the awareness that your life is about *you* as an independent person – not about living through the approval of others. You will have to learn and practice this new awareness to the point that it will rule out your old ways. Here is where reconditioning comes into play: you have to recondition your Sense of Self to a new program, one that focuses on the Self. Chapters 11 and 14 describe how to do that. You can find more information on this subject at www.healthysenseofself.com.

With a Restored Sense of Self, the behaviors you subconsciously used to identify yourself and that you perceived to be required for your survival are no longer needed or even desired. You no longer need to fill the inner sense of emptiness to "Feel-good-about-self," because the void is gone. Indirect Motivation loses its appeal, as Ego-References and Hidden Agendas are no longer important for your survival. You have replaced your Hidden Goals with your true goals.

Here is an example:

Your child has a performance coming up. You feel you need to go because you want to be a good mother. However, you have a conflict at work that you think cannot wait. If your motivation for either activity is rooted in realizing your Hidden Agendas, to get to "Feel-good-about-self" and satisfy your need for a Substitute Sense of Self, you are in trouble. With a Restored Sense of Self, you are better equipped to distinguish the priority between the activities, and you will not suffer or become upset if one of them doesn't get done. There is no agony, possibly just annoyance (a Quality-of-Life-level experience).

While you were dependent on a Substitute Sense of Self, you worked hard to do your best and avoid the ever-lurking (Fear of) Annihilation. Now, with a Healthy Sense of Self, you may still work on the same things, but the motivation is different. Indirect Motivation has become direct. The actions that you undertake have lost that extreme part of their emotional, Substitute Sense of Self–oriented charge, because now you (choose to) do them simply because you experience them as pleasant or enjoyable or because they need to be done.

You no longer have a Hidden Goal that keeps you spellbound, and therefore you no longer experience interferences as blocks on the road to a Hidden Goal. That means there is no longer any reason for anger or depression. You look at life with your own mind, through your own eyes, and in the awareness that it's your own inner compass guiding you. You know that your body is the home of your spirit and that your life is about *you*. You sense that you *are* already and that you are free to choose to *do* or *not to do* things based on your own Direct Motivation.

Addiction to Alcohol

There are many types of addiction: the use of alcohol and other substances, gambling, shopping, the Internet, work, and sex, among others. Due to the nature of my quest and background, I would like to zoom in on one of them: the addiction to alcohol. However, I invite you to apply what is being said below to any other addiction and you'll find out whether it is equally valid.

The degree of likelihood of becoming addicted to "Feeling-good-about-self" through achieving the anticipated desired outcome and getting approval depends on your type of motivation. With a Healthy Sense of Self, you are not very likely to go that route; it requires the Indirect Motivation that accompanies a Lack of Sense of Self. So it is with the addiction to drugs and alcohol. In this section, I would like to make it clear that I believe a Lack of Sense of Self is the root cause of people becoming alcoholics, ruining their lives, and ultimately succumbing to the ill effects of this addiction, which I do not think is a disease although it eventually turns into one.

Research in the field of addiction has yielded incredible results during the last decade. Many new treatment centers have been built, and there is a much deeper understanding of what substance abuse does to our brain chemistry. We know how our genetic makeup can be a decisive factor in the alcohol-related breakdown process in the liver; for example, some people lack certain enzymes that are necessary for that process. We now know how prolonged abuse of substances tears down the protective walls of our cells, which immediately increases our need of substance use. It is a very hard cycle to break. But how do people become alcoholics in the first place? The Disease Model[1] doesn't give an answer to that most important question. We need to find these reasons because only once we know why something happens can we make a change so it does not happen anymore.

Dual Problem

Dependency on a Substitute Sense of Self is an addiction in and of itself, and it follows the same rules as all the other addictions in that it can only happen when *you are not present to your Self.*

The same is true for an addiction to drugs or alcohol, all the while being aware that it destroys your body, your mind, and ultimately your life. Nobody in their right mind would let that happen. Nobody who is aware of being first and foremost a person, which implies understanding the body's need to recuperate from damage done by a certain amount of alcohol use, would cross that boundary on a regular basis. Only when your spirit has been prevented from fully taking possession of your body and learning to live with it and protect it, can you fall victim to this self-destructive behavior. When there is no Self that is sensed in your body and mind, there is no Self being activated. Now your body and mind fall victim to random, automatic behavior, which in the case of substance abuse leads to a huge complication.

The use of drugs or alcohol diminishes your willpower and your intelligence. Unfortunately, the addicted person has to overcome a dual problem: addiction leads to intolerable cravings that need to

[1] E. M. Jellenek fathered the disease concept of alcoholism, defining alcoholism as a medical disease with the purpose of liberating addicts from the stigma of being labeled as sinners and bad people. http://www.dualdiagnosis.org.

be dominated. But to be successful in mastering this addiction, they need to restore their Sense of Self. This, however, is not a task that someone with reduced intelligence and motivation can accomplish.

AA and other treatment institutions have proven to be quite successful in keeping people sober for a certain period of time. However, the success rates of twelve-step programs like AA and NA are notoriously difficult to maintain. Based on the organization's own 2007 random survey, 33 percent of the 8,000 North American members it surveyed had remained sober for over ten years. Twelve percent had been sober for five to ten years; 24 percent had been sober for one to five years; and 31 percent were sober for less than a year.[2] These numbers are not indicative of a satisfying success rate but could largely increase if help were actively offered to restore members' Senses of Self.

The Way out of Addiction

The SoS Theory claims that a Lack of Sense of Self is the root cause of every form of addiction. The addiction to substance abuse has a special place, as there is more to it than a Lack of Sense of Self. The alcoholic or drug addict loses the ability to control and adjust him- or herself because of the effect that the addiction itself has on that person.

Alcoholics can be compared to suicide bombers who give up their lives for a political cause or a religious belief. They can only do that when they do not have a sense of what is at stake: the gift of life (your Self). The preciousness of that gift, life, makes us all equal and therefore similar in our needs and wants. If you have never learned to connect with your Self and value your life, you do not know its value in the first place. You are not even really aware that you can lose it forever!

Implement Sense of Self Method in Treatment Centers

Therefore it would be great if the SoS Method could become a part of every treatment center's curriculum. Restoring the Sense of Self is a great first step in avoiding relapse. When people become aware of the

[2] Kevin Gray. "Does AA Really Work? A Round-Up of Recent Studies." *The Fix*. 01/29/12. www.thefix.com/content/the-real-statistics-of-aa7301.

preciousness of their body and mind, they are less likely to surrender it to addictions of any sort. When in recovery from alcohol or drug abuse, the person needs to truly feel that they have something to lose. That *something* is their Self.

Resources

For strong and effective guidelines for recovery from addictions, in general, I recommend the literature available from the Washington State Alcohol and Drug Clearing House (www.adaiclearinghouse.org), or from your local authority on this subject. I recommend the following for learning more about the addictive nature of substance abuse and its effects on the brain and lifestyle:

- *Staying Sober: A Guide for Relapse Prevention* by Terence T. Gorski and Merlene Miller (Thorofare, NJ: Independence Press, 1986)
- *Under the Influence* by James Robert Milam and Katherine Ketcham (New York: Bantam Books, 1984)
- *Beyond the Influence: Understanding and Defeating Alcoholism* by Katherine Ketcham and William F. Asbury (New York: Bantam Books, 2000)

There are many good resources out there about recovery. For substance abuse, which the SoS Method considers a complication of the addiction to a Substitute Sense of Self, you might also consider treatment in an addiction treatment program.

Compulsiveness

People are creatures of habit; we all know that. Some habits are harmless, and others turn into addictions or compulsions. Often, a very thin line separates a positive dedication from a negative addiction.

Compulsive Training

Music students – as well as other performers, such as athletes – at any age, are encouraged to practice more and more because they are made to believe that practice makes perfect, that is ... perfect practice.

As you become more seasoned in playing your sport or practicing your music, you may find out that dedicating a certain number of hours to training may open the possibility of becoming better in whatever you do. But it is not only the amount of time you train that counts, it is also the mindset and motivation behind it.

Unfortunately, not everyone has optimized these criteria.

You practice the way you are!

That means if you have a Healthy Sense of Self, you practice with a Healthy Sense of Self. You are operating from Direct Motivation and your efforts are of service to becoming a better player for the sake of becoming a better player. But the opposite is true as well: If you have a Lack of Sense of Self, your training strategy is focused on gaining a Substitute Sense of Self. By now, you can imagine what the result will be when playing ball or making music is used as a Vehicle. The outcome of the activity determines the degree to which you are able to feel safe from Annihilation. You may routinely practice until exhaustion sets in. Over time, this can lead to professional injuries due to muscle tension or overstraining.

My Own Dependency

My own practice habits as a professional bassoonist were pretty compulsive. Here is how that played out: In the year I started my long-term career with the Amsterdam Philharmonic Orchestra, I was going on my first major tour to Japan. We were to give a great number of concerts in many different cities. There was no time for practicing at all.

Our instruments were transported in a climate-controlled truck, and so three days before leaving, the roadies would collect our instruments. But I wanted to practice until the very last minute and was very concerned about not having my instrument available. I asked to see the managing director and explained my concern to him and that I wanted to be exempt from having to give up my instrument three days early. To my astonishment, he replied: "Don't worry about it. You'll be all right!" He was obviously familiar with a certain degree of compulsiveness, and it was considered something you had to learn to manage.

To apply the example to yourself, the activities described above can be replaced with any other activity that is relevant in your life, such as preparing for speaking engagements, acting roles, or presentations to board members.

Closing

The SoS Method claims that true and complete recovery from *any* addiction requires a shift from experiencing the Substitute Sense of Self through "Feeling-good-about-self" to the real, adequate, and healthy way of sensing your Self, which includes sensing your body and cultivating the inner knowing that you are your own person. This book now has come to an end. Your journey of curing your motivation continues. May you experience lots of positive changes in your own quality of life and become instrumental in helping as many others as you can to do the same. Together we can have an important and positive impact on our world!

Afterword

Reflections on the degree of difficulty when healing from an addiction to a Substitute Sense of Self ... and why it is worthwhile anyway!

Every day, my Sense of Self grew and more of "me" than just my mind started to trust that, one day, I would be able to completely let go of my need for a Substitute Sense of Self. I used a Substitute Sense of Self as a crutch for over sixty years because I didn't have anything else to hold on to when I lacked a Sense of Self, but now I see that it was fiction. I held this belief for such a long time that it was tough to let it go. Persistence and the appropriate tools, such as the exercises offered in the SoS Method, guided imagery, and EFT, helped me greatly along on my chosen path.

I hope these final thoughts inspire you to never give up working on overcoming what went wrong in your early childhood and adolescence. I say, "went wrong," but who am I to conclude that things really went wrong; maybe figuring out these things was meant to be part of your life's journey. Whether there is, or ever will be, for you or for me, a "happily ever after" is an unanswerable question. Improvement, though, is certain!

For me, it all started when, as a very young child, I felt I had to convince my mother that I was worth being taken into account. I believed that I had to live up to her expectations to make that happen, so I engaged in fulfilling those conditions that would lead to her approval, which in turn developed into my Early Childhood Survival Strategy. Over time, these strategies were buried deep down in my subconscious mind, where they ruled my entire existence as my ultimate motivator. On a conscious level, I was not aware of it, and it would take many years before I would fully grasp the scope of this problem and its haunting effect on my life.

When I started the process of healing myself from the dependency on a Substitute Sense of Self, I did not imagine that it was all about freeing myself from an addiction to parental approval, both in real life as well as internalized criteria. The memory of that surprise and my own body's lack of immediate cooperation with the changes that were being made for my personal well-being still shock me. After such a long period of denial and self-neglect, my system didn't recognize or accept any of my crucial discoveries at face value. One by one, I had to remove the building blocks of my survival strategy and tear down the wall that separated my real Self from living my own (real) life.

During the years I began implementing my Restored Sense of Self, the pull of the Black Hole was astonishingly strong. At moments, I would be caught off guard while (finally) having fun. Anything "good" that would happen to me on a Quality-of-Life Level was drawn into that void. The Black Hole co-opted anything positive and used it to fill itself up with a Substitute Sense of Self. This always immediately triggered great anxiety and insomnia. And when I was finally able to stay on track during the day, a relatively good night's sleep would erase the Restored Sense of Self that I had worked so hard to build up. Physical symptoms (migraines) or anxiety would kick in as soon as I woke up. I had to be utterly cunning to keep managing my own life and body during those moments, but I did! Day by day, it slowly got better. And then the improvements gradually set in to stay!

Hannibal took his elephants over the mountains in the year 218 BC; in all modesty, I do not believe that my efforts to heal myself were any less difficult to accomplish. I don't seek to compare myself to this great Carthaginian military commander but merely use this comparison to indicate how much effort it took me to reroute myself and uncover enough of my true Self to be increasingly true to it.

Here is a relevant quote from Kevin Toohey[1], which is based on one of C.G. Jung's insights in *The Autonomy of the Psyche*:

[1] As described in an article from Kevin Toohey's "The Frog Princess" as it appears in the book *Jung Talks, 50 Years of the C.G. Jung Society of Melbourne*, edited by Annette Lowe. Kevin Toohey is a Jungian analyst from Melbourne, Australia, and a former president of the Melbourne Jung Society. http://bit.ly/2zVAyFO.

"Psychologically, sometimes a destructive complex or affect is so destructive that it requires a heroic effort to turn away or escape. The magic carpet is the means by which this is affected. The carpet is a product of spinning. We can say it represents the story of individuation. At any one point in life, we often cannot see how the experience or threads of our lives form a tapestry that tells the story of Self. The escape from the destructive tendencies in the unconscious is made by comprehending thread by thread, the meaning of one's life experiences, and one's fate."

Presenting my work to the world goes together with my hope that people of all walks of life will be positively impacted and become aware of the need to examine their own presence in the world. Each of us owes it to our Selves to truly live our lives while being a true life-guide to our children. We all need to live in a way that allows us to get enough insight into what could be "unfinished business," acknowledge it, and do something about it. This better be before our offspring demand our attention, so we do not need to prove our right to exist through them or in spite of them.

Those of us who choose to become or already are parents have to be fully aware of the responsibility we take on when we decide to raise the next generation. For many of us, parenthood used to be a thing we "did" because it was expected of us. I wonder if humanity can sustain that approach. Wouldn't it be better if we all took the necessary steps to own such a great responsibility and work our way toward facilitating the development of a Healthy Sense of Self in future generations?

A Healthy (Restored) Sense of Self is what it takes to be your Self. Your children will follow your lead and develop their Sense of Self naturally. Once two entire generations manage to live their lives with a Healthy Sense of Self, our world will be a better place!

Glossary

Annihilation

A strong perception of being overlooked, not being seen and heard, not being taken into account, and not having any impact in one's environment, which is experienced as non-existing.

Black Hole

Metaphor for an intolerably terrifying emptiness or invisibility as experienced by a person with a Lack of Sense of Self who doesn't feel like (they are considered) a "real" person.
Like a force of nature, the Black Hole sucks in behavior and achievements that can potentially lead to *approval.* It fills itself with anything that serves as a Substitute Sense of Self, which immediately leads to anxiety about losing the Substitute Sense of Self.

Direct Motivation

Motivation that is ordinary, simple, and based in the present.

Direct Relationship with Self

A way of relating to your own being that includes body awareness, which means that you sense your Self without having to refer to achievements or other people's opinions about you.

Distorted Mirror

The process by which the primary caregiver is unable to effectively acknowledge their child(ren) as a separate being(s), as the caregiver is too wrapped up in their own problems and emotional neediness.
The child inevitably and naturally concludes that he or she *IS* the way he or she sees him- or herself reflected by the caregiver, which is, in the light of the child's mind, an understandable but incorrect conclusion that can have far-reaching negative implications.

Early Childhood Survival Strategy (ECSS)

Conclusion to take refuge in gaining approval, drawn instinctively by infants/toddlers/children when their needs of feeling acknowledged as separate (unique) individuals by their caretakers are not met. This process becomes the foundation for Indirect Motivation, which leads to an unhealthy way of experiencing the Self.

Ego-References

Subconsciously accepted requirements to feel and behave in certain ways and achieve certain results in order to feel approved of, as a substitute for a healthy way of experiencing the Self.

Enmeshment

An unhealthy relationship between child and primary caretaker. The child's identity remains under- or undeveloped and his or her motives stay geared toward getting the adult's approval, which leads to extreme dependence on approval.

Fear of Annihilation

Terror of being unheard by and invisible to others.

"Feel-good-about-self" (Fgas)

An emotional state (or thought) of relative well-being and safety based on the absence of feeling compelled to produce certain results at all costs, gained from succeeding to comply to the wishes of the caregiver, which leads to approval. It serves as a temporary and unhealthy substitute for a sincere sense of being alive (as a "real" person).

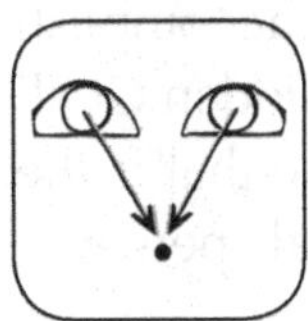

Focus Mode

Relaxed movements of the eyes, with the ability to stay fixed in the same place for extended periods, and which indicates a grounded mood or a person with a Healthy Sense of Self.

Healthy Sense of Self

The ability to experience and be present to your own person and to your own life and recognize both as uniquely owned by YOU. That includes the right to live and be as your Self and experience your innermost core as your ultimate home from where you live your life.

Hidden Agenda

A subconscious purpose that drives your actions or behavior, which is not the obvious, ordinary, expected purpose but the demonstration of the ability to perform an Ego-Reference to perfection, as a path to feel safe and on your way to achieving your Hidden Goal.

Hidden Goal

Your subconscious ultimate objective of getting the approval of your caregiver as an unhealthy substitute for feeling valued and related to (acknowledged) as a "real" person.

Hindrance

Any obstacle on your path to gaining a Substitute Sense of Self that frequently leads to anger or rage, which can be a gateway to violence or its counterpart, depression.

Indirect Motivation

The motive for doing or avoiding something is not what it appears to be; instead, the motive is to accomplish your Hidden Agenda and ultimately your Hidden Goal, which leads to a temporary emotional state that is the substitute for a lasting sense of being a "real" person.

Indirect Relationship with Self

Sensing yourself as a "self" through achievements or the responses of others, which gives you a temporary good feeling instead of a healthy abiding sense of being who you are.

Inner Conflict

Two or more competing and incompatible inner mandates to work toward experiencing a Substitute Sense of Self. This leads to high anxiety because the competition causes a no-win outcome.

Internalized Parental Voice (IPV)

The often-repeated verbal and nonverbal messages that parents, knowingly or unknowingly, transmit to their children becomes (almost?) hardwired in the child's mind so that it is perceived as an unquestionable truth (about and) by the child.

Lack of Sense of Self

Characteristic of a person who never developed a natural, ongoing inner knowing that he or she is truly alive as a "real," independent human being.

Magic Formula

A way of remembering the gist of the SoS Method: Move away from the addiction to "Feeling-good-about-yourself." First cross out the judgmental word "about" – don't be *about* your self – be yourself! Next cross out the word "good" – no need to point that out: *good* is your default state. What is left is: Feel your Self = sense your Self = have a Healthy Sense of Self!

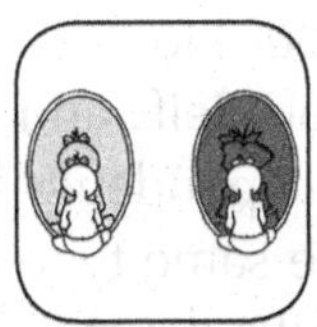

Mirroring

The mutual and subconscious verbal and nonverbal processes by which the primary caretaker conveys basic feedback to the child about whether the caretaker relates to the child as independently existing individual or as a means to fulfill the caretaker's emotional needs – this message functions as a mirror for the child and is accepted as the truth of who the child is.
The adequacy/inadequacy of the way this mirror functions is a decisive factor in the child's development (or lack thereof) of a Sense of Self of their own.

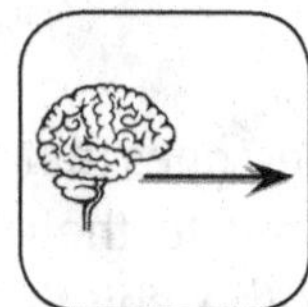

Motivation

In general, motivation is what creates an incentive or urge to do or avoid something. Motivation is the drive that determines behavior.

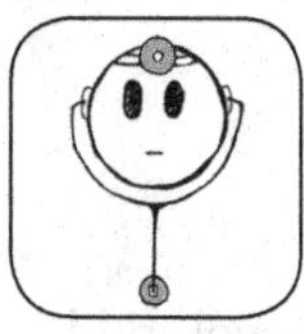

Motivation Check

A crucial (verbal) tool, which serves to a) detect your (Indirect) Motivation and b) record your Ego-References and Hidden Agendas, and to get insight what your Hidden Goal is.

Natural Sense of Self

The subconscious sense – developed normally in childhood – of being alive as a "real," definite person, with the unconditional right to exist as who you are, regardless of what others think, feel, or say about you.

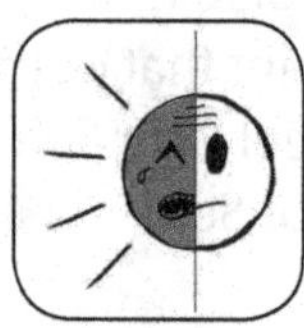

Quality-of-Life Level

A healthy level of experiencing life's events and responding to them with emotional reactions that are in sync with the degree of intensity of the actual effect of these events or behavior of others on your life.
It is indicative of a Healthy Sense of Self and distinguished from a (usually unaware) dependency on a Substitute Sense of Self where for the same type of events emotions are experienced that strike down to the level of your sense of existence-as-a-self.

Real Self (Authentic Self)

The totality of one's body, mind, and emotions and what comes with being a person is experienced in the healthiest, most integrated way as an independent and autonomous being; actions and awareness are based on living experience, not contaminated by pathological motives.* See also Natural Sense of Self.

*Not so much meant in a spiritual sense but more as a reference to the whole person you really are.

Restored Sense of Self

The end result of working with the SoS Method, which is being healed from the dependency on a Substitute Sense of Self and which consists of a steady awareness of being one's very own person who is free to live life based on one's own essence, preferences, abilities, and limitations.

There is an inner knowing of being separate from any parent or caregiver and free from any dependency on achievements or approval. There is an abiding sense of being (unconditionally) alive and "real."

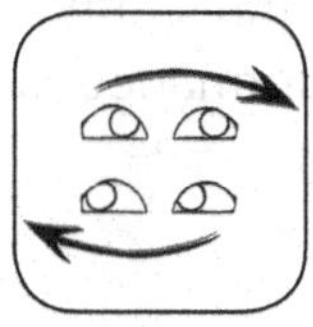

Scanning Mode

A person's eyes moving around restlessly, searching for opportunities "to Score," which would fill the need for approval and "Feeling-good-about-themselves." Scanning mode use of the eyes indicates activity aimed at achieving an unhealthy way to experience one's self.

Sense of Self (SoS)

A conscious and/or subconscious awareness of existing independently as a unique and potentially autonomous human being.

Substitute Sense of Self

A psycho-emotional structure that develops as the artificial backbone of the psyche of those children/adults whose caregivers relate to their children as an extension of themselves, and that leads them to develop a compulsive drive for achievement-based approval.

To Score

Being successful in using a Vehicle to improve on an Ego-Reference; a success that feels like gaining points toward the Hidden Goal,* which results in a "Feel-good-about-self" as a placeholder for the real-self experience.

*The Hidden Goal does not necessarily always have to be parental approval. It also can be the undoing of early childhood traumatic experiences, such as being bullied, not being accepted by peers, etc.

Vehicle

An action, activity or behavior used to display the performance of specific skills or character traits rather than the obvious, ordinary goal. The performance is ultimately aimed at getting approval (Fgas).

Acknowledgments

Questioning the role your caregivers have played in your life is uncomfortable for many people. Moreover, even though I had a hard time persuading my friends to read my manuscript and listen to my theory, those who ended up being touched by its content have been tremendously dedicated and helpful in producing this book. They are the ones who have taken care of the ten to twelve rounds of edits the material needed in order to be presented in a way that is coordinated enough to be understandable. Therefore, I can hardly say I wrote this book by myself.

Since 2008, numerous dedicated people have been involved, and I would like to thank them from the depths of my heart. Without you, this book would have stayed in Pandora's Box. Its content would have remained interesting to me but inaccessible to others, and very few people would have been able to make sense of it. Maybe no one would have wanted to open the box in the first place because the benefits would not have been clear and the content would have looked too scary. But thanks to all of your insights, effort, and time, we have here the verbalization of a solution to so many problems that now lies in the hands of the person suffering from them. Thank you all tremendously for seeing the big picture with me and spending your time and energy on getting my story and theory into shape so that others can benefit from it.

Let me begin with profusely thanking Alia Aurami, who was among the first to listen to what I had to say and verify the validity of it. Alia was also instrumental in writing up the first version of the Sense of Self Theory, which is still available at www.holispsych.com. Many people still find this first writing very useful and enlightening.

My heartfelt thanks go to Deborah Drake and Nora Smith, who have been consistently on my side as language sources and transformers of the conclusions I drew from my own challenges, making them more publically accessible. Thank you for never being bored or annoyed with the content, and thank you for your gracious patience to arrive at the point where we are now. In the early stages of Healthy Sense of Self, we did not work remotely. We worked together more often, and I happily recall the memorable circles of discussion about the jargon, about how to best choose the words, how to best describe them, and how to craft the best definitions. The nature of our jargon is a funny one as it turned out to be a subject with a life of its own. It never seemed to be finished, but in written text, you have to settle on something. So, thank you all for your valuable insights and also for staying true to your own opinions when we had to debate, at great length, until an agreement was found.

I thank my daughter Laura for her dedication and patience to producing the prototypes of what has become our brand, character, and illustration style. I am thankful to Marco Scozzi, who has picked up her style, trying to stay close while giving his own take on the artwork.

There were people who came and went over the last seven years whom I would also like to mention and thank: Lily Burns, Michael Maine, and Bookmasters.

Thanks also to Jolene Spath, Leighah Beadle-Darcy, Werner Vogels, and Kim Vogels. I want to specifically express my gratitude for the work done by my longtime friend Gianluigi Ottobrini in Novara, Italy. Thank you for translating the book into Italian; know that from our discussions, I learned so much, and it has greatly contributed to enhancing this book.

Thank you to Marielle Higler and Ilse Wortelboer for taking the material and translating it into Dutch, and discussing the issues that came up. See our Dutch website gezondzelfgevoel.nl.

Thank you to all the people behind those who helped me: their families, their friends, and their connections.

Special thanks to our beta readers. Your courage to be critical and honest about the material has made a noticeable difference. A tremendous thank you goes, once more, to the talented design team Vanessa Cucco and Marco Scozzi, who have stepped up to produce high-quality results in an amazingly short time.

You have made me feel that I am not alone in this intensive quest to make our world a better place. You have all made it possible for others to learn and benefit from my story.

And, last but not least, from a radical forgiveness point, I want to express my thanks to my mother for giving me this human experience.

Thank you.

Short overview of the Sense of Self Method

A Healthy Sense of Self is the felt sense of being your own person, separate from others. With a Healthy Sense of Self, you are free to be the unique human being you were born to be. It allows you to effectively become increasingly more independent through each stage of development. A Sense of Self (SoS) is cultivated from birth, but only when your primary caregivers truly see and acknowledge you as an autonomous being, as opposed to (unknowingly) considering you to be an extension of themselves or considering you to be a burden. A Healthy Sense of Self is profoundly significant because it is the foundation for living an authentic life, a life without shame, regret, or anxiety, as opposed to a lifetime of addiction to approval.

The Sense of Self Method is a self-help program that allows you to determine if you have a Healthy Sense of Self and, if one is lacking, helps you to build a Restored Sense of Self®. Restoring your Sense of Self ultimately leads to living and functioning as if you had a Natural Healthy Sense of Self. Chances are that, just like a person with a Healthy Sense of Self, you too will develop more inner peace and vitality, your relationship skills will improve, and your overall quality of life will greatly increase.

Abstract of the Sense of Self Method

Introduction

Insomnia and many other mental, emotional, and physical imbalances are part of a wide array of human suffering that share one root cause: a lack of sense of self. Restoring one's Sense of self dismantles many, if not all resulting aspects of ill health and lack of well-being.

The purpose of my studies was to discover the underlying cause of the sudden onset of insomnia that commenced after the birth of my first daughter (1985), as I resumed work as a bassoonist in the Amsterdam Philharmonic Orchestra.

My studies have resulted in multiple books and an online course about the Sense of Self Method. I developed this method to help people restore their sense of self and recognize that their motivation for doing or avoiding things often has nothing to do with who they really are and what they would want for themselves. Posing the question, "WHY do you do/want/avoid WHAT you do/want/avoid?" inspires people to look behind the scenes of their motivation. Then they start to see what drives them and envision the conclusion that being so estranged from their real self may have led to the symptoms of disease they are experiencing.

The intention of this abstract is to invite academically trained professionals, especially psychologists, to investigate the validity of my approach and, if deemed relevant, take steps to test my conclusions by conducting studies on a larger scale.

The Problem

At the time (1985) I sought treatment no relevant cure for insomnia was available in the medical field. I had to take matters into my own hands. My goal was to end my insomnia, restore my well-being, and get my life back on track.

In the process I noticed within myself an array of other issues, including but not limited to rage, fear of my own emotions, the need to manipulate other people and control circumstances, the lack of any spontaneous moments of happiness, as well as a workaholic behavior.

Through deep exploration into the subconsciously motivated mental and emotional reactions I displayed to daily challenges, I concluded these were all driven by a single factor: the urgent need to compensate for the absence of a Healthy sense of self.

This discovery led to my understanding that a myriad of other issues could be connected to that same root cause: difficulties in childrearing, relationship issues, insomnia, anxiety and depression, anger management issues, weight problems and eating DO, addictive behaviors, domestic violence, fear of failure, performance anxiety, loneliness, lack of empathy and compassion, the inability to work within or contribute to groups on the job or in the world at large.

And possibly: Alzheimer's disease and other forms of dementia, fibromyalgia, labelled disorders such as bipolar DO, ADHD, and many more.

The Method

I am not academically trained as a psychologist, but I consider myself a (self-made) motivation expert.

My method of collecting data and drawing conclusions has been performing ongoingly introspection, recording, and reviewing of my thoughts, feelings, and findings for over 30 years (1995 – 2015). Labelling my thoughts and feelings provided me with the tools to map out my inner processes and draw consistent conclusions. Asking the question, "*Why* do/did I do *what* I do/did?" and being brutally honest with myself has been instrumental in this approach.

Observing others to discover which essential piece of the puzzle they possessed that I was missing, helped me come to my conclusions about the overarching effects on behavior of a sense of self or the lack thereof.

The Results

I discovered that the various disrupting symptoms I experienced had one cause in common: a Lack of sense of self (LoSoS). A LoSoS is caused by inadequate Mirroring of the child by her caregivers. When a person is prevented from developing a Healthy sense of self in childhood, she becomes dependent on approval. Earning that parental smile makes her "Feel-good-about-herself". It gives her a fleeting moment of feeling worthy, which then is mistaken for a Sense of self. This cycle of dependency on approval for self-validation functions as a substitute for the missing connection to the Real self (Substitute sense of self (SSoS)).

Because of the life-and-death urgency to fill the void in the self-experience, a need develops to perform perfectly. This is particularly relevant for the self-imposed conditions a person with a LoSoS tends to use (and persists in using) to convince her caregiver that she is worthy of his or her attention. These conditions vary individually as they are founded on what one learns in childhood regarding the successes and failures in earning approval.

The dependency on approval, if not addressed, is carried over into adulthood and leads to an overwhelming amount of stress that can result in a great variety of mental, emotional, and physical symptoms.

Through guided introspection, the Sense of Self Method offers insight into the devastating consequences of motivations that are geared towards gaining a Substitute sense of self. It provides exercises in body awareness, visualizations, and self-affirmations as a path to a Restored sense of self.

Conclusion

What are the implications of this finding? Restoring one's sense of self is the answer to the seemingly unrelated array of problems and issues caused by a LoSoS. The moment one's focus shifts from the need to gain approval to experiencing unconditional self-acceptance, many of the symptoms disappear naturally.

Numerous benefits come with this approach because it enables people, to a large extent, to work things out for themselves. This results in fewer office visits, and, consequently, lower healthcare costs. Symptomatic treatment of ailments that result from a LoSoS seem to be a waste of time, money, and effort.

The immediate result of a Restored sense of self is less stress, better health and well-being, improved quality of life, and a higher degree of self-actualization. It also leads to more responsible and adequate child rearing for parents of young children. These positive changes are also reflected in fewer absences from work or school, and a greater sense of personal satisfaction.

If mine is a relevant finding, I would hope that more official, scientifically based conclusions will enable implementation of the Sense of Self Principle in the various modalities of healing. It is my dream to make Sense of Self counselors available in educational settings from elementary schools to universities and other institutes of professional education.

As a potential limitation I envision that my approach might, at best, be considered an extensive case study. However, it is not up to me to draw conclusions as I consider it immoral to withhold from the appropriate sources any information that might have the potential of being beneficial to the greater good.

About the Author

Antoinetta Vogels was born in 1946 in the Netherlands at the end of World War II. She vividly recalls listening to her father's stories about the horrors of the war, while walking with him through the ruins of his native city, Groningen. She made the firm decision, even as a young girl, that she herself had to do something *to make wars stop*!

Little did Antoinetta know that life would offer her an opportunity to contribute to the understanding of human behavior by having her grow up with a "Lack of Sense of Self," and therefore providing her with the task of figuring out what was "missing" in her life.

As an accomplished bassoonist in several professional classical orchestras in the Netherlands, Antoinetta was a disciplined performer who enjoyed the creativity and expression of her work.

Motherhood resulted in two lovely daughters and the sudden onset of severe insomnia, which forced her into early retirement from her musical career early. This is where Antoinetta's inner journey began in determining the underlying cause of the predicament that continued plaguing her for over twenty-five years: insomnia.

Antoinetta started out with continuous introspection. Next she began recording her thoughts and feelings, a process that enabled her to identify patterns of behavior, and ultimately led to her Sense of Self Theory.

Antoinetta's mission is to share how a Healthy Sense of Self is a crucial asset for each individual and for the world at large (Peace)!

Antoinetta lived in her homeland until 1995, when she moved with her family to Ithaca, NY. She later moved to Seattle, where she has been writing and speaking for almost a decade now.

Through her company, Healthy Sense of Self®, Antoinetta offers education and techniques that restore one's Sense of Self.

"A Healthy Sense of Self
is the backbone of the human psyche.
Without it a person skips his/her own life altogether."

Vision and Mission Statement of HealthySenseOfSelf®

Vision

Our Company strives to provide insight and deliver strategies that contribute to increase significantly the overall quality of life of the individual and ultimately of the world at large. HySoS helps in increasing or restoring a Healthy Sense of Self in the individual which immediately leads to improving health, productivity, success, well-being and peace. HealthySenseOfSelf® strives to expand this message in ever-increasingly diverse, effective, and well-utilized ways for ever-increasing numbers of individuals and groups so that this effect spreads outward in ripples, developing a momentum and life of its own.

Mission Statement

We believe that the world can be a better place and HySoS contributes to our envisioned world by developing and delivering both education and activities for making our Sense of Self healthier. Our specific ways of educating and providing activities for that purpose include, but are not limited to: offering information to individuals and to groups in the form of conferences, teleconferences, seminars and teleseminars, webinars online and/or real life –courses with potentially a Train-the-Trainers Program, educational speeches and presentations, podcasts, video's, radio and-TV appearances, articles in Journals, Newspapers and Magazines, a Newsletters, potentially our own Ezine. Our ultimate dream is: a HySoS –Foundation comprising of treatment and educational facilities, with national as well as international franchises.

HySoS strives to help people (re-)align with who they really are by strengthening or Restoring their Sense of Self®. Thus, we work specifically with parents, teachers, teacher-trainers, clergy, speakers, and others who influence many people, so we educate the educators for maximum scope of impact on the world. We also provide opportunities for both our employees and those we reach in other ways to gain full understanding and full benefits from this integrated non-medical method. We strive to be business as well as family, thus providing what's missing in many people's lives: a sense of purpose and home.

Overview HySoS Resources

Websites and Blogs:

https://www.healthysenseofself.com/

Website Netherlands:

https://www.gezondzelfgevoel.nl

Website Italy:

https://www.sanosensodise.it

Facebook:

https://www.facebook.com/Healthysenseofself

Facebook Netherlands:

https://www.facebook.com/GezondZelfGevoel

Facebook Italy:

https://www.facebook.com/SanoSensodiSe

Instagram United States:

https://instagram.com/healthysenseofself

Instagram Netherlands:

https://instagram.com/gezondzelfgevoel_nl

Twitter:

https://twitter.com/healthysos

Linkedin USA:

https://www.linkedin.com/in/annetvogels

Author's Amazon.com:

https://amazon.com/Antoinetta-Vogels/e/B00JBFU1SG

Author of:

- *Healthy Sense of Self - How to be true to your Self and make your world a better place*

- *Online Course: Introducing the Sense of Self Method*

- *The Sense of Self Help! Workbook*

- *The Motivation Cure - The secret to being your best Self*

- *A Guided Journal to a Healthy Sense of Self: Thoughts to Inspire Peace Within and Around the World*

- *How to overcome insomnia all by yourself*

Netherlands:

- *Gezond Zelf-Gevoel: Dé Methode om het beste uit Jezelf te halen*

- *Online Cursus: de Zelf-Gevoel Methode*

- *Werkboek voor de Zelf-Gevoel Methode (gebaseerd op de onlinecursus maar ook onafhankelijk te gebruiken)*

- *Het Gezond Zelf-Gevoel Dagboekje - Een inspiratiebron voor persoonlijke en wereldvrede*

- *Slapeloosheid - Hoe kom je er vanaf?*

Italy:

- *Diario Guidato a un Sano Senso di Sé: 120 pratici suggerimenti per riconquistare la propria vita*

Contacts:

- Email: contact@healthysenseofself.com

Netherlands:

- Email: info@gezondzelfgevoel.nl

Italy:

- Email: info@sanosensodise.it

Kirkus Review

Title Information

THE MOTIVATION CURE
The Secret to Being Your Best Self
Antoinetta Vogels
Healthy Sense of Self Publications (392 pp.)
$ 17.95 paperback
ISBN: 978-0-9887226-2-0; February 23, 2017

Book Review

An author offers a theory springing from her study of her psychologically neglected childhood and its lifetime of consequences.

The term "enmeshment" is used to describe a dysfunctional relationship with permeable and unclear boundaries that may lead to a damaging lack of autonomy. This is exactly what Vogels (*A Guided Journal to a Healthy Sense of Self*, 2014 etc.) experienced as a child with a mother who with held love and only granted approval with self-centered conditions. As the author grew, she began to realize this and how it contributed to her extreme anxiety and stress. She spent so much of her life, including her adult years, chasing potential parental approval that she never developed her own sense of self-worth. After studying herself for years, she has now composed her conclusions in this book as "The Sense of Self Theory & Method," intended particularly for those who suffered similar circumstances. Early on, she emphasizes the crucial role of the primary caregiver ("A Sense of Self is something that either develops or does not. That process depends mainly on the nature of the input from the primary caregiver... The people who are with the child from birth on are the ones who make the greatest impression on the individual"). Though not a licensed psychologist, the author certainly thinks and writes like one, and this volume is replete with definitions of terms and supporting examples. Vogels' "Sense of Self Theory" is incredibly well-articulated with insights that should resonate with those who endured difficult childhoods that led to thorny adult paths. The author also encourages new parents to center their children in their lives with an atmosphere of unconditional love. Unfortunately, the remainder of the work, namely the effects of lacking a sense of self and Vogels' recovery suggestions, loses some of the magic from the first section and includes some redundancies. Furthermore, it is likely that only those readers who fit the same mold as the author will find these parts especially useful. That said, Vogels' organization of the manual and her meticulous assessments are superb. Though her theory may still need perfecting, the concepts she writes about are vital and should be seriously explored in the world of psychology and human development.This book should help readers who have experienced a childhood deprived of parental acceptance break their approval-seeking habits and discover who they truly are.

Index

A

Acknowledgment
  approval and 87-88
  from caregivers 70-72, 88
Action stage of restoring Sense of Self 259-260
Addiction 231-33
  as challenge to restoring Sense of Self 231-33
  resources for recovery from 363
  to Substitute Sense of Self 112, 263-65, 363
Addictive behaviors, as effect of the Dependency on a Substitute Sense of Self 184-85
Affirmations. *See* Exercises and affirmations for Restored Sense of Self
Anger, as effect of the Addiction to Approval 192
Annihilation
  defined 43, 81, 371
  experiencing 81
  Fear of 79-81, 83-84, 259-260, 373
  Fearing the Fear of 86
Anxiety 347-48
Approval
  acknowledgment and 87-88, 138
  and Feeling-good-about-Self state 88
  as reward 122-23
  becoming hooked on 88-91
  enmeshment and addiction to 151-58
Asbury, William F. 363
Authentic Self (Real Self), defined 74, 377

B

Beattie, Melody 160n
Behavior
  addictive 184-85

NOTE: n after page number denotes footnote

fear of your 198-202
questioning your 120
Black Hole 338
as challenge to restoring Sense of Self 227-28
defined 80, 371
Blame, as challenge to restoring Sense of Self 234-35
Body awareness 273-75, 309-10
Body language 209-10
Brain tree 63-65

C

Caregiver. *See* Parent/caregiver
Castle of Enmeshment 87, 154-58
Child deprivation 106-9
Child neglect 107-8
Clemente, Carlo di 256n
Compulsiveness, as effect of Substitute Sense of Self–oriented Behavior 184-85, 208
Conscious Spiritual Self 327, 329-30
Conscious Thought-Form Self 76, 326, 328-29, 335-36
Contemplation stage of restoring Sense of Self 257-259
Conversations for transferring information or for enjoyment 296-99

D

Denial, beware of 230-31
Depression 86, 115-16, 131-32, 192, 354-60
Development
lacks in input in 59
metaphor for 58-65
sequence of 53-57
Direct Motivation 121
defined 121, 371
Indirect vs. 113-14
Direct Relationship with Self 282-85
defined 106, 371
Distorted Mirror 72-76
defined 73, 372

E

Early Childhood Survival Strategy (ECSS) 46, 95-97, 134
defined 90, 372
Eating Disorders 164

Ego-References 133, 135
conditions that become 138-40
defined 135, 372
examples of 142-44
fulfilling 104-5, 107, 269
Indirect Motivation and 336
Inner Conflict and 146-48
reactionary 142-43
recovering from 242-43
restoring Sense of Self and 230-31
stress in 233
Vehicles and 143-46
Emotional abuse 106-9
Emotional roller coaster 168
Enmeshment
addiction to approval and 153-60
Castle of 141, 156-160
defined 50, 372
Environmental input
in developmental sequence 53-57
lacks in 59
metaphor for 58-65
Exercises and affirmations for Restored Sense of Self 316-17
body awareness 310-11
reconditioning statements 273-75
holding onto Restored Sense of Self 316-17
in Maps for restoring your Sense of Self 349-50
listening to your body 310-11
Magic Formula 320-21
Motivation Check 245-46
self-awareness 220, 310

F

Fear
as challenge to restoring Sense of Self 234-35
as effect of the Addiction to Approval 241
map of 349-50
of change 202
of failure 202-3, 350
of not being able to function 201-2
of your behavior 199-201
of your emotions 198-99
Quality-of-Life 344
Fear of Annihilation 83-84
defined 81, 373
Fearing the 86
"Feel-good-about-self" (Fgas) State 332, 335, 337-38

approval and 82, 87-88
defined 98, 373
goal of 204-5
Indirect Motivation and 248-55
real feelings in 99
Feelings, real 99
Focus Mode, defined 373

G

Gorski, Terence T. 363
Gray, Kevin 362n

H

Habits, as challenge to restoring Sense of Self 229-30
Healthy Self
layers of 326
unhealthy vs. 337
Healthy Sense of Self (HySoS) 316
defined 31, 373
effects of 67
layers of 330
map of 346
See also Natural Sense of Self (NatSoS); Restored Sense of Self (Rest SoS)
HealthySenseOfSelf® 31, 44, 238, 254, 317, 333n, 354, 359
Hidden Agenda 75-77, 125-26
defined 120, 373
Hidden Goal vs. 128-29
Indirect Motivation with 119-20, 248-55
Hidden Goal 89
Annihilation and 87-88
defined 123, 374
Hidden Agenda vs. 128-29
Indirect Motivation and 248-55
Hindrance 75
defined 192, 374

I

Incarnated Self 326, 334, 335-36
Indirect Motivation 70, 122-23, 133
body language and 209-10
concepts of 248-55
defined 114, 374
Direct vs. 114

divided focus and 213
harmful effects of 214
Hidden Agenda with 119-20
layers of 334
patterns of 255
Sense of Self and 131-32
Substitute Sense of Self and 248-55
Indirect Relationship with Self, defined 100, 374
Inner Conflict
defined 144, 374
Ego-References and 144-46
Insomnia 86, 115, 352-54
Integrity, lack of 209-10
Internalized Parental Voice (IPV) 103-4
defined 25, 375

J

Jellenek, E. Morton 361n
Jung, Carl Gustav 368

K

Ketcham, Katherine 363
Korzybski, Alfred 22n

L

Lack of Sense of Self (LoSoS) 23, 327
characteristics of 42-43
defined 42, 375
detecting 43-44
in Maps for restoring your Sense of Self 346
stress and 346
symptoms of 44
Lipton-Dibner, Wendy 258
Lowe, Annette 368n

M

Magic Formula, defined 321, 375
Maintenance stage of Restored Sense of Self 257, 260-62
Maps for restoring your Sense of Self 343-50
inadequate mirroring in 346, 349
Milam, James Robert 363

Miller, Merlene 363
Mirroring 57, 67
  challenges of 76-78
  defined 68, 375
  distorted 72-76, 344-45, 372
  from caregivers 69-70
  in development of Natural Sense of Self 70-72, 344
  in Maps for restoring your Sense of Self 346
  map of 346
  vicious cycle in 78
Motivation
  defined 115, 376
  development of 113
  Direct (*see* Direct Motivation)
  Direct vs. Indirect 114
  discovering 112-13
  examples of 224-26
  Hidden Agenda as target of 119-20
  importance of knowing 115
  Indirect (*see* Indirect Motivation)
  overview 111-12
Motivation Check 245, 247
  defined 245-48, 376
Motivation Cure 111

N

Natural Sense of Self (NatSoS) 331-32
  comparison chart 159-72
  defined 42, 376
  environmental inputs and 58
  lack of 41-44, 375
  mirroring and development of 68-72
  Restored Sense of Self vs. 221-223
  Substitute Sense of Self as replacement for 28
  See also Healthy Sense of Self (HySoS); Sense of Self (SoS)
Nature vs. nurture 53-57

O

Ocular migraine 187

P

Parent/caregiver
  challenges of 76-78
  distorted mirroring by 72-73

importance of 47-48
mirroring by 69-70, 78
Pre-contemplation stage of restoring Sense of Self 257
Preferences, opinions, and feelings 290-91
Preparation stage of restoring Sense of Self 259
Present in here and now 285-87
Prison experiment 195, 196n
Prochaska, James 256n
Psycho-Emotional Self 326, 328-29, 336

Q

Quality-of-Life Level experience 224-26
Quality-of-Life Level fear 344
Quality-of-Life Level (QoL Level), defined 179, 376

R

Rage
in Maps for restoring your Sense of Self 346
Real Self (Authentic Self), defined 74, 377
Reconditioning Statements 274
accessing feelings, preferences, and opinions 290-92
awareness of senses 289-90
being grateful for all you have and receive 290, 305-6
body awarenes 301, 310-11
conversations for transferring information or for socializing 296-97
experiencing Self directly 282-85
present in here and now 285-87
relapse awareness 300-2
seeing others for who they are 292-95
sharing your life with others 303-5
think for your Self 287-88
Three M's of body awareness 278-79
work for the sake of the work 299-300
Recovery from addiction to Substitute Sense of Self 263
Relapse, awareness of 300-2
Restored Sense of Self (Rest SoS) 51, 220
achieving 239-43
as way out of addiction 362-63
as way out of depression 359-60
as way out of insomnia 353-54
benefits of 222-23
challenges to achieving 239
change process diagram, 262
comparison chart 159-172
defined 218, 377

exercises and affirmations for (*see* Exercises and affirmations for Restored Sense of Self)
feeling of 223-24
holding onto 316-17
Natural Sense of Self vs. 221
recovery from addiction to 263
stages of achieving 257-62
tools and time needed for 238
See also Healthy Sense of Self (HySoS)

S

Satir, Virginia 245, 261n
Scanning Mode, defined 164, 377
Scoring, defined 76, 378
Self
Conscious Spiritual 326, 329-30
Conscious Thought-Form 328, 334-35
defined 325-27
Direct Relationship with 105-6, 284-85, 371
Healthy vs. unhealthy 337
Incarnated 326-28, 334
Indirect Relationship with 100, 339-40, 374
lack of sensing 327
layers of 325-30, 334
think for your 287-88
Unconscious Spiritual 326, 327
See also Sense of Self (SoS)
Self-absorbed people, characteristics of 74-76
Self-contentment exercises 313
Self-esteem, Sense of Self and 340-41
Sense of Self (SoS) 331-32
as action 340
defined 24, 377
developmental sequence 53-55
importance of 46-47
Indirect Motivation and 131-32
input lacks in development of 58-59
lack of (*see* Lack of Sense of Self)
maps for restoring your Sense of Self 343-50
metaphor for development of 58-66
self-esteem and 340-41
See also Natural Sense of Self (NatSoS); Substitute Sense of Self (SSoS)
Sense of Self (SoS) Method
purpose of 27-29, 30-31
summarized in Maps for restoring your Sense of Self 345-50
summary of 44-46
Senses, awareness of 289-90

Sensing, defined 338-42
Shakespeare, William 267
Slipping back, as challenge to restoring Sense of Self 231
Smooth-floor syndrome 185-86
Social Self 77, 326, 329, 336
Solo syndrome 187-88
Spitz, Rene 57, 57n
Stress
  as challenge to restoring Sense of Self 237-38
  as effect of Substitute Sense of Self–oriented system 182-83
  as an effect of Substitute Sense of Self–oriented behavior 177-80
  in brain 231
  in Ego-References 227
Unconscious Spiritual Self 326, 327
Substitute Sense of Self (SSoS) 41, 131-32
  addiction to 192
  Black Hole and 79
  comparison chart 159-72
  defined 80, 378
  development of (*see* Mirroring),
  in Maps for restoring your Sense of Self 346
  Indirect Motivation and 248-255
  layers of 333-37
  Natural Sense of Self replaced by 220-21

T

Teasing thoughts 187-88
Three M's of body awareness 278-79
Tipping, Colin 235n
Toohey, Kevin 368, 368n

U

Unconscious Spiritual Self 326, 327-329
Unhealthy Self
  healthy vs. 337
  layers of 334

V

Vehicle 126-28
  define 127, 378
  Ego-References and, 141-44
  Indirect Motivation and, 248-255

W

Washington State Alcohol and Drug Clearing House 363
Work for the sake of the work 299-300

Z

Zimbardo prison experiment 195, 196n

Printed in the United States
by Baker & Taylor Publisher Services